# SHAKESPEARE SURVEY

# SHAKESPEARE SURVEY

## AN ANNUAL SURVEY OF
## SHAKESPEARIAN STUDY & PRODUCTION

### 7

EDITED BY
## ALLARDYCE NICOLL

*Issued under the Sponsorship of*

THE UNIVERSITY OF BIRMINGHAM
THE UNIVERSITY OF MANCHESTER
THE SHAKESPEARE MEMORIAL THEATRE
THE SHAKESPEARE BIRTHPLACE TRUST

CAMBRIDGE
AT THE UNIVERSITY PRESS
1968

Published by the Syndics of the Cambridge University Press
Bentley House, 200 Euston Road, London, N.W.1
American Branch: 32 East 57th Street, New York, N.Y. 10022

*Standard Book Number: 521 06420 1*

*Shakespeare Survey* was first published in 1948. For the first eighteen volumes it was edited by Allardyce Nicoll under the sponsorship of the University of Birmingham, the University of Manchester, the Royal Shakespeare Theatre and the Shakespeare Birthplace Trust.

*First published* 1954
*Reprinted* 1968

First printed in Great Britain
at the University Printing House, Cambridge

Reprinted in Great Britain
by William Lewis (Printers) Ltd, Cardiff

# PREFACE

The central theme of the present volume of *Shakespeare Survey* is that of Shakespeare's style. From the retrospective survey of contributions made to this topic during the past fifty years it becomes manifestly clear, first, that the interpretative investigation of the poet's language has recently attracted much attention, and, secondly, that there is still ample scope for further work in this field.

Associated with the initial 'Retrospect' are two other articles, the first suggesting ways in which the study of Shakespeare's language may be profitably pursued and the other exploring the methods by which he wrought his poetic instrument to serve dramatic purposes. A third article is concerned with an attempt to determine his spelling habits.

Textual and theatrical studies are, of course, fundamental for a consideration of Shakespeare's style. One contribution aims at indicating, in simple terms, the significance of modern bibliographical research; another seeks to determine the nature of Alleyn's histrionic method; still another discusses the relationship between audience and actors in the Elizabethan theatre; while a fourth presents important new documents concerning the players of the Red Bull Theatre. Not unconnected with these articles is a study of the imaginative impress made by Italy upon the dramatist.

In the series of studies of individual libraries an indication is given of the resources of the Birmingham Shakespeare Memorial Collection—from which has come our record of performances in the United Kingdom during 1952. The letters from our correspondents well show the continuing influence of the plays in the theatres of many lands.

For the next, the eighth, volume of *Shakespeare Survey* the central theme will be that of 'The Comedies'.

A.N.

*January 1954*

Contributions offered for publication in *Shakespeare Survey* should be addressed to:
The Editor, The Shakespeare Institute (University of Birmingham), Stratford-upon-Avon.

# CONTENTS

[*Notes are placed at the end of each contribution. All line references are to the 'Globe' edition, and, unless for special reasons, quotations are from this text*]

# LIST OF PLATES

# FIFTY YEARS OF THE CRITICISM OF SHAKESPEARE'S STYLE: A RETROSPECT

BY

M. C. BRADBROOK

There is no question relating to Shakespeare as a writer which does not involve his style. His only art was that of dramatic speech: his thoughts and beliefs are known only through his art: he left no equivalent of Milton's *De Doctrina* or Boswell's private papers. Yet on this central problem comparatively little has been written. It is too vast and intimidating; critics evade it for topics of characterization, theatrical conditions, philosophic implications; or they nibble at a corner—imagery, punctuation, Euphuism. In Ebisch and Schücking's *Shakespeare Bibliography* (1930), nineteen pages out of nearly three hundred suffice for Language, Vocabulary, Prosody and Style; C. H. Herford's little sketch (1925) does not include the subject, 'Mind, Art and Personality' being his nearest approach.[1] The earliest definitions of Shakespeare's style— Webster's "right happy and copious industry", Heminge and Condell's "easiness", the tributes of Jonson, Milton and Dryden have not since been matched in comprehensiveness and assurance. Restoration poets showed their views of Shakespeare's style by the freedom with which they 'improved' him; the adaptations of Rowe and Otway, Davenant and Tate and of Dryden himself are documents in the history of criticism (see Hazelton Spencer, *Shakespeare Improved*, 1927). Many editors of the eighteenth century allowed themselves almost comparable liberty of emendation, erasing such unheroic nouns as "hats", "fishes" or "blanket". Dr Johnson's pronouncement is representative: "The style of Shakespeare was in itself ungrammatical, perplexed and obscure." The Romantics exalted Shakespeare, but even the criticism of Coleridge revealed the dangers of personal judgements in matters of style, as in his notorious pronouncement upon the Porter's scene in *Macbeth*. It was the great achievement of nineteenth-century scholarship to refound the criticism of style upon a basis of historic knowledge: the twentieth century has widened and deepened this knowledge until a division between linguistic and literary criticism has reopened: the present need is for a synthesis of aesthetic judgement and scholarly insight, of taste and learning.

## GRAMMAR AND LEXICOGRAPHY

Fifty years ago, the study of Shakespeare's style was in the hands of philologists, for the last half of the nineteenth century had seen the rise of a new science of language. The work of James Murray and Henry Bradley, which culminated in 1928 with the last volume of the *Oxford Dictionary*, reinforced by the scholarship of Germany and Scandinavia, focused attention upon Aussprache, Wortbildung and the like. This was the Industrial Revolution of Shakespearian studies, this the generation that constituted scholarship on a professional scale; the age of the 'Variorum Shakespeare', a monument that time has to some extent surprised.

The linguists did their work once for all. The *Oxford Dictionary* cannot be superseded though it may be corrected; more specialized works may appear, such as the *Early Modern English Dictionary* projected by the University of Michigan; but Abbott's *Shakespearian Grammar* (1869), Schmidt's *Lexicon* (1874: revised by Sarrazin 1902), Wilhelm Franz's *Shakespeare-Grammatik* (1900: revised 1909, 1924, 1939), and Onions's *Glossary* (1911) can never grow outmoded. Nevertheless, the direction of linguistic studies has changed. Studies of dialects and of contemporary speech, the whole science of phonetics with its international alphabet, such concepts as phonemes, morphemes (not that they are always accepted by linguists of the older schools) with the emergence of semantics and semasiology have shifted the emphasis from literary language towards observation and record. The change may be paralleled by the shift in the field of anthropology from Frazer's great assimilative collection based on classical reading as well as on modern science towards field work which requires specialized medical, linguistic, agricultural and psychological training. Such development has been made possible only through the achievement of the first generation. It is thanks to Abbott that such readings as these, 'emended' in the Globe text, now stand:

His tears runs down his cheeks like winter drops... (*Tempest*, v, i, 16)
There is no more such masters... (*Cymbeline*, iv, ii, 371)
We had droven them. (*Antony and Cleopatra*, iv, vii, 5)

Yet Abbott and even Franz leave room for further annotations upon such lines as:

If trembling I inhabit then, protest me
The baby of a girl, (*Macbeth*, iii, v, 105–6)

as a glance at the New Arden edition of *Macbeth* will show.

These scholars were still ruled by classical theory, especially in prosody; their interest in words was etymological first and foremost; Eilert Ekwall's *Shakespeare's Vocabulary, its etymological elements* (1903) may fitly represent the earlier contribution of Uppsala. The chapter on Shakespeare's English in *Shakespeare's England* (1916) was written by Henry Bradley with emphasis on pronunciation, orthography and grammar; it concludes with a survey of colloquial English and of dialects in which older views of the predominance of London English are still discernible. The modern view is that while the transition from Middle to Early Modern English began sooner than was formerly supposed, the standard language was still only incipient and that the three dialects upon which London English drew were by no means assimilated to a norm. Shakespeare wrote to be heard and not to be read: his tongue had the flexibility and careless ease of the popular stages, rising from colloquialism to high astounding terms but depending always upon the ear of the auditory—as richly variable as it was copious and voluble.

In a chapter on Shakespeare in his *Growth and Structure of the English Language* (1905), Otto Jespersen anticipated the general trend. He discussed the scope of Shakespeare's vocabulary, and his use of language to individualize character—a trait on which Pope had commented in his time and which has been examined with sensitive acumen recently by Arthur Sewell. Shylock is instanced as an example. Shakespeare's boldness of sentence structure, his readiness to adapt and use new words and his taste for the 'unpoetic' language of ordinary life are likewise noted.

Fifteen years later, in his *History of Modern Colloquial English*, H. C. Wyld amplified and confirmed some of the views of Jespersen.

Studies in Shakespeare's dialect have appeared ever since Wright's *Dialect Dictionary* (1898–1905) opened up this field. Among them are those of Appleton Morgan and Baker. Another such is being at present undertaken by H. E. Collins. Law terms, sea terms, sports and other specialized subjects have been investigated by professionals and amateurs, with the general result that Shakespeare is found to be apt rather than exact, though well furnished with all kinds of diction.

## ORTHOGRAPHY, PRONUNCIATION AND PROSODY

These three topics are closely related; in these fields linguists and bibliographers have to some extent collaborated. Pollard followed up *Shakespeare's Fight with the Pirates* (1917), in which he discussed his author's idiosyncrasies of spelling and punctuation, as traceable from the texts, with an article upon 'Elizabethan Spelling as a Literary and Bibliographical Clue' (*The Library*, 4th Series, IV, 1923). The work of Greg, McKerrow and Dover Wilson has shown how closely a knowledge of printing practice and of palaeography is related to emendation: Shakespeare's spellings may identify a good text, the peculiarity of his hand guide the editor past a misprint (always, however, the problems of the playhouse intrude). The text of Jonson's plays, prepared by himself for the press, illustrates by contrast the complexity of Shakespeare's. There was perhaps no final text of *Hamlet*: what we have may represent genuine alternatives. As there may have been two or more pronunciations of a word open to Shakespeare, so there may have been two ways of acting Brutus's reception of the news of Portia's death. An open choice between alternatives must be accepted if Shakespeare's art is to be glimpsed with the lambent glow of life upon it. Except in the narrative poems, his style was not that of a bookman: his plays, for good or ill, had something of the fluid life of ballads, as the 'Bad' Quartos (whatever their origin) make plain.

Punctuation, like spelling, is no longer taken as within the editor's discretion. Alfred Thiselton first propounded the theory that Elizabethan punctuation was rhythmic rather than syntactic: Percy Simpson maintained this view in his *Shakespearian Punctuation* (1911) and stoutly defended it, as Dover Wilson also did in the first volume of the Cambridge New Shakespeare (*The Tempest*, 1921). The historical background has recently been investigated in an important article by Walter J. Ong, S.J. (*PMLA*, June 1944); in 1945 Peter Alexander, in *Shakespeare's Punctuation*, illustrated the relation of stops to style by an analysis of the Quarto and Folio versions of "What a piece of work is man!". He thinks Shakespeare's punctuation, in those texts nearest to his manuscript, is intended for the actor, not for the reader: "what Shakespeare thought suitable for the public and Lord Southampton can be studied in his *Venus and Adonis and Lucrece*". Once again we penetrate beyond the printed page to a colloquial style: but even punctuation intended for the reader will have conventions different from those of today.

In matters of pronunciation, opinion has shifted since the days of Franz and of Wilhelm Viëtor, who in 1906 published two volumes on *Shakespeare's Pronunciation*, with translations into phonetic script. The older scholars were challenged by the late R. E. Zachrisson of Uppsala (*Shakespeares Uttal*, 1914; *The English Pronunciation at Shakespeare's Time*, 1927), and more recently by Helge Kökeritz, who also attacks the English phonologist Daniel Jones. Kökeritz's work has appeared in various periodicals but his book *Shakespeare's Pronunciation* (1953) sums up his views comprehensively. He stresses the variant pronunciations open to Shakespeare; he believes with Zachrisson that Elizabethan pronunciation was much nearer to modern speech than is generally allowed. Revivals of the plays in what was taken to be original speech must thereby forgo some of their most attractive effects.

Kökeritz derives his evidence largely from puns, of which he has made a special study, and by which he claims to have solved "not a few textual cruces". Evidence on elision and stress can be gathered from song books, and an important article on this subject by E. H. Scholl appeared recently (*PMLA*, March 1948). Metrical studies, which are closely related to this subject, have been infrequent, and prosody has been left to general students of language, such as T. S. Osmond (*English Metrists*, 1906; *A Study of Metre*, 1920) and Sonnenschein. In her *Elizabethan Lyrics* (1951), however, Catherine Ing has a section on Shakespeare's songs.

Milton Crane's book on *Shakespeare's Prose* (1951), which relies upon earlier work by G. F. Krapp, Morris Croll and W. Hendrickson, surveys Shakespeare's work in relation to that of other Elizabethan dramatists. But it was journalists like Nashe who influenced him most deeply, with their acute sense of an auditory to be captivated, their variety, range and flexibility. Perhaps the most useful hints towards a study of language are not to be found in considering Euphuism, the doublet, or other traditional topics, but in glimpses towards the general development of the language afforded in Owen Barfield's *History in English Words* (1926), G. H. McKnight's *Modern English in the Making* (1928) or F. W. Bateson's *English Poetry and the English Language* (1934).

## VOCABULARY, READING AND THE POPULAR STYLE

The growing specialization of linguistic studies has meant that language and literature are too often taught separately; this has been particularly unfortunate for students of Shakespeare. Comparatively few students of language would wish to confine themselves to a single author, especially one with so complicated a textual history. A holograph of that semi-literate Stratford yokel whom Baconians delight to dishonour would be more tempting to them. Studies of the vocabularies of individual writers other than Shakespeare are even rarer, though the value of these to Shakespearian studies cannot be over-estimated. One such volume, A. H. King's *The Language of Satirized Characters in Poetaster* (1941), will indicate some of the possibilities: H. C. Hart and A. C. Partridge have worked on the vocabularies of Jonson and Shakespeare.

Recent criticism of Shakespeare's language and style shows a distinct cleavage between that stressing the colloquial and popular elements, and that emphasizing the influence of rhetorical theory, the practice of other writers, and Elizabethan doctrines of poetry. The first, developing from the work of Zachrisson and Wyld, was favoured by the general literary taste of the inter-war years, when colloquial and unpoetic language was the vogue, and James Joyce was experimenting in the novel. The second type of criticism, developing on the academic side from work into the history of ideas by Arthur Lovejoy and his school, is proving much to the taste of research students in search of subjects. Here too the general return to formality—that "rage for order" which has led Eliot from *The Waste Land* to *The Four Quartets*, and has elevated the later as against the earlier Yeats—may have helped to transform Shakespeare from a Protean entertainer of Elizabethan prentices to a hierophant, fully armed in the panoply of symbols and allegory.

A third view, originating with Croce, and with Lascelles Abercrombie's *Plea for the Liberty of Interpreting*, would cut out all historic considerations. This is the view of the New Critics in America, but the doctrine has not been for export only. In particular the great body of criticism devoted to Shakespeare's imagery has been largely written without reference to the historic context of the plays, and to the differences between Shakespeare's English and that of today. Such critics may claim to have learned Elizabethan English by the direct method—which is one of the best ways of learning it; but a direct knowledge from reading only will lack some fullness of life, especially for the understanding of a popular dramatist, as a purely linguistic approach will also miss nuances only to be gained by a knowledge of the theatre.

An unlearned, though not uneducated, Shakespeare, adapting himself to the needs of the common stages, was bound to be influenced by his audience. Hence recent works dealing with the audience are frequently concerned with style and structure; as for example S. L. Bethell, *Shakespeare and the Popular Dramatic Tradition* (1944) and Alfred Harbage, *Shakespeare's Audience* (1941), each of which, in different ways, adds a stereoscopic depth to the plays. The riches of popular speech are gathered up in W. G. Smith's *Oxford Dictionary of English Proverbs* (1935) and in Morris P. Tilley's *English Proverbs of the Sixteenth and Seventeenth Centuries* (1950); posies and mottoes were collected by Joan Evans in *English Posies and Posy Rings* (1931). George Gordon, in *Shakespeare's English* (1928) dealt chiefly with new words, as did H. C. Hart in *Stolne and Surreptitious Copies*, and in two articles on Shakespeare's vocabulary which appeared in the *Review of English Studies* in 1943. Gladys Willcock, in *Shakespeare and Elizabethan English* (in *A Companion to Shakespeare Studies*, 1934) provides the best short introduction to the subject: if her essay is compared with Henry Bradley's (written eighteen years earlier) the growth of emphasis on popular elements will be evident. Miss Willcock's and Miss Walker's preface to their edition of Puttenham's *Arte of Poesie* (1936) dilates at more length upon courtly style. On other occasions, Miss Willcock, E. C. Pettet and Alwin Thaler have stressed Shakespeare's conscious artistry (Shakespeare Association Pamphlet, 1934; *Essays and Studies*, 1949; *PMLA*, December 1938), whereas Hardin Craig sees him as working by rule of thumb (*Studies in Philology*, April 1942).

F. P. Wilson in *Shakespeare and the Diction of Common Life* (1941) stressed the value of puns, images and proverbs, three of the most frequent subjects for discussion in the following decade. His article on 'Shakespeare's Reading' (*Shakespeare Survey*, 1950) again suggests that Shakespeare learned through talk and popular channels as much as through books. The extent to which Shakespeare's speech has captured general interest may be illustrated by citing half a dozen articles which appeared recently: those of Kenneth Muir in *The Cambridge Journal* (May 1950) and M. M. Mahood in *Essays in Criticism* (July 1951), both on the pun: those of D. S. Bland in *Shakespeare Survey* (1951) and Maurice Evans in *The Cambridge Journal* (April 1951), both on colloquialisms: and two by L. S. Cormican on 'Medieval Idiom' in *Scrutiny* (Autumn 1950 and Spring 1951). None of these are by professed linguists, and some suffer from an inattention to the facts of linguistic history, but all are concerned with Shakespeare's speech in terms of his particular time and profession.

The effect of Shakespeare's contemporaries upon his style has been a topic of controversy since Malone's day. His imitation (followed by his parodies) of Euphuism and Lyly's comedy has not proved a very fruitful subject although forty years ago it was not an unpopular one. Shakespeare's supposed imitation of Beaumont and Fletcher in his last plays or the influence of Marlowe and the University wits upon the early histories are bound up with questions of the Shakespearian canon. The disintegrators, whose work in the early years of this century forms one of the curiosities of critical history, relied heavily upon arguments from style to support their case for collaboration or botching. The works of J. M. Robertson, once thought worthy of refutation by Chambers or Greg, are now hardly read at all. It is at present fashionable to claim even *Titus Andronicus* for the canon, and Hardin Craig has defended 'Shakespeare's Bad Poetry' (*Shakespeare Survey*, 1948). A far more objective use of literary tests than former critics used has recently enabled A. C. Partridge to make out a case for collaboration in *Henry VIII* (*The Problem of 'Henry VIII' Reopened*, 1949). By a strict examination of grammatical idioms (the obsolescent expletive *do*, the literary *hath*) and of Shakespeare's anacolutha, Partridge evolves an effective system of checking, based on his previous work on Jonson's vocabulary. This book is a rare example of literary-linguistic interplay.

Meanwhile, in the Cambridge New Shakespeare, Dover Wilson continues to postulate revision and rewriting of many of the plays, largely upon the evidence of conflicting styles. This rewriting, however, he quite often allows to represent Shakespeare's own second thoughts.

An annotated edition of Shakespeare is of course the best test of the swing of critical taste: the Cambridge Shakespeare was started over thirty years ago, and the new Arden edition is circumscribed by need to retain its old format; which also, to some extent, affects the volumes of the New Variorum. The differences which the last fifty years have made to editorial policy will, however, need no emphasizing to those acquainted with any of these works.

### RHETORICAL THEORY AND ELIZABETHAN DOCTRINES OF POETRY

Advocates of the popular Shakespeare stress his debt to the Bible, the Prayer Book, the Homilies, the medieval drama and folk literature. Critics with a bias towards the history of ideas investigate his debt to Wilson, Puttenham and the Ramists. Hardin Craig voted for Wilson, Thaler for Sidney: Miss Frances Yates in her study of *Love's Labour's Lost* (1936) saw Shakespeare the "villanist" opposed to the "artsmen" whom he satirized in Holofernes and Armado. Modern poetry itself has now returned to formality, and rhetoric is no longer a term of abuse. The history of W. B. Yeats's use of the word, for example, is enlightening, especially in the light of his dramatic practice. The more rhetorical of Shakespeare's contemporaries, Jonson and Chapman, Tourneur and Marston, enjoy popular favour at the expense of Heywood, Fletcher and Massinger, the nineteenth century's choice. T. S. Eliot has explored the possibilities of dramatic rhetoric in his plays and advocated it in his criticism. This revolution in general literary taste has reinforced the new understanding of Elizabethan critical theory which scholars, mainly American, have instituted. The most extensive contributions have been made by T. W. Baldwin, who in *William Shakspere's Five Act Structure* (1947), *Small Latine & Lesse Greeke* (1944) and *The Literary Genetics of Shakspere's Poems & Sonnets* (1950) has amply demonstrated the extent to which Shakespeare could draw on a knowledge of Latin authors and on classical and modern systems of rhetoric, grammar and logic. For the Elizabethans, poetic theory and rhetorical theory were closely combined; the Orator as hero was no mere figure for bookmen in days when a man might have to rely on his own efforts to plead for his life; the practice of listening to sermons and court cases meant that even the uneducated would have a trained ear, and the series of experiments by which the Elizabethans evolved their great literary forms in the nineties had been planned by poets like Gascoigne and Spenser, by the practice of noblemen and travellers, and by popular journalists such as Nashe and Greene. Baldwin himself is not concerned with the general literary development of the Elizabethan age, but with its educational grounding: in fact it is sometimes doubtful whether Shakespeare is illustrating the history of ideas or the history of ideas is illustrating Shakespeare. Nevertheless, his work ensures a full appreciation of the precise theoretic and literary aids which were open to Shakespeare: it answers the old query of the nature of his reading.

In a study which rests upon Baldwin's work, *Shakespeare and the Arts of Language* (1947), Sister Miriam Joseph C.S.C. investigates in detail Shakespeare's use of schemes, figures, topics of invention, argumentation, pathos and ethos. She is concerned simply to record and tabulate the extent to which the practice of rhetoric and logic may be illustrated from the works of Shakespeare, and neither to estimate its relative significance nor to survey its development: she has done for him what E. K. did for Spenser: "a pretty Epanorthosis and withal a Paronomasia" etc. Others have explored Shakespeare's use of particular devices, such as the Oration (Milton Boone Kennedy, *The Oration in Shakespeare*, 1942) or the Monologue (Warren Smith, *Shakespeare Association Bulletin*, October 1949). A. Sackton has also examined the works of Jonson from a rhetorical point of view (*Rhetoric as a Dramatic Language in Ben Jonson*, 1948), and has written (*University of Texas Studies*, 1949) on the Paradoxical Encomium in Elizabethan Drama. A comparative study of rhetorical figures in Elizabethan poets may eventually be expected, but much remains to be done. The literary quarrels of Harvey and Nashe, the Poetomachia, and the value of parody—especially in Shakespeare's own works—would all be relevant here. One of the chief needs is a full study of the learned poets, Chapman and Jonson.[2]

The formidable scholarship of Rosemond Tuve in her *Elizabethan and Metaphysical Imagery* (1947) is not directed specifically upon Shakespeare: she is concerned with the history of aesthetic theory and its relation to the non-dramatic poets of Shakespeare's day, but her discussion of the concept of decorum, the garment of style and the doctrine of "ut pictura poesis" is bound to affect the reading of all Elizabethan poetry. She represents the extreme Right in critical scholarship, and speaks for the "Artsmen". The relation of poetic theory to the practice of the popular stages (and indeed of poetic theory to poetic practice at any time) is a subject that inflames the passions; Miss Tuve's views have not been unchallenged, and the dramatic genre in any case raises special problems which have not yet been fully worked out. Certainly the older views of a primitive dramatic structure, as put forward by Stoll and Schücking, now lie in considerable danger. One of the by-products of the new interest in rhetoric has been its effect upon modern conceptions of Elizabethan acting. Alfred Harbage, who favoured a formal type of acting, has been followed by Bethell and B. L. Joseph, who in *Shakespeare's Acting* (1951) virtually identified the actor's art with that of the orator.

In exploring the various kinds of Elizabethan drama—history, comedy, tragedy, pastoral and the rest of Polonius's catalogue—the rhetoricians have helped especially to a better understanding of the problem plays. *Measure for Measure* has emerged as fully "doctrinal" according to the best Elizabethan prescriptions from the scrutiny of Roy Battenhouse and Elizabeth Pope. The study of *Hamlet* in relation to other revenge plays, which was begun by Thorndike and Stoll and carried on by Lily B. Campbell, Percy Simpson and Fredson Bowers, depends partly on the continuity of theme, and partly on stock phrases, recurrent images and lines. Continuity of doctrine is inseparable from traditions of style in Revenge drama, for this was a pragmatic literary definition, one evolved within the theatre itself. The work of Dover Wilson, Tillyard and Lily B. Campbell on the English histories, if it is chiefly concerned with the recovery of older patterns of thought and belief, is also dependent partly upon the Elizabethan view of the moral end of poetry. Comedy has received least attention, but E. C. Pettet, in his little book on *Shakespeare and the Romance Tradition* (1949) discusses Shakespeare in relation to the romantic comedies of Lyly and Greene. *In Shakespeare and Spenser* (1950) W. B. C. Watkins compares the two poets in their use of common themes and images, and their common interest in the craft of language. Like Tillyard and others, Watkins sees in Shakespeare the continuing influence of late medieval literary forms.

## SYMBOLISM, IMAGERY AND AMBIVALENCE

It may be said that while exploration of theatrical conditions was the outstanding feature of Shakespearian criticism in the first three decades of this century, the exploration of language and style has been gaining ground since that time and now predominates. Of this study, one of the most important branches is the examination of imagery, sometimes in historic terms, but more often in Crocean independence of time, place or background. An investigation of similes and metaphor was anticipated as long ago as 1794 by Walter Whiter, it was foreshadowed by Coleridge in some of the most famous chapters of *Biographia Literaria*, but not developed. Suddenly, about 1930, several works appeared, all dealing with related aspects of this subject. In her little pamphlet, *Some Recent Research in Shakespeare's Imagery* (1937), Una Ellis-Fermor described the first stages of the movement. Spread and development of interest has led the intrepid explorers into the paths of psychology, anthropology, mythology and Jungian metaphysics: image-clusters, or unconscious associations of words have been tracked down: Shakespeare's fellow-dramatists have been put to the question: there has been a vast deal of repetition and much disagreement. (As Kenneth Muir noted, two critics will interpret the disease imagery of *Hamlet* in totally different ways.)

One of the earliest works on these lines was George Rylands's *Words and Poetry* (1928), which had as subtitle to Part II, 'Notes and Quotations preparatory to a study of Shakespeare's diction and style'. While citing parallels from Marlowe, Spenser and others, Rylands was not really concerned with Shakespeare's contemporaries or even with himself *qua* Elizabethan—rather as one who contained in himself the seed of development, and was not of an age but for all time. His article, 'Shakespeare's Poetry' in *A Companion to Shakespeare Studies* reaffirms the position, showing Shakespeare's progress "from conceit to metaphor".

The work of Caroline Spurgeon, beginning with a couple of essays in 1930 and 1931, culminated in her book *Shakespeare's Imagery and what it tells us* (1935). It was preceded by writings of Colin Still, F. C. Kolbe and Elizabeth Holmes, and contemporary with those of Wilson Knight and Wolfgang Clemen. (*The Wheel of Fire*, 1930; *The Imperial Theme*, 1931; *The Shakespearean Tempest*, 1932 by Knight; *Shakespeares Bilder*, 1936 by Clemen.)

Many criticisms have been levelled at Miss Spurgeon's book as being too tabulated, too close to the card index, and for the way in which poetry is used as an aid to build a picture of Shakespeare the man; but her death cut short Miss Spurgeon's work when it was yet uncompleted. Yet *Shakespeare's Imagery* remains, as a first survey, indispensable to students of the subject. Its chief contribution was the concept of imagery as undersong, seen at its most potent in the main tragedies, but traceable throughout Shakespeare's work. Miss Spurgeon's friend and successor Una Ellis-Fermor has worked out some of the implications in *The Frontiers of Drama* (1945).

Wilson Knight saw the plays as constituting a single vast design, held together by certain symbols. Imagery, action and character are all parts of the design. His writing had therefore a unity, and a fiery quality which stimulated readers to enthusiasm or to violent disagreement. For Knight each play embodied a vision of the mystery of things: Shakespeare was in the exact sense a metaphysical poet, whose last plays were the consummation of all his art. With this impassioned conviction, Knight essayed a close scrutiny of the text: he traced imagery from great central statements like the soliloquies of Hamlet and Macbeth down to evanescent hints in the speech of minor characters. His influence has been far-reaching: it is behind much of the work of the so-called 'Cambridge school' and much modern American criticism. Few will go all the way with Knight; but in his elucidation of the problem plays and the final romances, he decisively changed the course of critical thought.

Wolfgang Clemen's book, translated in 1951, was primarily a study in the chronological development of Shakespeare's use of imagery, and differed in this respect from the books of the two preceding writers. Each play is approached in the manner dictated by its own form: thus, in *Hamlet* and *Othello* imagery is studied as it serves to distinguish character: in *Antony and Cleopatra* and *King Lear* the use is more complex, the variety greater, and the world of the play more entirely created and displayed through this means. Clemen is in search of "a truly organic method of understanding the images". Where Caroline Spurgeon aims at comprehensiveness, Knight at exaltation to a poetic rapture, Clemen is both sober and sensitive, and though the effect of his book was not so startling, it may in the long run become less dated. In her *Jacobean Drama* (1936) Una Ellis-Fermor applied this method to the final plays and Tillyard followed suit with his volume on *Shakespeare's Last Plays* (1938). S. L. Bethell and D. Traversi have both studied *The Winter's Tale* at length (the latter more particularly in his *Approach to Shakespeare*, 1938). The students of leading themes and recurrent images were not long content with a merely literary approach. To read the plays through theme and imagery was an invitation to all kinds of doctrinal irrelevances. Shakespeare has always had the power to attract to himself the whole mind of his readers, and the generosity to accommodate their most irrelevant interests; this mode of reading releases the fantastical student from some of the limiting effects of plot and character, not to mention the exigences of stage production. *The Winter's Tale* as vegetation myth, *Hamlet* as dramatization of the Oedipus complex, the resolution of the problem plays as if they were dreams of a patient undergoing psychoanalysis, and of the romances as the fine flower of a World Congress of Faiths—such were the aberrations of the wilder disciples.

During the 1930's Shakespeare the playwright was sunk in Shakespeare the poet: this may have been in reaction from the great emphasis laid upon theatrical conditions in the preceding two decades. Imagery and theme are also, however, the binding forces in the work of the most influential poets of the day; and as Browning's age saw in Shakespeare a great delineator of

B

character, so the age of Eliot and Yeats saw him as the poet of tempests and music, of the king and the beggar man, of blood and sunlight, his creed expressed in Ulysses's speech on order and degree, but his practice more amply mirrored in the scenes upon the blasted heath in *King Lear*. Paradox, dichotomy and ambivalence, polarity and integration were favourite terms of the new critical diction. Since the students of imagery were Crocean in their disregard of the life and thought of Shakespeare's day, they found themselves directly opposed to the rhetoricians: in America this has developed into a controversy between the New Critics who advocate an aesthetic-psychological approach to literature and more traditional students of 'background' and the history of ideas. These last may engage (Irish-fashion) in a quiet little battle on their own. See, for example, F. R. Johnson in *English Studies Today* (ed. Warner and Bullough, 1951): he takes on Mrs Forest, who had taken on Miss Campbell and Co. The conflict is by no means limited to Shakespearian studies. A general statement of the position is given in Lionel Trilling's 'The Sense of the Past' (*The Liberal Imagination*, 1948). Both schools have their own type of pedantry; both risk the substitution of explanation for interpretation. The increasing numbers of research students must yet each be provided with a subject; the increasing number of university teachers who march under the banner 'Publish or Perish' must attempt to survive. *The American Scholar* for the summer of 1951 contains a wicked parody by 'Thomas Kyd' of New York City (now of Harvard) in which the "laminated imagery" of *Antony and Cleopatra* is resolved into "the Chaos Pattern, the Bed-clothes Pattern, the Insect Pattern, the Alcoholic Beverages Pattern and the Card-Game Pattern". (For parody from the opposite camp see Hereward T. Price, *Construction in Shakespeare*, 1949.) The lessons of the Marprelate controversy have not been lost, it seems. Recent development of criticism through imagery may be most profitably studied in the work of Cleanth Brooks, R. B. Heilman, the late Donald Stauffer in America: in England, Roy Walker, with some of the fiery enthusiasm of Wilson Knight but with a more developed interest in presentation, has written of *Hamlet* and *Macbeth*. Frank O'Connor in *The Road to Stratford* (1949) gaily trails his coat, reviving that sinister figure, the collaborator—who turns out to be Henry Condell—and indulging in a reckless game of parallel citations: but he applies to the plays a true theatrical sense, and the lively challenge to professional scholars of an artist is nowadays as welcome as it is rare.

In the early work of I. A. Richards, a technique of "practical criticism" was worked out by which individual poems could be analysed closely in terms of the reader's experience. I. A. Richards's most distinguished pupil is William Empson, whose *Seven Types of Ambiguity* appeared in 1930. Here, and in his two other books, *Some Versions of Pastoral* (1935) and *The Structure of Complex Words* (1952), Empson deals with certain passages from Shakespeare, especially in *Henry IV*, the *Sonnets*, the four main tragedies, *Timon* and *The Tempest*. Multiple meanings are sought through syntactical ambiguities, puns and paradoxes: the implications of key words ("fool" in *Lear*, "honest" in *Othello*) are explored with the ruthless ingenuity of a mathematician in search of every possible variation. At times Empson's mixture of sensitiveness and virtuosity can produce really startling interpretations: he is as deeply dyed with Freud as the imagists are with Jung, and his liveliness and dexterity are particularly suited to an analysis of dramatic speech. In his last book he shows some concern for the historical evolution of meanings, but on the other hand he is not trained as a historian of language and some shots go wide.

His influence has been widespread, and inevitably he has come into conflict with the more historically-minded students of literature. He and Miss Tuve have exchanged a few remarks in various reviews and she has recently (1952) set out a full-length refutation of one of his most dashing shockers, the analysis of Herbert's 'Sacrifice' in *Seven Types of Ambiguity*. Here Empson's taste for ambivalence (a word he put into circulation) has certainly exposed him to fire.

F. R. Leavis, L. C. Knights and others who during the last twenty years have written in the Cambridge periodical *Scrutiny* have dealt with Shakespeare in a manner related to that of Empson and Richards. A few sentences from an early essay of Knights may indicate the line of approach. "*Character*—like *plot, rhythm, construction* and all our other critical counters—is merely an abstraction from the total response in the mind of the reader or spectator...our duty as critics is to examine first the words of which the play is composed, then the total effect which this combination of words produces in our minds." "A Shakespeare play is a dramatic poem." "*Macbeth* is a statement of evil." "*Macbeth* has greater affinity with *The Waste Land* than with *The Doll's House*." Such a method—delicate, concentrated and concerned always to reach the evaluative judgement—has great possibilities. It has also, especially when applied to drama, its own limitations.

Only through examination of particular passages could a true history of poetic and literary language, that is to say a history of style, be achieved. It would require control by historic and linguistic disciplines. It would require also to treat these disciplines as servants, not as masters. Such a history is far more easily communicated by word of mouth—for reading aloud is an essential part of it—than it ever could be transmitted in book form.

A teacher in a training college recently said: "My dilemma is this—shall I teach the students to read, or shall I give them the background?". This is the dilemma upon which the study of Shakespeare's style is at present impaled, and a comprehensive and interpretative work is the first need. The time is ripe for a volume which should stand with Chambers on the stage, with Pollard and McKerrow and Greg on the texts.

## NOTES

1. In referring to the "terrifying accumulation of discussion and elucidation of Shakespeare's language" (below, p. 12), Miss Willcock has measured by implication the yet more terrifying accumulation upon other Shakespearian topics.

2. Some important studies of Chapman, still unpublished, were produced at a Symposium on his work organized by Professor D. J. Gordon at the University of Reading in March 1952. The range of this poet's work and interests would tax the learning and imaginative sympathy of any individual. Mention may be made, however, of the pioneer study of Jean Jacquot (*George Chapman*, Paris, 1951), though its interest is not primarily in style. The student of Jonson has now an invaluable instrument in the completed *Works* as edited by Herford and Simpson, the last volume of which appeared in 1952. Hallett Smith's *Elizabethan Poetry* (1952) is a valuable study of non-dramatic poetry from the rhetorician's point of view and in his British Academy Annual Shakespeare Lecture for 1951, *Shakespeare's Poetic Energy*, George Rylands stressed the connections between Shakespeare and the non-dramatic poets of his time.

# SHAKESPEARE AND ELIZABETHAN ENGLISH

BY

## GLADYS D. WILLCOCK

Shakespeare's language is proving one of the most germinal topics in present-day Shakespeare studies and there is a stimulating variety of approach. For those who have wearied of the incessant detective work expended on the Elizabethan setting and in attempts to probe Shakespeare's life-history, certain new tendencies and principles in literary criticism offer a refreshing alternative to the historical approach and seem to set the poet free from the bondage of Time and Change. Yet the language is basic and this language is Elizabethan. Wherever the critic ends, he must begin from a recognition of the Elizabethan factors in the language; he may, indeed, as in the recent rehabilitation of the pun, be moved to exploit them. In what follows I shall try to illustrate these Elizabethan factors and I have before me two primary objects or beliefs: first, the necessity of keeping continually in mind the *oral* aspects of Shakespeare's language, originally conceived in the mind for an actor's voice and published to the world on an actor's lips; and, secondly, the conviction that the best solvent of pedantry is not less knowledge but more—that the more we know of the Elizabethan mind as it worked on and through language the more difficult it becomes to rivet on to Shakespeare certain modern pedantries.

It is a stimulating approach to the subject to form in the mind some conception of the terrifying accumulation of discussion and elucidation of Shakespeare's language summarized in an up-to-date bibliography and then to turn back to the impressions which this same language made on his contemporaries and immediate successors. A few brief but very well-known passages will be sufficient:[1] "an absolute *Iohannes fac totum*" who "supposes he is as well able to bombast out a blanke verse as the best of you"; "sugred Sonnets among his priuate friends"; "a happie imitator of Nature...a most gentle expresser of it...what he thought, he vttered with that easinesse, that wee haue scarce receiued from him a blot in his papers"; "Nature her selfe was proud of his designes, And ioy'd to weare the dressing of his lines"; "an open, and free nature...an excellent *Phantsie*, brave notions and gentle expressions: wherein he flow'd with that facility, that sometime it was necessary he should be stop'd;" "sweetest Shakespear, fancies childe, [warbling] his native Wood-notes wilde"; "whilst toth' shame of slow-endeavouring art, Thy easie numbers flow".

These "easie numbers" now require a library of exegesis for their interpretation. To a very large extent the reason lies, of course, in the 'now'—in time which antiquates antiquities. But this is by no means the whole explanation. That a poet need not be 'easy' to contemporaries and difficult to posterity needs no labouring. A more interesting clue lies in the fact that the emphasis on nature and ease comes with the Jacobean and early Caroline quotations—that is, with the passage of the first interval of time. It is the first achievement of perspective; it is, I believe, a recognition of Shakespeare's Elizabethanism, an Elizabethanism which he relinquished more reluctantly than other poets and dramatists born in or near his decade, such as Chapman. The quotations show the Elizabethan impression of confidence, 'sweetness', versatility merging into the Jacobean sense of easy flow and gentle expression, of Nature almost untrammelled.

The comparison with Nature may be held to imply a recognition of range; apart from this there is no hint of appreciation of the Shakespearian sweep from native woodnotes to the fierce dispute betwixt damnation and impassion'd clay—almost as if the plays from about 1601 to about 1609 failed to modify the impression made by those written before and after. Though the shaking of the stage under Shakespeare's 'buskin' is not overlooked, these comments may well seem to us deficient in explicit appreciation of Shakespeare's tragic language. Whatever may be the explanation of this, there can be no doubt that the impact of Shakespeare on those who could see his plays while his own fellow-actors were still on the boards left the impression of Nature herself at work, and for my present purpose it is interesting to note the predominating extent to which this impression is translated into terms of language: "gentle expression", "easie numbers", "woodnotes" etc. The eighteenth century, with its social orientation and growing sense of human potentialities, translated the same conviction of Nature into terms of character and understanding of life. The nineteenth century greatly complicated the responses to Shakespeare and the connotations of the word 'Nature' underwent subtle but far-reaching alterations. The complication is proceeding apace. Shakespeare is made to respond to every 'ology' as it appears, but we remain in easier moods habituated to the older notion and may therefore on turning back to the early critics miss some of their tone and quality through forgetfulness of the revolutions that lie between. The revolution in linguistic conditions is at least as drastic as any other.

When the Jacobeans, speaking of Shakespeare, juxtaposed 'Nature' and 'ease' it is clear that they recognized in his language to an especial degree the quality of spontaneity. It is a quality that is often ascribed to the Elizabethan language at large. Augustan critics complained of its licence; modern critics of a genial and expansive turn are attracted by its scope and liberty and will write as if it were an inspiring linguistic jungle, with Shakespeare as the Bandit King thereof: "in the rankness and wildness of the language he found his opportunity".[2] I must leave on one side how far the whole Elizabethan period can ever be brought under one generalization and examine this jungle theory.

The hierarchical organization of society, the all-penetrating concept of 'Degree', must have had important consequences in language as in social and personal life. Speech must have followed behaviour and been correspondingly formalized and subject to conventions. There were, of course, the unbuttoned moments, but Elizabethan letters and many recorded scraps of conversation show continual 'my lordings' and 'your gracings' between equals, with the appropriate adaptations of diction and sentence-structure, and children were expected to express themselves with almost grovelling servility. Many people listened to elaborate linguistic virtuosity in sermons and public orations and expected language in general to rise to its occasions. The artificial and the rhetorical aroused no instinctive distrust. These social or public conventions not only governed and modified style; they must have strengthened the hold of convention on language in general. They lessened incentive to 'cut the cackle'. When blunt speech might be dangerously impolitic as well as impolite many men must have practised assiduously how by indirections to find directions out. It would be an interesting calculation to assess from letters, dedications and state papers how much Elizabethan energy went into linguistic windlasses and assays of bias. All this must have maintained a wide gamut of social tones; it conduces to that impression of range left on us by Elizabethan speech. It has a pretty obvious bearing on the

B *

language of the dramatists and the tracing of it lends a new interest to Shakespeare's chronicle plays, where he runs through a wide range of social types from king to common soldier and where there are frequent state occasions and much parleying between rival parties and bandying of honorific titles. The audience, so far as we can tell, expected to hear the appropriate language for all this and seems to have put no pressure on the dramatist to sacrifice language to action. It is true that there is textual evidence showing that plays were frequently shortened for acting by docking the speeches—this is the simplest theatrical method of meeting time limits—but plenty was left. That influential sections of the audience came to the theatre prepared to distribute their attention pretty evenly between language and action is indicated not only by protracted passages of verbal play but also by the continued popularity of the *tirade*, or lyric or epic set speech, from Kyd to Beaumont and Fletcher. This is all, of course, stage-language, but the pervading sense of Degree in the background of life must have provided nuances and contrasts which we fail to catch. However we divide our interest and sympathy in *Henry IV* between the blank verse of battle and policy and the prose of Eastcheap, I doubt if, without a little effort of the imagination, we can recapture the quality to the first Elizabethan listener of Falstaff's opening words to Prince Henry:

> Now, Hal, what time of day is it, lad? (*1 Henry IV*, I, ii, 1)

This was emancipation with a vengeance, as 'romantically' out of the ordinary as Caliban's "the isle is full of noises" (*Tempest*, III, ii, 144).

When we turn to the language of books we are, of course, faced with a more extensive body of evidence. Histories of the language sort out the principal factors that contribute to the language that Shakespeare was to inherit and use: the growing interest in the vernacular, learned and popular influences, particularly the influence of Latin, the expansion of vocabulary, the contributions of the poets, translators and travellers. The general impression is one of vigour, range and growth. But, as we saw in considering the spoken language, range, if it be a range of conventions, is not the same thing as liberty; it is certainly not 'wildness'.

It is not necessary to look far before finding evidence in the period leading up to Shakespeare for the domination in the literary language of convention, artifice and studied complication. A few names and notions will recall the trend of things during Shakespeare's adolescence: Wilson's *Arte of Rhetorique* (1553) and its numerous successors, Gascoigne's *Certain Notes of Instruction concerning the making of English verse* (1575), Puttenham's *Arte of English Poesie* (1589); among the 'notions': Imitation, Decorum, Art in its Elizabethan sense.

The Elizabethan Arts of Rhetoric are not to be thought of as the pedantic diversions of a few schoolmasters. Latin rhetoric was, of course, a school and university subject, but it was the deliberate and expressed object of the producers of the vernacular rhetorics to bring the subject from the school to the world, and there is no doubt that the world, in so far as that was literate, welcomed it. The Art was offered to adult men and women not only as a guide to the improvement of English but as a means of enhancing the enjoyment of the spoken and written word. The word 'Art' in titles and texts is to be given its full Elizabethan concreteness. 'Art' was 'Craft'; the *Arte of English Poesie* was a manual of prosody and rhetoric for the budding poet. Educated Elizabethans could quote glibly enough the tag *poeta nascitur non fit*, but they were by no means minded to leave heredity to work unaided.

Lyly's *Euphues and his England* will enable a half-century of taste and strenuous cultivation of language to be crystallized in a paragraph:[3]

Among a number of ladies he fixed his eyes upon one, whose countenance seemed to promise mercy and threaten mischief, intermeddling a desire of liking with a disdain of love: showing herself in courtesy to be familiar with all, and with a certain comely pride to accept none....But such a one she was as almost they all are that serve so noble a Prince; such virgins carry lights before such a *Vesta*, such nymphs arrows with such a *Diana*.

This is not jungle language. We can more aptly compare it to an Italian garden, complete even to the mythological statuary disposed at the end of brief vistas.

This paragraph shows clearly how prominent in this rhetoric-shadowed language was the scheme as well as the trope—indeed in Lyly's prose the patternings and sequences of words are more assiduously practised than the mental transferences which to-day take first place as figures of speech. In the poets there is naturally a better balance between scheme and trope and in Shakespeare the master-trope of metaphor plays from the beginning the major role. Nevertheless, the love of patterning is conspicuous in all those plays which overlap with the work of the University Wits:

> Ay, but she's come to beg, Warwick, to give;
> She, on his left side, craving aid for Henry,
> He, on his right, asking a wife for Edward.
> She weeps, and says her Henry is deposed;
> He smiles, and says his Edward is install'd.     (*3 Henry VI*, III, i, 42–6)

In such a passage the very thinness of the substance and the prosiness of the names emphasize the exploitation of the absorbing interest in patterned language to get dramatist and actor through intractable chronicle material.

Shakespeare's early plays, particularly the Histories, reveal a certain fluid distinction between types of elaborate diction in addition to the obvious formal distinction between verse and prose. Kings and princes, ambassadors, papal legates and bishops, councillors and barons conduct their affairs in a language which is heightened by every device cultivated at that period: striking metaphor, bold simile, high-astounding terms, mythological allusions, replacement of the small change of language (such as pronouns) by names and synonyms, the grandiloquence of honorific titles. The minor tropes and the schemes play their part (as has been shown) but the dominant impression is that of pomp and amplitude. The marching and countermarching are done to this language; it is the medium of leadership, policy and business. It can be called the 'language of estate'. Ordinary citizens will use it when they are, as it were, caught up in the machine of state: *1 Henry VI* opens with a dead march and the Duke of Bedford declaiming

> Hung be the heavens with black, yield day to night!
> Comets, importing change of times and states,
> Brandish your crystal tresses in the sky,
> And with them scourge the bad revolting stars....

But dukes have no monopoly of such language. In *2 Henry VI*, IV, i, a sea-captain notices that night is coming on:

> The gaudy, blabbing and remorseful day
> Is crept into the bosom of the sea;
> And now loud-howling wolves arouse the jades
> That drag the tragic melancholy night.... (1-4)

and in *Richard II* (III, iv, 29) a gardener bids his mate

> Go, bind thou up yon dangling apricocks....

On the other hand, more strongly patterned language tends to occur in emotional contexts, in lyrical and reflective passages. Henry VI and Richard II in royal elegiac mood use a wide selection of the figures of Amplification patterned by appropriate schemes such as Anaphora:

> So many hours must I tend my flock;
> So many hours must I take my rest;
> So many hours must I contemplate;
> So many hours must I sport myself.... (*3 Henry VI*, II, v, 31-4)

Strong feelings such as scorn or indignation will often find pointed schematic expression:

> For I am sick and capable of fears,
> Oppress'd with wrongs and therefore full of fears,
> A widow, husbandless, subject to fears,
> A woman, naturally born to fears.... (*King John*, III, i, 12-15)

The patterns are used to strike the note of love. In *King John*, II, i, in a long scene of estate, a citizen of Angiers, who in the rest of his speech shows himself a master of the language of estate, promotes the match between Blanch and the Dauphin in a few lines of Euphuism cut into lengths of blank verse:

> If lusty love should go in quest of beauty,
> Where should he find it fairer than in Blanch?
> If zealous love should go in search of virtue,
> Where should he find it purer than in Blanch?
> If love ambitious sought a match of birth,
> Whose veins bound richer blood than Lady Blanch? (II, i, 426-31)

The patterning of love-language can naturally be more abundantly illustrated from the comedies. Corresponding to the language of estate we have here a full and diversified style varied by whatever figures serve the turn and adapt it to the palace, the 'orchard' or the street. This is the diction of dukes and counts, of well-to-do fathers and mothers. It is the young men, particularly when falling in or out of love, whose feelings sweep them into the schemes:

> And why not death rather than living torment?
> To die is to be banish'd from myself;
> And Silvia is myself: banish'd from her
> Is self from self: a deadly banishment!
> What light is light, if Silvia be not seen?
> What joy is joy, if Silvia be not by?...

> Except I be by Silvia in the night,
> There is no music in the nightingale;
> Unless I look on Silvia in the day,
> There is no day for me to look upon;  (*Two Gentlemen*, III, i, 170–81)

The young people in these plays might be said to speak more conventionally than their elders; at least they display a more obvious artifice, and this artifice they pursue, not because they do not have feelings but because they have. Here undoubtedly Shakespeare is striking a note of fashion; we are linked with the sonneteering world. Hyperbole, lyricism, we expect; we should call them 'natural'. We find both, but built into controlled movements and patterns, which, however rapidly Shakespeare's pen constructed them, carry the association of a stylized Court, not of a jungle.

If we pause here to ask how this use of language—of which *ars est celare artem* could never have been said—gave rise to notions of nature and ease or of unfettered wildness, there are, of course, several answers. First, I have been considering only one aspect of Elizabethan use of language at a particular turn in its evolution. I have dealt only with Shakespeare's early plays and everyone knows that his style underwent a gradual but fundamental revolution. This chronological development, however, must have been very largely masked from the Jacobeans. Secondly, language is not the whole matter. Thirdly (the only reason I can develop here), the qualities which we, as it were, *translate* as spontaneity, even wildness, are conveyed in Shakespeare and in other writers by the zest with which their exacting games were played, by the range of tones and consequent variety, and by the spendthrift energy. A very large proportion of Elizabethan vigour flowed into language; it flowed not only from men-of-letters but from speakers and listeners. The dramatic language of the Marlowe-early Shakespeare phase can only be fully understood and appreciated as a co-operative effort of poet and audience. Language was the principal approach to Art; language the most widely-apprehended introduction to Design. However much enthusiasm lightened labour, the effort was there—in the acquisition, the learning from Arts and manuals, in the Imitation of models and of each other, in the practised listening and aural dissection of the elements of fine speaking. It was because this approach to Art sought to unite grave affairs, even passion, with open artifice and verbal play that the Augustans fell foul of it in Shakespeare's case and missed the element of Art. This gives a particular interest to some opinions of Ben Jonson omitted from my earlier list. They come in very relevantly here. Jonson in many ways prepared the ground for the Augustans, but he knew the living, working and talking Shakespeare. On the subject of Shakespeare, Nature and Art he speaks with two voices. To Drummond he confided that Shakespeare wanted Art; to his commonplace book he confided the wish that he had blotted a thousand lines—which is to the same effect. When he was composing the commendatory verses prefixed to the First Folio, the exigencies of the occasion compelled him to stiffen the analogy with Nature by finding proofs of Art. He found them in this field of language—in the wrestling with, the conquest of, expression:

> he,
> Who casts to write a liuing line, must sweat,
> (such as thine are) . . . .

Undoubtedly Shakespeare 'sweated' rapidly; the evidence for this is unimpeachable. But in that truly characteristic language, in which Jonson saw the mirror of Shakespeare's "minde and manners", there was *work*, the exertion of strength, the adaptation of means to end.

The discipline and conscious elaboration associated with the rhetorical side of Elizabethan speech are, of course, only one aspect of the development of the language. Even here the delight accompanying achievement has brought us close to the idea or quality of spontaneity. From other linguistic fields the conditions of freedom and variability then prevailing may now be illustrated.

During the mid-Tudor period Saxon purists had endeavoured to stop the recruitment of the language by adaptations from foreign and ancient languages. For a time they were astonishingly influential, but by the eighties the Saxon shield-wall had everywhere given way and the foreigners were swarming through the breaches. Coinage now became rampant. We think of Shakespeare as a prolific and daring coiner of neologisms, but every writer of any pretensions to range or substance was busy adding to the stock. Shakespeare took what he wanted where he found it, but was not concerned to build up a specifically poetic diction, which is one of the reasons why his words went home to men's business and bosoms. All this has been abundantly illustrated in many books and articles on Shakespeare's language and I wish to do no more here than to recall it and set it in its place. There were elements of redundancy and confusion in it, in Shakespeare as in his contemporaries, but in such a heyday of expansion the chaos might easily have been greater. That it was not, I attribute to the long, slow growth of a certain critical sense in language during the mid-Tudor period. When the barriers went down the expansion was led by men who had acquired the feel of the language and acknowledged some responsibility.

When we turn from vocabulary to other fields of language, we find striking differences between the sixteenth-century state of affairs and ours to which less justice is generally done. The points which I shall collect now will be found all to relate to one central problem, Uniformity, or the validity of any idea of Correctness as applied to Elizabethan speech.

There is a tendency to look back upon the Elizabethan period as a golden age of language, and perhaps rightly if we limit the period to a generation or so born within ten years of 1560. In the works of Shakespeare and Bacon we have a superb use of the English medium—indeed, the supreme use in our history. In letters, state papers, even depositions in law courts, in anecdotes and *obiter dicta* of men well known and men obscure we are often astonished by a rhythm, a choice of picturesque phrase, a subtlety of sheer verbal approach, which incline us to think that the relations between a poet and his public then must have been very different from those of which poets complain today. It was, I have no doubt, easier, though not necessarily more prosperous, to be a poet then. No admirer of this excellence, however, would deny that its distribution was patchy. There is an enormous body of Elizabethan writing which is, except for professional purposes, unreadable. The conditions of the time were, so to speak, providentially adapted to nourish the genius of men of the calibre of Shakespeare, Bacon and Donne. They left smaller men to flounder as they could. The anonymous lyrics of the song-books show, indeed, how the alternative traditions, discipline and techniques of music guided the lyrical impulses of otherwise undistinguished men into graceful and spirited form. Large-scale works, however, particularly in prose, will generally strike the modern reader as 'thick'—dense with pressure of vocabulary and allusion, with parentheses and piled up clauses. A good deal has been made of the lack of a standard prose style, such as the English have possessed since the time of Dryden, though the definition of a standard style is often left a little nebulous. By a standard prose style must be meant a flexible but normalizing habit setting general limits to the endurable length of sentences, favouring certain preferences as to usage and structure, restraining excess in figure and parenthesis and, above all, establishing a certain nexus between prose and the educated spoken language. A prose that could serve this turn was early achieved by Shakespeare, but the spoken dramatic prose existed in too distinct a category to be of benefit in the world of books. And his contemporaries, in any case, did not want a 'standard' prose as defined above. It would have meant throwing half the delights of *elocutio* overboard; they would not have wanted it because the idea of Uniformity in the linguistic field was as yet alien.

This statement may seem to conflict with the known facts that grammarians and orthoepists had, since the mid-century, been airing their views on the writing and pronunciation of English, and that Puttenham in the *Arte of English Poesie* had recognized the existence of a standard form of English. Of the orthoepists, some were men of academic and social weight like Sir Thomas Smith, friend of Cheke and Ascham; others were men of vigorous and even original minds like Mulcaster; many were, however, men of narrow experience and unrealistic outlook whose writings merely darken counsel. There is no evidence that they formed a sufficiently coherent body of doctrine to impose any unifying influence on the living and growing organism of speech. Mulcaster is the most interesting and best-informed writer on the contemporary language after Puttenham, with, for a schoolmaster of those days, a truly remarkable capacity to accept the facts of the English language as they were. A number of authors, major and minor, passed through his hands at St Paul's and Merchant Taylors', but no common impress can be traced in them, and his most important pupil, Spenser, as soon as he emerged from tutelage, took an independent line. Undoubtedly the chief interest to us of these 'linguists' is the testimony they collectively afford to the growing preoccupation with all sorts of language questions during the early and mid-Elizabethan periods. It is quite true that some of them are looking for an authority to impose uniformity, and draw up rules—this was especially the case with the classical prosodists—but in doing so they make it abundantly clear that no such authority existed and that the times were unpropitious to it.

Puttenham's well-known remarks in his chapter 'Of Language' in Book III of the *Arte* leave us in no doubt as to the conditions prevailing and fit admirably with other evidence. He prescribes for the poet a standard language—"the vsual speach of the Court, and that of London and the shires lying about London within xl. myles, and not much aboue". His distinction is not, of course, purely regional: a little earlier the poet has been told to follow generally "the better brought vp sort...men ciuill and graciously behauoured and bred". Here, we may say, there is a centralizing influence and standardization is clearly on the way. In the field of the literary language Puttenham does no more than acknowledge the results of a process which had been in progress for a century and a half. The state of affairs which had prevailed in the fourteenth century, when two great poets such as Chaucer and the author of *Gawain and the Green Knight* wrote, not only two markedly different styles, but in different dialects, was past. Elizabethan books retain little dialectal colouring and even the manuscripts, showing far greater variability, do not carry many dialectal signs of place of origin or scribal history. But it is important to be clear how much is covered by Puttenham's 'standard'. First, it is intended only to hold for the written language and accepts for this the London dialect of educated people: that is, the vocabulary, the inflexions and grammatical usages of that district and class. Secondly, it has no reference to style and structure. It was compatible with the utmost individual stylistic variation. Thirdly, to Puttenham this language is not the prescription of any authority nor governed by any 'rules'. He does not claim that it is to be adopted because it is the best type of English in all respects. Purer English was *spoken* north of Trent; nevertheless the writer must use Southern. The ramifications of Court business in those days, the position of London, gave it currency and it was this currency that decided the matter. What we have here then is a very much tempered uniformity; the nature and title of the London standard were based upon the facts as they were, upon convenience and usage. The Universities "where Schollers vse much peeuish affectation of words out of the primatiue languages" are not to exercise pedantic interference. And how tempered this uniformity is becomes more obvious when one considers the flexibility of usage testified to by good Elizabethan authors, the variability they maintained in their manuscripts and the co-existence of other factors all tending to maintain the open door in language.

One of these factors was the not yet broken strength of the oral tradition. The tyranny, the drugging influence, of print, were still in process of development. The oral tradition of language had its discipline of *quality* in speakers of rank or capacity and on public and private occasions of any moment, but only a minority of pedantic minds as yet envisaged for it a discipline of *uniformity*. Puttenham is again perfectly explicit on this point. The poet, he says, is not to take the "termes of Northernmen, such as they vse in dayly talke, whether they be noble men or gentlemen, or of their best clarkes" because the poet is *writing* Southern in order to secure currency; the northern terms do not in themselves "in dayly talke" imply any inferiority social or cultural, for clearly they are heard on the lips of noblemen, gentlemen and scholars. There was therefore a recognized bilingualism—a local speech for the tongue and a modified standard language for the pen. Puttenham assumes that whatever a county magnate writes or speaks in Town, at home among his servants and country folk, he will use the home-grown speech. It happened to get recorded of Sir Walter Raleigh that he maintained his Devon 'burr' at Court, but this is not to be thought of as an isolated instance of local patriotism. He was doubtless often answered in equally distinctive Yorkshire or East Anglian. Still less must the Westcountry doric as spoken by him be brought under the present limitations of 'dialect' or 'the countrified'. A man using dialect would speak with all the range, subtlety and power conferred on him by his intellect, imagination and experience. It is impossible to think of Raleigh's Devon as yokel's speech.

There is, so far as I know, no evidence as to how far actors in Shakespeare's time standardized their elocution. Their base was London, their patronage they found in the Court. Recent efforts "to get closer to Shakespeare" by producing his plays according to Elizabethan pronunciation rest on the assumption that there was for the actors *an* Elizabethan speech, though it is recognized, of course, that actors, professional chameleons, will adapt themselves to the classes and types they represent, refined or boorish as the case may be. But the evidence just cited shows that even the courtly world did not judge by 'accent'. What it is safe to say is that actors coming up (like Shakespeare) from the provinces would have had to make their tones and delivery pleasing and intelligible to their audiences in City and Court.[4]

For rustic effects the Elizabethan theatre had a conventional stage-Southern (or South-Western) of which Shakespeare makes temperate use as in the dialogue between Edgar and

Oswald (*King Lear*, IV, vi). In the group of plays in which Falstaff lives and dies, Shakespeare draws more variously than elsewhere on acoustic effects from different 'accents': French, scraps of schoolboy Latin, broken English, different regional brands of 'English', pre-eminently the Welsh. Shallow's "How a good yoke of bullocks at Stamford Fair?...How a score of ewes now?" (2 *Henry IV*, III, ii, 42, 55) suggest that he was expected to sound as well as look the typical squireen, speaking to family, friends and household as Puttenham expected such a man to speak. All this, if well done, is good comic business at any time.

In the field of orthography we can again trace some wishful thinking on the subject of Uniformity. Orthography was a burning topic with most Elizabethan writers on language. There was a more urgent desire to reform this branch of language than any other. English spelling was even then felt to be a reproach as well as an inconvenience. Views were freely expressed. As is well known, a very considerable degree of standardization was carried out by the end of the century and greatly accelerated in the next. But this was in no way the work of those with 'views' but of the printing houses, simplifying their problems in the quiet pursuit of business. The spelling in Elizabethan printed books is, by and large, compositors' spelling, and though it is moving towards conventions we accept today, the standardization is, even in the most carefully printed books, very far from complete. Everyone can recall how not only long new words, but the simplest and commonest, can be spelt in two or three different ways on the same page. It is only when we turn to authors' own manuscripts that we can appreciate the extent of the normalizing achievement of the compositors. In their manuscripts authors continued to spell 'phonetically', or, rather, personally, and consequently it is from manuscripts of the period that invaluable evidence has been obtained as to the current pronunciation. Punctuation in the manuscripts is also frequently erratic or inadequate and we have therefore to accept the fact that the punctuation in the printed books is also in the main the contribution of the compositors.

It is well known that Shakespeare's grammar soon began to give trouble to his editors. Some First Folio texts, in this as in some other respects, are already less Shakespearian than the earlier good quartos and much less so than the unblotted papers which his fellows received from the poet's hands. It is in the Second Folio, however, that the first marked step towards a 'reforming' of Shakespeare's grammar is taken. The reason cannot be that English syntax and usage had taken a sudden leap between 1623 and 1632. The chief explanation is, doubtless, that the Shakespearian *corpus* was now regarded as a *book* in a world where the broad Elizabethan bases of the Shakespearian spoken word had begun to contract. From 1632 onwards the text of Shakespeare underwent a long slow process of modernization in grammatical usage as in orthography, a process reflecting the evolution of taste and linguistic theory and custom in the English world at large. When a more historical perspective became possible the process was tardily reversed and Shakespeare's language has begun to recover its natural and legitimate Elizabethanism. We now record a superior amusement at some of the almost incredible things said about Shakespeare's ignorant and untutored language at the end of the seventeenth century. Whatever our response to the puns and conceits, we remind ourselves strenuously that the best taste of the period relished them. All schoolchildren know that they must accept but not imitate the double comparatives and double negatives. Shakespeare's relative constructions gave considerable trouble to his eighteenth-century editors, partly, as we now see, because the language under the pressure of Dryden's later usage, of French and Latin and of the generally diffused idea of Correctness, was undergoing a spasm of denial of its own traditions. Numberless so-called 'corrections' have been made because editors forget on matters of detail, though they know well enough in general, that the plays were composed to be spoken, not read, and used rightly therefore the variability, the ellipses, the turns of colloquial speech.

On many points we have learnt, then, to accept Elizabethan usage and we are no longer quick to stigmatize as signs of ignorance or poetic licences constructions which our modern grammatical analysis rejects. On some points of accidence and syntax, however, we can still find editorial hesitation or refusal. An example is provided by third person plural present indicatives levelled under forms which to us are singular. The Globe editors accept "The Riches of the Ship is come on Shore" (*Othello*, II, i, 83, Folio version), fortified perhaps by their knowledge that "riches" is derived from the French *richesse*, a singular noun; in any case the "is" is felt to be right. On the other hand they reject Gonzalo's "My old bones akes" (*Tempest*, III, iii, 2) and print "ache" (with some loss of flavour?); likewise the Cambridge New Shakespeare, with the Note: "compositor's grammar". So it may have been, but it *was* 'grammar' in the sense of being a widely-used variant of the commoner form without -s. The inflexion is in the strictest sense Elizabethan since examples can be found in the Royal letters and we cannot hastily withdraw it from the range of acceptable variations, prompted sometimes purely by the poet's ear in search of effects it relished.[5]

Custom was the only guide the Elizabethan possessed. Tudor zeal in linguistics lagged noticeably behind in the syntactical field—there is no body of work on accidence or syntax to compare with the Arts of Rhetoric or the discussions of pronunciation or orthography. When the Elizabethan practised construction he did it as an exercise in rhetoric. Classical and renaissance rhetoric had provided a place for consideration of the vices of speech including breaking Priscian's head, and the Elizabethan Arts mostly do likewise, but this purely negative side of their task interested their authors little, and, in any case, they had not the apparatus to expose 'bad grammar' at large. Their illustration of errors tends to be thin and conventional. This can be brought home by contrasting with the proportions assumed by the exposure of errors in Fowler's *Modern English Usage* the two slight chapters (Book III, xxi and xxii) in which Puttenham dismisses the subject. In these he finds something to say on barbarism or foreign speech, tautology, ambiguity etc., cites an example or two of abuses of order which may be considered related to construction, and polishes off Solecismus, or actual grammatical error, in six lines of which the wording shows that he has not troubled to detach this topic from his text-book source so as to make it a branch of English linguistics; he provides not a single example.

We should be chary of imputing to the Elizabethan any habit of grammatical analysis such as we make in answering syntactical questions, however little grammar of the parsing variety we have learnt at school. When he had learnt to read the vernacular from his hornbook he was taught at school nothing further about his own language at all. If there was one thing of which, as a result of mid-century discussions, he was convinced, it was that "our language wanteth grammar". In the theatre he would listen to much verbal play and to a good deal of linguistic satire. But the dramatist pilloried "derangement of epitaphs", affectations, pedantries. He spent few shafts of wit on bad grammar.

It may be objected that the learning of Latin would supply any reasonably intelligent Elizabethan with a more than sufficient sense of accidence and syntax which could be applied, *mutatis mutandis,* to the native language and that it might indeed lead to the importation into English of superfluous grammatical distinctions and categories. So it did, ultimately. But I doubt if even those Elizabethans who had a fair reading and speaking knowledge of Latin gained thereby any strong sense of grammatical rules or the sort of syntactical analysis in which editors of Shakespeare were trained. To the humanist, the classical languages were primarily not intellectual disciplines *per se,* but gateways to knowledge—of life, of philosophy, of history, of science, of oratory. Writers on education from Erasmus onward expect us to visualize the Tudor infant scampering through his grammar in a few months in his eagerness to get to the 'pretty' fables of Aesop or the 'sweet' Bucolics of Virgil. The *Royal Grammar* catered (in theory) for no more than three months at the rules. This reduction of grammar did not pass without protest. There are wails from Skelton onwards as to the banishment of Priscian and Donatus, who were to most Elizabethans merely reverend traditional names. Upper-class boys learnt their Latin on a 'direct method' through daily intercourse, and at the Universities Latin was, in the regulations, the only spoken language. Many less fortunate boys must have been so badly taught that their dim notions of the rules could only have muddled them. Shakespeare allows his Holofernes to know when Priscian has been a little scratched. In *The Lady of May* Sidney is more merciless to his Rombus, who is as innocent of the distinction between nominative and accusative as many a Smith minor. Apart from the oral approach, the key to the attainment of Latin was translation and re-translation, imitation and yet more imitation. It was perfectly natural therefore that the Elizabethans should apply the same method to the solution of such problems as they recognized in their own linguistic task, that they should concentrate on acquisition and enrichment by imitation and leave to the future all the pruning, unifying, regularizing, summarized in the notion of 'correctness'—a state of affairs which constituted a particular turning-point in our language, unlikely, I think, to be repeated. In language it was possible to combine a maximum of Art with a minimum of inhibition.

It was undoubtedly the liberties which he appeared to take with language that greatly sharpened the idea of Shakespeare as Nature's poet which the age of Dryden passed on to the age of Pope in a far extremer form than it had been received from Jonson. In the Restoration period Shakespeare was pictured as sitting down to write, wrapped in a cloud of unknowing, cascading from bombast to puns, mixing metaphors and confounding his parts of speech, but miraculously, by a combination of genius and luck, producing magnificent plays. "His words like casual atoms made a thought." [6] He just wrote and then himself wondered "how the devil it proved such wit". Jonson knew better than this.

Of course, Shakespeare, as a great and original maker of poetic speech, took liberties even beyond Elizabethan amplitude. But, as is shown by the critical pointers scattered through his plays (particularly those of Elizabethan date), he was always alert and aware on the subject of language. He would certainly not be cold towards the ardent patriotism which warmed and animated the Elizabethan pursuit of the Arts of communication. There seems something 'providential' in his emergence on the crest of the Elizabethan wave. He would have been a supremely great poet at any time, but if he had been born ten years later, he would have missed a stimulating collaborator—the Elizabethan speaker and listener. Seizing upon both art and liberty he soared to the happy valiancy in which no other poet has equalled him. From this springs that Elizabethanism which the Jacobeans recognized and expressed after their own fashion. He did not create the conditions in the theatre which gave him his opportunity, and his success in his own manner did not preserve in other men this Elizabethanism even to the chronological close of Elizabeth's days. Ten years later would have brought him too near to Ben Jonson, and after Jonson nothing was exactly the same.

The anonymous Restoration critic from whom I quoted before blandly asserted of Shakespeare "He did not know what trope or figure meant". It is one of the most untenable statements about Shakespeare that have ever been made. Shakespeare could not have avoided this knowledge. He began to write in a literary world revelling in schemes and tropes. Analysis and parsing may have been unknown, but the Elizabethan had been taught, or had absorbed, an alternative analysis. He knew what to do with a paragraph or a stanza offered to his eye or ear. He was avid for words, he loved to identify figure and device, to mark the chimes and echoes. He made demands on language and expected to be satisfied. Where conditions differed remarkably from those prevalent today was in a widespread willingness to take a great deal of trouble with language. If, after the next fifteen minutes' talk of a politician on the wireless we read, or better still, contrive to hear, some of the debating speeches in *Troilus and Cressida* or *Coriolanus*, remembering that originally these were intended for immediate apprehension by the ear, the contrast should bring home what I have urged as to Shakespeare's co-operation with a linguistically intent and active national mind. Shakespeare's stature may or may not be enhanced thereby; in any case, it does not need enhancing, but the Elizabethan listener may gain a cubit.

## NOTES

1. With the exception of the penultimate quotation from *L'Allegro*, the passages from which these extracts are taken will be found in E. K. Chambers, *William Shakespeare* (1930), II, 188 (Robert Greene), 194 (Francis Meres), 230 (Heminge and Condell), 209 (Ben Jonson), 210 (Ben Jonson), 235 (Milton).

2. George Gordon, *Shakespeare's English* (Society for Pure English, Tract 29, 1929).

3. *Euphues and his England*, ed. Croll and Clemons (1916), p. 290.

4. The phonology of Shakespeare's language has been exhaustively treated in *Shakespeare's Pronunciation* by Helge Kökeritz (Yale University Press, 1953). For Shakespeare's use of dialect see p. 35.

5. For other Shakespearian examples, see Abbott, *A Shakespearian Grammar*, p. 235; for a brief discussion and some non-Shakespearian examples, see H. C. Wyld, *History of Colloquial English* (Blackwell, 1936), p. 340.

6. Prologue to *Julius Caesar* (1672). It has been attributed to Dryden, but this seems completely untenable.

# THE POET AND THE PLAYER

BY

## GEORGE RYLANDS

A born dramatist is an artist who sees figures moving and hears voices blending. His pigments and clay are flesh and blood, his instrument the human voice. With a limited time and a restricted space he manœuvres two or more human beings in such a way as to compel from other human beings the attention thay would give to a contest at chess, at tennis, or in the ring. He is at once stump orator, puppet-showman and ventriloquist. He feels and thinks in terms of the ear and the eye. It is the momentary picture and the fleeting phrase that count. The audience must carry away certain visual and certain auditory memories. In poetic drama the ear supersedes the eye.

The cardinal part of the dramatist's problem, Granville-Barker asserts, is how to provide for the collaboration of the actor. "Collaboration it has to be. Interpretation understates the case." The character is re-created in terms of the actor's personality. In the history of the stage this collaboration often appears to be less an alliance than a rivalry and the great periods of renaissance and development, according to Granville-Barker, have almost invariably been dominated by dramatists who knew so much of actors and acting that they had no illusions left about them. "Their way of dealing with this rivalry has been to provide for the actor, perhaps what he liked to do, but always with far more of it than he could easily manage to do, and sometimes with what it was apparently quite impossible to do." The audience is the third factor or sharer in the world of illusion. In this triumvirate the playwright is Octavius Caesar, Mark Antony stands for the players, and the audience (at the worst) is Lepidus. They must collaborate also. After playing Hamlet in Manchester on 26 April 1847, and taking special pains to communicate "the very spirit and feeling of the distracted sensitive young man", Macready noted in his diary:

I did not feel the audience responded to me. I did not on that account give way, but the inspiration is lost; the perfect *abandon*, under which one goes out of oneself, is impossible unless you enjoy the perfect sympathy of the audience; if they do not abandon themselves to the actor's powers his magic becomes ineffectual.

What a metempsychosis! The soul migrates from the dramatist to the actor, from the actor who "goes out of himself" to the audience.

The dramatic imagination sees and hears. The audience remember a picture, a gesture, an intonation, a pause. In the study with Shakespeare's plays upon our knee, critics, commentators, editors ranged upon the shelves, the drama stands still. We skim and skip and halt and cogitate. Like Orpheus we look back and the poet's shadowy figures dissolve in the day-dreams of our egoism. But in the theatre the curtain rises and falls night after night; the stage-manager knows the playing time within a couple of minutes. *Volat irrevocabile verbum.*

The effects are momentary. "Mr. Kean's attitude", writes Hazlitt, "in leaning against the side of the stage before he comes forward to address Lady Anne, is one of the most graceful and striking ever witnessed. It would have done for Titian to paint.... His manner of bidding his friends good night, after pausing with the point of his sword, drawn slowly backward and

25

forward on the stage as if considering the plan of the battle the next day, is a particularly happy and natural thought. The concluding scene in which he is killed by Richmond is the most brilliant of the whole. He fights at last like one drunk with wounds; and the attitude in which he stands with his hands stretched out, after his sword is wrested from him, had a preternatural and terrific grandeur, as if his will could not be disarmed, and the very phantoms of his despair had withering power to kill." The same actor was *seen* at his finest after the murder of Duncan. "The hesitation, the bewildered look, the coming to himself when he sees his hands bloody, the manner in which his voice clung to his throat and checked his utterance, his agony and tears, the force of nature overcome by passion, beggared description. It was a scene which no-one who saw it can ever efface from his recollection."

Mrs Siddons in Lady Macbeth's speech "Hie thee hither" used to elevate her stature, to smile with a lofty and uncontrollable expectation, and with an arm beautifully raised in the air to draw the very circle she was speaking of ("the golden round") in the air about her head as if she ran her finger round the gold. As Constance she was at once passionate and dignified, and when she wildly seated herself upon the ground exclaiming

> Here I and sorrows sit;
> Here is my throne, bid kings come bow to it,

the effect was electrical. She used to pace up and down as the eddying gust of her impatience drove her, and all her despairing and bitter words came with double force from her in her career. Garrick copied nature for the representation of mad Lear in which his genius was most movingly revealed. He imitated the expression and action of a friend who had gone out of his mind after letting his child of two years, which he was dandling and fondling at an upper window, fall to the flagged area below. Garrick "had no sudden starts, no violent gesticulation...he moved his head in the most deliberate manner; his eyes were fixed or if they turned to anyone near him he made a pause and fixed his look on the person after much delay; his features at the same time telling what he was going to say before he uttered a word". When Ellen Terry played Ophelia she went to the madhouse to study wits astray:

I was disheartened at first. There was no beauty, no nature, no pity in most of the lunatics. Strange as it may sound, they were too *theatrical* to teach me anything. Then just as I was going away I noticed a young girl gazing at the wall. I went between her and the wall to see her face. It was quite vacant, but the body expressed that she was waiting, waiting. Suddenly she threw up her hands and sped across the room like a swallow. I never forgot it. She was very thin, very pathetic, very young, and the movement was as poignant as it was beautiful.

The visual is as important for the representation of the humours as of the passions. Charles Lamb recalls how Bensley threw an air of Spanish loftiness over the part of Malvolio. "He looked, spake, and moved like an old Castilian.... With what ineffable carelessness would he twirl his gold chain!" And on the countenance of Dodd, the perfect Aguecheek, you could see "the first dawn of an idea stealing slowly...climbing up little by little, with a painful process, till it cleared up at last to the fulness of a twilight conception—its highest meridian".

Profoundly concerned as the dramatist must be with the eye of the spectator—he must have that flair for the thing seen which was so notable in some of the imaginative foreign films of the old silent days—yet it is our ears that he must borrow, especially if he is a poet as well as an orator. "Whatsoever is commendable in the grave orator is most exquisitely perfect in him", John Webster tells us in his 'Character of an Excellent Actor'. Shakespeare's Burbage had "all the parts of an excellent orator animating his words with speaking and speech with action". B. L. Joseph has shown that rhetorical delivery, in which the Elizabethan schoolboy was trained and which lawyer, politician, and divine practised, is the clue to their stage playing. *Vox, vultus, vita*—voice, countenance, life—from these three springs flows a certain visible eloquence which is at once "an eloquence of the body and comely grace in delivering conceits and an external image of an internal mind". Delivery or expression is at once audible and visible. How salutary if Mulcaster, Headmaster of Merchant Taylors', could rise again to teach our actors *vociferatio* or the exercise of the voice! The grammar-school boy of 1612 was exhorted from his first day "to pronounce everything, audibly, leisurely, distinctly, and naturally, sounding out specially the last syllable that each word may be fully understood". Attend, all ye who list to enter the portals of Broadcasting House!

And so, when Webster tells us that the Excellent Actor "adds grace to the poet's labours; for what in the poet is but ditty, in him is both ditty and music", he anticipates the dramatic criticism of Bernard Shaw whose very first Shakespearian notice declared: "it is the score not the libretto that keeps the work alive and fresh; and this is why only musical critics should be allowed to meddle with Shakespeare".

"For voice, eye, action and expression, no actor has come out for many years at all equal to him." Such was Hazlitt's first impression of Kean; and Leigh Hunt, looking back in 1831, could say that "he is unquestionably the finest actor we ever saw". Saw and *heard*. In 1814 Hazlitt placed his recitation of "Farewell the tranquil mind" with the scene in *Macbeth* after the murder as the two finest things Kean had ever done. Hunt who thought the speech "Had it pleased heaven..." the finest passage in the finest performance on the stage, records in 1831 that the delivery of the "Farewell" was as beautiful as ever—perhaps had a still more touching melancholy. "His repeated farewells with the division of the syllables strongly marked, fare well, were spoken in long lingering tones like the sound of a parting knell. The whole passage would have formed an admirable study for a young actor, in showing him the beauty of sacrificing verbal painting to a pervading sentiment. It was right to give emphasis to the word farewell, because the speaker is taking leave of all his felicities, and has the strongest sense of doing so; but Mr Kean gave no vulgar importance to the plumed troop and the big wars as commonplace actors do; because the melancholy overcomes them all; it merges the particular images in the mass of regret." "The tone of voice in which he delivered this speech", says Hazlitt, "struck on the heart and the imagination like the swelling notes of some divine music." Once more we look forward to Shaw who says of *Othello*, "tested by the brain it is ridiculous, tested by the ear it is sublime".

The words do not convey ideas: they are streaming ensigns and tossing branches to make the tempest of passion visible. The actor...must have the orchestral quality in him.... It is of no use to *speak* "Farewell the tranquil mind"; for the more intelligently and reasonably it is spoken the more absurd it is. It must affect us as 'ora per sempre addio, sante memorie' affects us when sung by Tamagno.

Kean possessed without doubt the orchestral quality, the organ music, the *vox humana*. More remarkable as pointing the distinction between study and stage is the recollection by an

American poet of the effect Kean could produce, not by a soliloquy, not by the single line or word even, but by a mere ejaculation:

A man has feelings sometimes which can only be breathed out...there is no utterance for them in words. I had hardly written this when the terrible and indistinct "Ha!" with which Mr Kean makes Lear hail Cornwall and Regan as they enter in the fourth scene of the second act came into my mind. It seemed at the time to take me up and sweep me along in its wild swell. No description in the world would give a very clear notion of the sound.

Such virtue in a single 'Ha'! *Blackwood's Magazine* noted the electrical effect produced by Kean in the transition from "Bid them come forth and hear me" to "O are you come?" In *Richard III* the frequent and rapid transition of his voice from the expression of the fiercest passion to the most familiar tones of conversation was admired by Hazlitt who reports that this artifice was imitated and caricatured by others. Laurence Olivier has achieved transitions of this kind with success, but modern audiences are all too frequently addressed in "the familiar tones of conversation": it is the orchestral quality, the swelling notes of some divine music, the streaming ensigns which we desiderate.

This is the heart of the problem. How are music and meaning, sound and sense, conversation and versification to be reconciled? "Speak the speech, I pray you, as I pronounced it to you, trippingly on the tongue: but if you mouth it, as many of your players do, I had as lief the town crier spoke my lines." If the Prince composed "Thoughts black, hands apt, drugs fit and time agreeing", did he really expect Lucianus to pronounce it trippingly? And if "Indeed indeed, sirs, but this troubles me" or "Now might I do it pat, now he is praying, And now I'll do't" comes easily off the tongue, is there to be *no* mouthing of

> 'Tis now the very witching time of night,
> When churchyards yawn and hell itself breathes out
> Contagion to this world.

In *Hamlet* (it would seem) Shakespeare is leading a revolution. The watchword (as in all aesthetic revolutions) is "Back to Nature". That he had a tenderness, despite his Pistol parodies, for the robustious periwigged style of "Feed and be fat, my fair Calipolis" is revealed in Hamlet's Marlovian recitation; but from *Hamlet* onwards, although he is always experimenting, marauding, and extending his conquests, versification fits character, mood, or situation more and more closely. The rhetorical and ornamental become means to an end, until in the first two romances style at moments has the upper hand. In the history of Shakespearian playing the pendulum swings between the declamatory and the colloquial, the prophetic and the pedestrian. "The players", said Dr Johnson sitting with Garrick in a tavern after the play, "have got a kind of rant with which they go on without regard either to accent or emphasis". We cannot believe it of Garrick himself. "On the stage he was natural, simple, affecting." It cannot be true of Betterton, of whom Cibber said that he never heard a line come from him in tragedy wherein "his judgment, his ear and his imagination were not fully satisfied'. In Leigh Hunt's view, Garrick's nature displaced Quin's formalism and in precisely the same way Kean displaced Kemble. Kemble was "literally a *personation*—it was a mask and a sounding-pipe". We suspect Macready of having been a rhetorician like Kemble, his rhetoric interspersed with passages of violence and rage. (Shaw's father said that Macready played Coriolanus like a mad bull.) Henry Irving, whose Shakespearian productions were to be seen rather than heard, conquered his stammer but played tricks with his mother tongue which drove Henry James to frenzy—even "the impossible Mr Daly" noted the absurdity of Irving's sudden rises and falls of tone. With Ada Rehan and Ellen Terry (whom James found too natural) and Forbes Robertson and F. R. Benson's introduction of the Oxford accent, nature gradually but relentlessly thrust artifice out of the stage-door. Bernard Shaw was the indefatigable and peremptory propagandist of the change, contending that Shakespeare is a word musician and that if you let him do the work himself all will come right:

To our young people studying for the stage I say, with all solemnity, learn how to pronounce the English alphabet clearly and beautifully from some person who is at once an artist and a phonetic expert. And then leave blank verse patiently alone until you have experienced emotion deep enough to crave for poetic expression, at which point verse will seem an absolutely natural and real form of speech to you. Meanwile if any pedant proposes to teach you to recite, send instantly for the police.

This is sanguine to say the least—and fallacious. Shaw attacks the elocutionist of his day, not because he encouraged declamation but because he deplored sing-song and broke up verse to make it sound like insanely pompous prose. The sing-song way for Shaw is the right way but we must not misunderstand him. "Mere metric accuracy is nothing. There must be beauty of tone, expressive inflection, and infinite variety of nuance to sustain the fascination of the infinite monotony of the chaunting." This recalls the American poet's remark on Kean's Lear. "Read any scene and see how few words are there set down and then remember how Kean fills it out with varied and multiplied expressions and circumstances."

Granville-Barker shared Shaw's confidence in leaving verse and language to speak for themselves. We are too apt to value his five Series of *Prefaces* for their analysis of dramatic form, revealing Shakespeare as a conscious artist in his "conduct of the action". But Granville-Barker had a more original and valuable contribution to make. For him as actor, producer, and playwright, "the speaking of the verse must be the foundation of all study": "Here is the touchstone by which all interpretation must first and last be tried"; "Verse was his supreme dramatic resource"; "the master-medium of his stage-craft". Verse heard not read.

All poets presumably test their lines by ear as they write them, if not by speech. But with Shakespeare dramatic *writing* was for convenience of record merely; his verse was not only conceived as speech, it was to be so born and only so meant to exist. He provided music for an orchestra of living individual voices that he knew. As nearly as might be he spoke through his actors. It is the mere notation of this once-living music which remains.

His advice concurs with that of Shaw. Leave it to Shakespeare.

The speaker—for it is of course a question of speech—who sets to work upon a finger-tapping basis of rule and exception, with account to be taken of the use of extra syllables, of the curtailed or overrun line, of weak endings and the like, will soon find himself at a feeble and tangled halt. Let him rather acquire an articulate tongue, and unfailing ear for the pervading melody and cadence of the verse, let him yield to its impetus, and—provided, of course, that he knows more or less what it is all about—Shakespeare can be trusted to carry him through.

Let him, by all means, we agree: but the proviso if not odious, as Millamant would say, is formidable. Shaw and Granville-Barker were prose dramatists. Our most eminent contemporary poet could say ten years ago, with his successes in the theatre still before him, that

we still have a good way to go in the invention of a verse medium for the theatre; a medium in which we shall be able to hear the speech of contemporary human beings, in which dramatic characters can express the purest poetry without high-falutin' and in which they can convey the most commonplace message without absurdity.

Eliot insists that the music of poetry cannot exist apart from meaning and that it must be latent in the common speech of its time. He himself as a schoolboy and apprentice to poetry could not remember the technical terms of metric and scansion; but he allows that the analytic study of abstract forms and the classification of lines with different numbers of stresses and syllables may prove useful as "a simplified map of a complicated territory". The best training for a poet is to become so engrossed in a particular poet as to be able to produce a recognizable derivative.

Amidst all this talk of declamation and sing-song and colloquial speech, of scansion and tempo and stress, what are the actors to do, to justify Granville-Barker's faith that they can train their ears and tongues and train our ears to the whole great art of Shakespeare's music making?

First, I would say let them devote more time to the English poets other than Shakespeare. By frequent memorizing of the divers kinds—lyric, elegiac, epic, didactic—the relation between sound and sense (which differs radically between Donne and Pope, Milton and Tennyson, Shelley and Blake, Wordsworth and Crabbe), the potentialities of rhyme and rhythm, of acceleration and pause, the fluid and the formal, the decorated and the direct, can be felt, assimilated and understood. Shakespeare's line is the decasyllable which rhymed and unrhymed, in sonnet and stanza and ode, in couplet and quatrain, is the staple of English poetry. This leads to my second point—scansion. Are we to rant or wail or sing or pontificate or gossip or state or argue? Shall we emphasize or ignore or counterpoint the five foot iambic structure? The answer is that there is a time for all these things. But the actor can seldom learn a passage in Shakespeare without being unconsciously influenced by the associations which adhere to it—the footlights, the crowded house, thronging thoughts of Garrick and Gielgud. The beginner cannot spout Shakespeare even in his bath without the *arrière pensée* of a professional career. Shakespeare is for him first and foremost a dramatist rather than a poet. The potentialities of the blank verse line can therefore be studied more selflessly and aesthetically, in Milton,

> Blind *Thamyris* and blind *Mæonides*,
> And *Tiresias* and *Phineus* Prophets old.

> Rocks, Caves, Lakes, Fens, Bogs, Dens, and shades of death,

or Tennyson

> Myriads of rivulets hurrying through the lawn,

or Yeats

> Once a fly dancing in a beam of the sun,

or Eliot

> Harry telephoned to me from Marseilles,

before graduating to a technical investigation of Shakespeare, who will reverse the iambic movement in

> I am dying, Egypt, dying; only...

or conceal the ending in

> The inevitable prosecution of
> Disgrace and horror,

or expand and overcrowd in

> These dangerous unsafe lunes i'the king, beshrew them,

or relax lyrically in

> The night to the owl and morn to the lark less welcome,

or divert us with a curiosity

> Hoo! hearts, tongues, figures, scribes, bards, poets, cannot
> Think, speak, cast, write, sing, number: hoo!

He will redispose the five links of the chain; whether by cutting in half—

> Beautiful tyrant! fiend angelical!

or by division in thirds—

> Unhousel'd, disappointed, unanel'd,

or quartered—

> Bounty, perseverance, mercy, lowliness,

or criss-crossing the five feet—

> Insisture, course, proportion, season, form,

or pushing the counterpoint to an extreme,

> Wrong right, base noble, old young, coward valiant.

There are moments recognizable from their rhythm where the poet takes over from the dramatist:

> There is a history in all men's lives...
> There is a tide in the affairs of men....
> There is a willow grows aslant a brook....
> There is a cliff, whose high and bending head....

In Othello's priestlike speech before the sacrifice of Desdemona forty monosyllables fall like the waterdrops of Chinese torture before the crowning grandeur of "monumental alabaster". In Ulysses' oration on Degree on the other hand Shakespeare frequently changes gear and the speaker must be capable of rapid acceleration, of sudden declension and arduous ascent.

Such things as these are known to Macaulay's schoolboy, but have they been pondered and assimilated until they become the second nature of our provincial Romeos, Richards and Perditas? What percentage of the audience at Stratford or the Old Vic know when a syllable is dropped from, or added to, the line? Yet such an audience in the concert hall pride themselves on their aesthetic shudder when the executant is out of time or tune.

To master the single line is easy: but the line is part of the paragraph, the paragraph of the speech, the speech of the sequence, the sequence of the movement which fills two acts or three. How rarely our producers, even when they make a fine showing and sounding with a particular scene, relate that scene in tone and pace and colour, for contrast and development, to the scene that goes before and the scene that follows after. Then again, on the stage Shakespeare's blank verse is vaguely believed to be the same in 1592, 1602 and 1612. The major point at issue is the breach or the observance of the line length. "The verse will always respond better to a dramatic than a prosodic analysis", says Granville-Barker of *Hamlet* very rightly. *Hamlet* is the turning-point. In 1592 brave Talbot, "new embalmed with the tears of ten thousand spectators", who imagined they beheld him fresh bleeding, assaults the fortress of Bordeaux thus:

> How are we park'd and bounded in a pale,
> A little herd of England's timorous deer,
> Mazed with a yelping kennel of French curs!
> If we be English deer, be then in blood;
> Not rascal-like to fall down with a pinch,
> But rather, moody-mad and desperate stags,
> Turn on the bloody hounds with heads of steel
> And make the cowards stand aloof at bay:
> Sell every man his life as dear as mine,
> And they shall find dear deer of us, my friends.
> God and Saint George, Talbot and England's right,
> Prosper our colours in this dangerous fight!

That is plain sailing before an invigorating breeze; but when the voyage from *Henry VI* to *Henry VIII* is accomplished, we find ourselves lifting and sinking on tumultuous billows or at anchor in a choppy sea:

> He was a man of an unbounded stomach,
> Ever ranking himself with princes;
> One that, by suggestion, tied all the kingdom:
> Simony was fair play;
> His own opinion was his law.
> I'the presence he would say untruths;
> And be ever double both in his words and meaning:
> He was never, but where he meant to ruin, pitiful.

The passage is printed as *vers libre*, the line length equated to the sense length, because it reveals the method of late Shakespearian verse. A reader will think twice before he can dispose of it as verse and it is too often spoken as printed here. And what are we to make of this?—

Thou told'st me when we came from horse the place was near at hand. Ne'er longed my mother so to see me first as I have now. Pisanio! Man! Where is Posthumus? What is in thy mind that makes thee stare thus? Wherefore breaks that sigh from the inward of thee? One but painted thus would be interpreted a thing perplexed beyond self-explication: put thyself into a 'haviour of less fear, ere wildness vanquish my steadier senses. What's the matter?

This is in fact blank verse and not (as printed) a rather incompetent specimen of prose. It supports Eliot's contention that dramatic verse is dependent upon common speech. If the Imogen is aware, as she utters it, of the metrical pauses—subconsciously aware—if the pauses at the line endings last but a split second, the speech will be projected into the auditorium. As blank verse it is in motion, as prose it stumbles and stands still. "All dramatic speech", writes Granville-Barker,

must have in it something of the enhancement of poetry...the enhancement may be cunningly condensed within seemingly commonplace talk. But there it must be. If speech is to be made to carry in the theatre it must have in it some quality equivalent—for a comparison—to the effective length of a well-bowled cricket-ball. Nor in Shakespeare's theatre of all others can this poetic enhancement be surrendered.

Let us simplify. In the first half of Shakespeare's career the verse is sufficiently regular to justify most variations and concealments, the disappointment as well as the fulfilment of expectation. From *Hamlet* to *Macbeth* the regular and the irregular tend to alternate and cancel out. It should be difficult to go wrong. From then on, the virtuosity is such—his style may be his mistress or a maid of all work, various as Cleopatra, empress and slut—that no actor can afford with his inward ear to forget the beat. The Jacobean actor and his audience were so habituated to the rhythm and structure of blank verse that *they could not help keeping time*. Emphasis and nuance depend upon the instinctive acceptance of the norm. Against it Shakespeare can underline or high-light a word or phrase, whether at the close or the opening of a line. "The language should always seem to feel though not to suffer from the bonds of verse", wrote Coventry Patmore; and he points out that the confinement of metre makes the very deformities of phrasing beautiful, one of its noblest functions being to produce "these exorbitancies on the side of the law". "What in prose would be shrieks and vulgar hyperbole is transmuted by metre into graceful and impressive song." This process is the converse to that already noted by which metre gives lift and length and poetic enhancement to commonplace speech. As Shakespeare became more experimental and more expert in his handling of line and sentence length, of verse paragraph, of stress, pace and rhythm, so his language became more audacious and eccentric, his grammar more telegraphic, his panache more splendiferous. All the more essential therefore in the latest plays to hang on to the blank verse line as a drowning man to a spar and let the imperious surge of conceit and metaphor break over one's head. Academic studies of Shakespeare's imagery take little or no account of the repercussions on his imagery or on single words, familiar or strange, caused by the *pace* at which the passage is moving and the *position* assigned to it in the line. Pace indeed is the beginning and end of the matter; as Ellen Terry learnt in the hard school of the old stock company:

Pace is the soul of comedy, and to elaborate lines at the expense of pace is disastrous. Of course it is not a question of swift utterance only, but of swift thinking.... *Vary the pace*. Charles Reade was never tired of saying this, and, indeed, it is one of the foundations of all good acting.... All my life the thing which has struck me as wanting on the stage is *variety*. Some people are 'tone-deaf', and they find it physically impossible to observe the law of contrasts.

33

Ellen Terry (who acted with Charles Kean in 1856) is still a living memory. We can link her advice with a recollection of Augustus Hare, whose grandmother taught him to read aloud, herself having been instructed by Mrs Siddons. "She gave me the lessons she had received, making me repeat the single line, 'The quality of mercy is not strained', fifty or sixty times over, till I had exactly the right amount of intonation on each syllable, her delicate ear detecting the slightest fault." With these two actresses, the natural and the sublime, each a mistress of gesture and expression, we return to our starting-point and a restatement of the theme. The dramatist sees figures moving and hears voices blending. He imagines in terms of mime, not motivation; not of psychology but the memorable phrase; not of an analytical process but an inevitable sequence of moments. Our producers and players today—and our audiences—care overmuch for the eye and all too little for the ear.

Poets, it has been said, learn from poets; prose writers from conversation. A poetic dramatist learns from both, as Shakespeare and T. S. Eliot have done. Every actor must do the same. As he steps on to the stage, as he falls asleep after the play is done, his prayer should be:

> Sphear-born harmonious Sisters, Voice, and Vers,
> Wed your divine sounds, and mixt power employ
> Dead things with inbreath'd sense able to pierce.

Lives there a thing with soul so dead as a matinée audience at Midsummer?

# SHAKESPEARE'S ORTHOGRAPHY IN *VENUS AND ADONIS* AND SOME EARLY QUARTOS

BY

## A. C. PARTRIDGE

When the word *orthographie* came into English via French in the late Middle Ages, it meant 'right writing'. As late as 1640 Simon Daines in *Orthoepia Anglicana* so defined it, and distinguished it from *orthoepie*, or 'right speaking'.[1] Most of Daines's section on Orthography deals with capital letters, punctuation, elision, etc. Grammarians of an earlier generation, such as Hart and Bullokar, seemed to give to orthography a more restricted meaning (one favoured by the *New English Dictionary*), viz. "that part of grammar that determines the value of letters, individually or in combination, in making sounds or words". This was nothing more nor less than spelling, which Hart and Bullokar realized needed reform and regularity. They failed in their proposals because writers and printers ignored them as the figments of pedants,[2] and it was eventually the more practical consideration of haste during the polemic activity of the Civil War that compelled the printers to systematize.

Along with developments in spelling went changes in pointing or *distinction*. In sixteenth-century England punctuation was lacking in the subtleties of Western European practice. In ephemeral English works, such as plays, punctuation was at first almost entirely impressionistic. When piracy or economic pressure compelled theatre-companies to part with the rights in their plays, speed in getting their wares to market was, for the publishers, a primary consideration; and there was neither time nor reason for the printer to revise punctuation. But in subsequent editions, if such plays as *Richard II* are a guide, dramatic punctuation was gradually superseded. Printers of the last quarter of the sixteenth century had learnt much from Continental texts, especially editions of the classics and Latin grammarians, and had acquired a logical system of punctuation, founded largely on the grammarian Ramus (Pierre de la Ramée) and the printer Aldus Manutius, whose *Interpungendi Ratio* appeared in 1566. At the beginning of the seventeenth century English writers who were also classical scholars, such as Bacon and Jonson, followed this lead; and so did scribes like Ralph Crane, who made privately commissioned copies of works. Independently the technique of punctuation was often carried to extremes of fussiness, for example the use of the co-ordinating comma in Ben Jonson, and the varieties of elision and parenthesis in Ralph Crane. While the editing of plays was poor in textual accuracy, a more sophisticated orthography became a general feature of all published works intended for the new and rising generation of readers.

Except in a technical or historical sense, the term orthography is now little used; spelling and punctuation are separate conventions. But in the sixteenth and seventeenth centuries their functions to some extent overlapped. For instance, elided letters or syllables could be indicated equally by a modification of spelling or by punctuation. Before 1600, care in the use of the apostrophe to mark elisions and contractions was observed mainly by printers and scribes who exercised it in such works as would reach a scholarly or aristocratic circle. Plays, when Shake-

speare became associated with the drama, were non-literary works, but employed many contractions, which were achieved at first by the simple omission of letters. But at the turn of the
century plays had begun to acquire prestige as poetry. As metrical accuracy became important,
marks of elision began to increase, where before they had been largely taken for granted.
Jonson was a stickler for the carefully pointed elision, and after 1600 the newer dramatic orthography of his plays was remarkable for its range of colloquial and contracted forms of all kinds.

The study of orthography in the thirty years 1593–1623, which covers the period of earliest
publication of Shakespeare's works, should account for all aspects of the graphic representation
of words, both in verse and prose. It is unsatisfactory to think of orthography as 'correct
writing', implying spelling or other conventions that did not really exist. There is, perhaps,
a *sensus communis* or common denominator of correct usage to be extracted from the experience
of this age; but it is very small and obvious. If on the other hand orthography is held to imply
external grammatical authority (i.e. a system such as Bullokar's or Hart's), English has never
submitted kindly to it. I prefer, therefore, to convert a rather vague term to preciser use by
defining orthography as 'that part of writing, peculiar to author, scribe, editor or printing
house, which is concerned with accidentals such as spelling, punctuation, elision, aphesis, syncope
and contractions generally'. This definition has the merit of dealing with actualities, viz. literary
works, the product of an individual or a house, often of both.

Because the printing-house has, in fact, tampered with Shakespeare's orthography, a reconstruction of his methods of writing has been regarded, until recently, as an extravagant, if
not impossible, proposal; but sporadic attempts have been made on the Continent and in
America, in such publications as *The Library*, and in the pretty game of textual emendation.
Recovery cannot indeed be reduced to scientific method, like the reconstruction of a dinosaur
from a few fossil bones. But it may be more systematic than has been supposed, if the examination is confined to evidence contained in the printed quartos believed, on good bibliographical
grounds, to be based on Shakespeare's manuscripts. In what follows I have dealt mainly with
the earliest Quarto, *Venus and Adonis* (1593); but conclusions have also been drawn and citations
made from *Richard II* (1597), *Romeo and Juliet* (1599) and *Hamlet* (1604), especially the first.
These four quartos represent, respectively, the press-edited text, the fair copy, the foul papers,
and the blundering compositor's literal version—valuable in different ways for determining with
reasonable probability how Shakespeare composed his lines.

The printer of the 1593 Quarto of *Venus and Adonis* was Richard Field, a Stratford man and
it is thought a friend of Shakespeare. In 1579 Field was apprenticed to Thomas Vautrollier,
a Huguenot who had been admitted to the Stationers' Company in the very year of Shakespeare's
birth. During the next twenty years Vautrollier became a printer of considerable standing,
printing besides musical, grammatical and religious works, North's translation of *Plutarch's
Lives*, Ovid's *Poems* and Bright's *Treatise of Melancholie*. On the master printer's death in 1588,
Field married his widow and acquired his business. W. W. Greg in 'An Elizabethan Printer
and his Copy'[3] shows that Field was a printer of authority and readily edited the copy of
Harington's translation of *Orlando Furioso* (1591), as regards punctuation and spelling. Fripp in
'Shakespeare's Pronunciation'[4] points to at least one important reason why Field had to shorten
Shakespeare's spellings: he printed the concluding couplet of each stanza of *Venus and Adonis*
to the right of the quatrain, and had difficulty in avoiding 'tucked in' lines. He undoubtedly

'improved' Shakespeare's orthography, and took some care with the general set-up of the verse lines and the metrical elisions, probably because the poem was in honour of the Earl of Southampton. Field in the care of his printing had an eye to the patron and the literacy of his public.

The dedication to the Earl is brief, personal and in prose; the printer had no reason to depart from Shakespeare's manuscript, from which both this and the dedication of *Lucrece* seem to be set up. These dedications and the First Quarto of *Richard II* are perhaps the most careful representations of Shakespeare's orthography extant. They show considerable conformity in the use of accidentals in carefully prepared texts, which may explain the actors' conviction that the master never blotted a line. But this conviction must have been based on Shakespeare's fair copies, not on the foul papers; because the evidence of the plays set up from the latter is clearly to the contrary. This makes it advisable to divide the copy for Shakespeare's manuscript-based quartos into at least two primary categories: 'fair copies', such as *Richard II*, and 'foul papers', such as *Romeo and Juliet* (Second Quarto).

A distinguishing feature of the writing of the dedications is the absence of syncope in the spelling of weak past participle inflexions, e.g. *pleased, praised, honoured, deformed* in the dedication to *Venus and Adonis* and *assured* and *lengthned* in that to *Lucrece*. The single exception is *vntutord* in line 7 of the dedication to *Lucrece*, which was due to the compositor's justifying his line. The full spelling in prose does not imply pronunciation of inflexional *e*, as it normally does in Shakespearian verse, where a more precise orthography is necessary for metrical reasons. Otherwise the printer could not have dropped the *e* in *vntutord* or preserved the Shakespearian spelling *vnpolisht* (*Venus and Adonis*, Dedication, line 2), in which the poet conformed to the phonetic practice of the time in converting *-d* to *-t* after unvoiced stem-finals. In the printing of past participial endings the dedications to *Venus and Adonis* and *Lucrece* conform to the practice of the *Authorised Version of the Bible*.

*Venus and Adonis* differs from the manuscript-based quarto plays in the care of its printing, the attention paid to marks of elision, its use of poetical contractions, forms and vocabulary, and sometimes in its spelling. Shakespeare lies behind the editorial practices of Field, and the following analysis aims at distinguishing the author's orthography.

## (a) SPELLING

1. Shakespeare preferred full spellings, such as *sonne, proppe, woorde, heere, hee, cheekes, ecchoes, onelye, dooth, goe*. Where the modern shortened form is found, it is commonly the correction of the printer. Fripp's reconstruction of passages from *Venus and Adonis* and *Lucrece* in the Shakespearian spelling is conjectural, but probably not very wide of the mark. He may be right in attributing such spellings as *wo* and *fy* to Field's compositor, though the former occurs twice in the first two Acts of *Richard II*. Fripp shows how space compels the compositor on occasion to introduce & for *and* or to do away with final *-m* or *-n* by placing the nasal abbreviation stroke above the preceding vowel.

2. Shakespeare probably preferred final *-ie* (occasionally *-ye*) to *-y*, e.g. *dutie, onelye, laie*, and *-ll* for *-l* at the end of a word, e.g. *hopefull, portall*. Also such spellings as *hie* for *high, noyse* for *noise, deaw* for *dew, shewes* for *shows, chaunt* for *chant, ougly* for *ugly*, to name only a few. Many of his spellings are indeed pronunciation spellings; hence the forms *ake, seruill, quier*,

*daine*, the intrusive *d* in *frendzies* (of line 740), and the omission of silent *b* in such words as *nums* (892) and *lim* (1067); but in line 1146 *dūbe*, & for *dum*, and probably shows the hand of the compositor.

3. In words of French origin, sibilant *c* (e.g. *centinell*, 650) is a common feature of Shakespeare's spelling; but words such as *honour* are indifferently spelt *-or* or *-our*, with a slight preference for the latter.

4. Interesting rarities, such as the spellings *sacietie* (19)=satiety, *ceaze* (25), *sullein* (75), *atturney* (335), *murmour* (706), *skorne* (1084) are found on every page. Such forms are unorthodox, but it would be dangerous to describe them as individualisms. Spellings equally unusual occur in the *Authorized Version of the Bible*, and some of Shakespeare's most curious orthographies are paralleled in the *Book of Common Prayer*.

5. Shakespeare shared the taste of his printer for visual rhyme, hence the rhymes *nye/eye*, *thine/eine*, *despight/night*, *donne/sonne*[5] (=sun, 749–50), *Nuns/suns* (=sons, 752–4), *togither/whither*, *confesse/decesse* (=decease), *feare/seueare*, *conuaide/aide*.

### (b) SYNCOPE AND ELISION

By the early sixteenth century, syncope of *-e-*, in preterite and participial endings of weak verbs, was probably universal in colloquial speech, except in endings *-ded* and *-ted*. By the end of the century the full orthography *-ed*, or the conventional verse elision *'d*, had become the vogue of the printers, after both voiced and unvoiced stem-endings; but, prompted by a desire to spell as they pronounced, some writers and printers assimilated the *'d* to *t* after unvoiced stem finals. All varieties of ending are found in *Venus and Adonis*, e.g.

| | |
|---|---|
| a well proportion*e*d steed (*proportioned* trisyllabic) | (290) |
| rubi-colou*r*d portall | (451) |
| And all amaz*'d*, brake off | (469) |
| this black-fac*'t* night | (773) |

On the evidence of Field's treatment of Harington's script, the dedications to the two early Shakespeare poems, and the orthography of *Richard II*, it would appear that the marks of elision in *Venus and Adonis* are the work of Field's compositor, but that the second quotation (451) is exactly as Shakespeare wrote it. The printer even inserts the quite unnecessary apostrophe in such past participles as *wreak't* (1004), while Shakespeare in line 2 of the Dedication to *Venus and Adonis* presumably wrote *vnpolisht*, and in the poem itself *laught* (4), *blusht* (33), *pusht* (41), *stuft* (58), *kist* (59), *Forst* (61), *vnaskt* (102), *blest* (328), *ceast* (919), etc.

In prose, it seems that Shakespeare's early practice was to write the full ending *-ed* if the stem-final was voiced, with a preference for the assimilated ending *-t* if the stem-final was unvoiced. In verse, as *Richard II* testifies, he simply omitted the *e* if he preserved the normal syncope of speech, and inserted it if he wanted the extra inflexional syllable; in the latter case there could not be assimilation to *-t* after unvoiced stem-finals. This simple orthography obviated the dotting of his manuscript with marks of elision, which, as he realized, even the printers were using sporadically. In fact, Field's compositor inserted marks of elision only where they occurred to him; frequently enough to suggest a deliberate intention of improvement, but not as yet, in view of the date, a very urgent one. Sometimes the compositor replaced an elided *e* to justify his line, sometimes through prose habit and carelessness. Lapses naturally also occur on the part of the author, and are found even in Jonson's Folio of 1616.

After stems of weak verbs ending in a vowel or vowel-sound Shakespeare seems to have employed the full spelling *-ed*, pronounced *-d*, e.g. *wooed* (97), *swayed* (109), *borrowed* (488), *glewed* (546). A typical pentameter in Shakespearian orthography (save for *top*) is line 1143:

> The bottome poyson, and the top ore-*strawd*,

where *strawd*, instead of *strawed*, appears as the nearest possible spelling to a visual rhyme for *fraud*.

Orthographical inversion often takes place where the stems of weak and strong verbs end in unstressed *-en* or *-er*; and I am inclined to believe that syncope of *e* may have taken place before *n* and *r* of the suffix, instead of in the inflexional ending itself, e.g. *fastned* (68), *battred* (104), *gathred* (131), *falne* (monosyllabic, 354). *Proportioned* in line 290 may indeed imply a final syllable [∫ned] rather than modern [∫ənd]; for orthographically syncope appears to have implied elision of *e* only, so that for French *io* the full spelling had to be retained.

A further proof that marks of elision are a sophistication unpractised by Shakespeare at this time is, I think, to be found in such forms as *curt'sie* (=courtesy 888), *Ne'er* (1107), the plural *mouth's* (695) and the third person singular present indicatives *tell's* (587), *fall's* (594), *esteem's* (631), *root's* (636), *crop's* (1175). The apostrophe in these verbs and in *mouth's* marks elision of the original inflexional *e*, a point with which a writer like Shakespeare a decade before 1600 can scarcely have been concerned.

If in 1593 a manuscript poem had to be press-edited in an Elizabethan printing-house, consistency was hardly to be expected. By 1604, however, when Field came to print Sir William Alexander, Earl of Stirling's, *Paraenesis* and *Aurora*, the niceties of elision were well-established, and even to some extent cultivated by Shakespeare himself, as appears in the Second Quarto of *Hamlet*, printed in the same year. In this play Roberts's prentice compositor appears to have left us a fumbling transcript. But while dramatic orthography, in such matters as punctuation and elision, had been considerably tightened and regularized under the influence of Jonson's newly-printed 'humour' plays, the verse orthography of court poets had also improved through the stimulus of better printers, such as Field. The copy of the Earl of Stirling's poems presented to the printer must have been much more precisely pointed than that of Shakespeare's *Venus and Adonis* and *Lucrece*. In *Paraenesis* elision is on the whole carefully marked, especially of *e* in past-participial endings. In these endings *t* is not substituted for *'d* after unvoiced consonants. The poem was dedicated to the King, and it is reasonable to suppose that the copy would have been as near letter-perfection as possible. In this aspect of elision a laxer orthography is noticeable in *Aurora*, a collection of miscellaneous poems.

## (c) POSSESSIVE GENITIVE

The apostrophe before *s* was not employed by Shakespeare and his contemporaries. Where it occurs sporadically, as in Ben Jonson,[6] it is simply a mark of elision of *-e* belonging to the old masculine genitive singular inflexion *-es*, applied in Standard English to all genders and declensions by the end of the fourteenth century. This elision resembles that of the plural *mouth's* indicated above. But usually spelling sufficed to show that, in colloquial speech, owing to the unstressed nature of inflexions, the *e* had for some time been dropped, except after *-ch* and *-s*, or other sibilant or affricative stem-finals. The same syncope occurred in the third person singular present indicative of notional verbs, where, in the spoken language, the Northern inflexion *-es* had superseded the Southern *-eth* (cf. Field's orthography *tell's*, *fall's* above). The necessity for employing these marks of elision was not appreciated by most printers, and Jonson drew attention to it in his definition of *Apostrophus* in Book II, chapter I of his *Grammar* (the form *apostrophe* was first used by his friend Howell in 1642). But in practice Jonson mainly insisted on the mark of elision for the possessive genitive in proper names of Romance-language origin ending in a sounded vowel, e.g. *Every Man in His Humour*, I, i, 140, "*Prospero's* invention". In the case of other nouns, whether in the genitive singular or nominative plural, he was apparently indifferent to the use of the apostrophe. But Jonson's use of the possessive genitive, in all its possibilities of variation and substitution, is pedantically learned, whereas Shakespeare's is extremely simple, consisting of the uniform addition of *s* for singular and plural possessives, and the absence of any inflexion whatever if the nominative already ends in *s*, e.g. *Venus and Adonis* (261), "*Adonis* trampling Courser". The latter was, of course, a metrical consideration. Field's compositor preserves Shakespeare's orthography for all possessive genitives.

## (d) PUNCTUATION

There is no reason to suppose that Shakespeare's punctuation in *Venus and Adonis* was more elaborate or different in intention from that of his plays. The poem can certainly not have been pointed by Shakespeare as it appears in Field's printed version, for there are practices that do not occur again, except in *Lucrece*. To what extent Shakespeare's printed stanza verse employs a different system of punctuation from that of the plays appears in the following analysis.

The stanza scheme of *Venus and Adonis* consists of a quatrain followed by a couplet. About half of the couplets are loosely attached to the quatrain, being marked off only by a comma. The other half are self-contained, and are then commonly separated by a colon; less commonly by a full-stop, semicolon or question-mark. Enjambement at the end of the quatrain occurs only five times, and in two of these the stop has apparently been omitted by the author or printer, viz. at lines 406 and 1006. This conclusion is derived from the evidence of stops in the 199 stanzas of the poem. Wherever a colon is used at the end of the quatrain, modern editors are at a loss what to do, sometimes converting it, sometimes retaining it; the former when the stop coincides with some sense relation between the parts, the latter where the pause is clearly a metrical one. All but seventeen lines of the poem are end-stopped, but a metrical pause is often inserted in the form of a comma where logical syntax does not require it, e.g.

> The studded bridle on a ragged bough,
> Nimbly she fastens                                              (37–8)

Probably the comma here conforms to Shakespeare's practice, and indicates inversion of the normal order to emphasise "Nimbly". But there is much comma-pedantry, mainly syntactical, which I believe is Field's.

It is clear from the poem as a whole that the comma, especially at the end of a line, is over-worked, and that by modern standards a longer stop, such as a semicolon or colon, is often called for.  But the use of the semicolon as an intermediate time-stop, with co-ordinating effect, was not understood until Jonson used it with logical precision; and the colon seems to have been largely reserved for metrical or rhetorical function, to mark off elocutionary units of a poetical passage or speech.  Another function of the colon, possibly the work of Field's compositor, is to mark off a simile, especially if it is followed in the next line by the word "so", e.g.

> Like a diuedapper peering through a waue,
> Who being lookt on, ducks as quickly in:
> So offers he to giue what she did craue                    (86–8)

Both the colon and "So" are here resumptive.  In lines 815 and 928 a semicolon is substituted in this function.

In the stanza lines 751–6 the resumptive semicolon at the end of line 754 was misinterpreted in the Boswell-Malone Variorum Edition of 1821 and by succeeding editions, such as the Cambridge, Globe and Oxford:

> Therefore despight of fruitlesse chastitie,
> Loue-lacking vestals, and selfe-louing Nuns,
> That on the earth would breed a scarcitie,
> And barraine dearth of daughters, and of suns;
> Be prodigall, the lampe that burnes by night,
> Dries vp his oyle, to lend the world his light.

This is, on the whole, good Shakespearian orthography; but the editors have destroyed what I believe is the poet's intended sense by substituting a comma for the semicolon after "suns" and a colon for the comma after "prodigall". Venus's exhortation to "Be prodigall" is addressed, not to the vestals and other religious orders, but to Adonis, whom she adjures not to follow their example.  Possibly the editors see "Be" at the beginning of line 755 as an indicative plural, not as an imperative, which vitiates the sense further. To secure the true meaning, "Therefore" must be taken with "Be prodigall" four lines lower; "despight...suns" provides a long interpolation, and the purpose of the semicolon is to mark its end and pick up the imperative. This is a kind of rhetorical pointing, just as the semicolon in line 516 and the comma in line 774 are gesture stops. Whether the semicolon after "suns" in line 754 represents the precise quality of stop employed by Shakespeare is doubtful. The mass of evidence in the manuscript-based quartos suggests that he used four stops mainly in his writing, the comma, colon, period and question-mark; though he probably used the semicolon here and there for special situations, where none of his regular stops was suitable.

It is notable that exclamation marks are used only three times in *Venus and Adonis*, twice when the exclamation, indicative of emotion, is inserted between parentheses (lines 38 and 635), and once faultily in line 985:

> O hard beleeuing loue how strange it seemes !
> Not to beleeue, and yet too credulous:

where the mark should come either after "love" or "credulous", and has been inserted after "seemes" by the printer. For both Shakespeare and Jonson in his early quartos,[7] a lesser time-stop, such as a comma, usually sufficed after a simple interjection, as at lines 95 and 505–6; but where an exclamatory sentence or phrase began with an interrogative word, it was common to end with a question-mark, e.g.

What though the rose haue prickles, yet tis pluckt? (574)

The use of parentheses in the poem also suggests the sophisticating touch of the printer. It occurs

(i) When a sentence, usually to indicate the speaker, is inserted in the actual words of a speech. This obviates the modern use of inverted commas for the speech, a device not yet discovered by the printing trade; e.g.

Thrise fairer then my selfe, (thus she began)
The fields chiefe flower, sweet aboue compare (7–8)

The comma after "flower" is a metrical pause, probably Shakespeare's.

(ii) When a casual reflection, sometimes in the form of an exclamation, is interposed in the narrative; e.g.

The studded bridle on a ragged bough,
Nimbly she fastens, (ô how quicke is loue!) (37–8)

Brackets, circumflex accent and exclamation-mark are here the work of Field's compositor, and might be that of a modern printer. Yet the Globe edition unnecessarily improves to

fastens:—O, how quick is love!—

which has nothing to commend it.

## (e) CAPITALS

Simon Daines, in his *Orthoepia Anglicana* (1640), has the following interesting statement on the use of capital letters:[8]

The pronoune, or word (I) must alwayes be written with a great letter; so must every proper name, or peculiar denomination of every individuall: as all the Attributes of God Almighty, the names of Angels, Saints, and evill spirits; the titles given by the Heathens to their faigned Gods and Goddesses; the names of men and women of all sorts whatsoever; the names of moneths, winds, rivers, Cities, townes, Islands and Kingdoms: the particular name of any peculiar dog, horse, or beast of any kind soever: The first word of every verse, at least Heroique: any letter set for a number, as you had in the beginning of our Orthoepie: Any letter standing for any such, or the abbreviation as we there mentioned. Lastly, all names or Titles of Magistrates, Arts, Offices, and Dignities, in what respect soever taken. In these, I say, altogether consists the use of Capitall Letters, in all other we use onely the smaller.

It is probable that, in the employment of capital letters for nouns other than proper names, there was some sort of printers' convention. Wyndham in 1898 gave a useful classification of substantives that were normally capitalized[9] by the printers of Shakespeare's poems, and with some modification the list will do for the nine quartos of plays based on Shakespeare's manuscript and printed by 1604. My own list has the following dozen categories:

1. Personifications and images, especially if based on classical statuary, mythology and emblems; e.g.

> His *Art* with *Natures* workmanship at strife,      *(Venus and Adonis*, 291)
>
> Or like a *Nimph*, with long disheueled heare,      (147)
>
> Ouer my *Altars* hath he hong his launce,      (103)

2. Names of animals, birds, fishes, insects, plants, trees and flowers, especially if used in fables, emblematically, proverbially or typically; e.g.

> But this foule, grim, and vrchin-snowted *Boare*,   *(Venus and Adonis*, 1105)
>
> Even as an emptie *Eagle* sharpe by fast,      (55)
>
> like a dried *Hering*      *(Romeo and Juliet* (Quarto 2), II, iv, 39)
>
> As *Caterpillers* do      *(Venus and Adonis*, 798)
>
> an emptie *Hasel* nut      *(Romeo and Juliet* (Quarto 2), I, iv, 67)

3. Names of precious stones and substances; e.g.

> in shape no bigger thē an *Agot* stone,
>      *(Romeo and Juliet* (Quarto 2), I, iv, 55)
>
> Or *Iuorie* in an allablaster *(sic)* band,      *(Venus and Adonis*, 363)

4. Names of arts, sciences and public entertainments; e.g.

> The setting Sunne, and *Musike* at the close,
>      *(Richard II* (Quarto 1), II, i, 12)
>
> And we meane well in going to this *Mask*,
>      *(Romeo and Juliet* (Quarto 2), I, iv, 48)

5. Names of religions and their institutions, etc.; e.g.

> ere I last receiude the *Sacrament*      *(Richard II* (Quarto 1), I, i, 139)
>
> Which is the god of my *Idolatrie*   *(Romeo and Juliet* (Quarto 2), II, ii, 114)

6. Names of diseases, ailments, etc.; e.g.

> Full soone the *Canker* death eates vp that Plant
>
> The *Pox* of such antique lisping affecting phantacies
>      *(Romeo and Juliet* (Quarto 2), II, iii, 30; II, iv, 29)

7. Terms of cosmology, heavenly bodies, time and geography of the earth; e.g.

> blacke *Chaos* comes againe
>
> Shone like the *Moone* in water seene by night
>      *(Venus and Adonis*, 1020, 492)

Let two more *Sommers* wither in their pride,

(*Romeo and Juliet* (Quarto 2), I, ii, 10)

A *Bay* in Brittaine          (*Richard II* (Quarto 1), II, i, 277)

8. Terms relating to kingship, chivalry, statecraft, and government; e.g.

Adde an immortall title to your *Crowne*

By that, and all the rites of *Knighthoode* else,

Most mighty *Liege*, and my companion *Peeres*,

(*Richard II* (Quarto 1), I, i, 24, 75; I, iii, 93)

the forefinger of an *Alderman*      (*Romeo and Juliet* (Quarto 2), I, iv, 56)

9. Professions, trades, occupations; e.g.

Being *Iudge* in love, she cannot right her cause     (*Venus and Adonis*, 220)

Made by the *Ioyner* squirrel      (*Romeo and Juliet* (Quarto 2), I, iv, 66)

Like shrill-tongu'd *Tapsters* answering everie call,

(*Venus and Adonis*, 849)

10. Technical terms (e.g. (*a*) Heraldic, (*b*) Printing and publishing trade, including book, volume, reader, (*c*) Rhetoric, (*d*) Duelling, etc.):

Now is he totall *Gules* horridly trickt       (*Hamlet*, II, ii, 479)

Oh thou the earthly *Authour* of my bloud

(*Richard II* (Quarto 1), I, iii, 67)

ah the immortall *Passado*, the *Punto* reuerso, the *Hay*

(*Romeo and Juliet* (Quarto 2), II, iv, 26–7)

11. Personal appellations and family relationships; e.g.

Nurse, commend me to thy *Lady* and *Mistresse*,

(*Romeo and Juliet* (Quarto 2), II, iv, 182)

He is our *Coosens Coosin*       (*Richard II* (Quarto 1), I, iv, 20)

12. Foreign words not yet felt to be naturalized; e.g.

Even from the tounglesse *Cauernes* of the earth,

Before this out-darde *Dastard*?

we shall see / *Iustice* designe the *Victors* chiualrie

(*Richard II* (Quarto 1), I, i, 105, 190, 203)

That this system is apparent in all the manuscript-based quartos of Shakespeare printed by different houses before 1604, is not evidence in itself that he himself conformed to the convention in his writing. Autograph manuscripts of plays of the previous decade are rare, and point to negligent use of capitals by authors, both in respect of these categories, and at the beginning of verse lines. There is no ground whatever, except chance, for supposing that the capitalization of substantives before 1600 and even as late as 1610 indicated dramatic or elocutionary emphasis.

Percy Simpson's treatment of emphasis capitals in *Shakespearian Punctuation* (1911) is based upon the practice of the Folio of 1623, and by the latter date capitalization had so increased that it is possible to accept the emphasis thesis, with the proviso that *not all* capitals emphasize. I suspect that the influence of scribes, such as Ralph Crane, who cultivated the majuscules as an ornamental feature of his calligraphy, had much to do with the practice of capitalization. Crane and Jonson account for many editorial practices of the First Folio, and their influence probably began to be exerted in the second decade of the seventeenth century. About this time there was a considerable importation into literary works of foreign words and technical terms, also capitalized; and if one adds the influence of Continental, especially German printing, the stage would logically be reached when it became convenient and time-saving for the printers to capitalize practically all substantives, and to italicize those of foreign origin. This is, in fact, the situation at the end of the seventeenth century. Though printers varied, the peak period for the use of capitalized substantives extends roughly from the Restoration to the middle of the eighteenth century.

## (*f*) Contractions

It is not here possible to give an account of the use, development and orthographical representation of Shakespeare's contractions and colloquial weakenings. There is not a clear division between verse and prose uses, nor between forms found in literary productions, such as *Venus and Adonis*, and those employed in plays; though naturally exclusively poetical prepositions, adverbs and conjunctions such as *twixt, tween, ere, nere, oft* and *where* (=whether) predominate in the poems. Apart from these, there are 26 contractions in *Venus and Adonis*, proclitic *t* for *it* (14), proclitic *th'* for *the* (2), *'s* for *is* (4), and *Ile* for *I shall* or *will* (6). These four kinds are again in use in *Richard II* and *Romeo and Juliet*. The most notable additions in the early plays are colloquial weakenings of pronouns and prepositions: *s* for *us*; *a* for *he*; *yee, ye* and *y'* for *you*; enclitic *'t* and *th* for *it* and *the*, *i* or *y* for *in* (in the expression *ifaith, yfaith*), and *a* for both the prepositions *of* and *on*.

In *Romeo and Juliet* (Quarto 2) *a* for *he* is used by Mercutio, Capulet and Romeo familiarly, but by the Nurse only when angered, and mainly in the disapproving *quotha*; in fact *a* in this expression may stand for any weakened personal pronoun (for instance *you* in II, iv, 124). *Ye* for unstressed *you* is used principally, but not always, by the racier speakers, such as Mercutio and the Nurse.

Two interesting weakenings are erroneously indicated by elision in *Richard II*, probably not by Shakespeare himself:

Sweare by the duty that y'owe to God, (I, iii, 180)

Metre here requires *you* or the full unstressed form *ye*. Elision is marked because of the juxtaposition of two vowels.

Oh had't beene a stranger, not my child, (I, iii, 239)

The apostrophe indicates weakening of the pronoun to [ət], not actual elision.

*They* and *them* are the invariable orthography of Shakespeare himself; he does not favour the contractions *th'* and *'hem* of Jonson or *'em* of Fletcher. He observes the full form *them* not only in the poems, but in the plays, as is clear from the manuscript-based quartos. He probably felt

45

that the accusatives *'hem* and *'em* would obtrude by reason of their frequency, without providing the metrical advantage of a decreased syllable. Even in the weakened double ending of the rhyme *betweene them/seene them* (*Venus and Adonis*, 355–7) Shakespeare retains the dignity of the full form, where Fletcher in his plays would have reduced to *'em*.

*Weele* and *theile* in the plays of the nineties are analogous to *Ile* in *Venus and Adonis*, but the modern orthography *'ll* for *shall* and *will* does not occur. Nor does *'m* for *am* and *'ld* for *would*; but contraction was probably achieved by slurring or light pronunciation in the following verse lines, where the full orthography appears:

> She *would* be as swift in motion as a ball
> Ifaith I *am* sorrie that thou art not well.　　(*Romeo and Juliet*, II, v, 13, 54)

This raises the question what Shakespeare's orthography would have been in the later plays of the Folio, in fact all after *Hamlet*. After the accession of James I, Shakespeare's Company enjoyed the special favour of royal protection, and the publishers of the later quartos, *Lear*, the *Sonnets*, *Pericles*, *Troilus and Cressida*, and *Othello*, all appear to have obtained their copy by the back door. Consequently these quartos are not very reliable evidence. But the Folio texts of *Coriolanus* and *Antony and Cleopatra* are thought to be based on Shakespeare's manuscripts, and there appears an almost new dramatic orthography, replete with contractions and elisions of all kinds, such as *a'th*, *and't*, *in't*, *to't*, *to'th'Capitoll*, *upon's*, *th'fire*, *wee'l*, *they'l*, *y'are*, *hang'em*, *ha's*, *ta'ne*. Two explanations are possible for this, the first that Shakespeare had absorbed from others a different technique, and had developed it independently. This, I think, must be accepted as probable; for he was willing to learn, had in discourse possibly discussed these matters with Jonson, and may have realized the freedom and flexibility in dialogue which the extended system of contractions and elisions conferred. The second possibility (equally likely) is that the foul papers Shakespeare originally produced were either copied or edited by the Company's scribe before Heminge and Condell handed the copy to the publishers, or possibly the copy was edited by the publishers themselves.

What Shakespeare wrote in the forms illustrated in the preceding paragraph can only be conjectured. It is reasonable to suppose that he was, by now, using marks of elisions, at any rate in such difficult orthographies as *ath*, *int*, *tot*. These reduced combinations were so frequent, so much a part of the texture of the verse, and so important for correct rhythmical interpretation, that he probably inserted marks of elision where they were necessary to avoid misreading. But in these minutiae he nodded frequently, and many of the punctuation-marks must have been the result of confused and over-zealous editing.

To sum up this mass of discrete evidence is difficult; but the general features which emerge and can be checked by constant reference to the Quartos thought to be based on Shakespeare's manuscripts, are clear. Shakespeare's spelling was old-fashioned in its attachment to full-spellings and its curious blend of Tudor, individual and pseudo-phonetic representations. His mind must have been well stored with books written and printed in a previous generation; and when he became fully absorbed in the business of writing and producing plays, he apparently had little time to read and to keep abreast with the newer developments in printing and orthography, until his contact with Ben Jonson about the turn of the century. When Field received his manuscripts of *Venus and Adonis* and *Lucrece* he had no scruple in editing what he found, because Shakespeare's orthography seemed to him arbitrary. In *Richard II*, Shakespeare or a careful amanuensis appears to have made a fair copy of his play, for its orthography is the key to all that is characteristically his in the other good quartos. It is one of his most carefully prepared dramatic texts, another being *Hamlet* (Quarto 2). His punctuation was always light, and probably employed the semicolon rarely and the exclamation mark not at all; commas did general service for shorter stops, and colons tended to mark off the elocutionary and rhetorical units of the actor's delivery, so as to secure smoothness and dramatic significance in the important speeches. Syncope and obvious elisions he obtained mainly through the spelling; he did not dot his copy with apostrophes, and never used this symbol for the possessive genitive. If an unstressed extra syllable occurred in a familiar word or colloquial combination, he relied on the actor to slur it, as he would in everyday speech; elsewhere he envisaged a light pronunciation or half-syncope for metrical variation—which is what he meant by speaking the speech "trippingly on the tongue".[10] I imagine that he used capital letters regularly after full-stops, for proper names and titles of dignity, and possibly for emblematic and classical images. I think it possible that, in marginal verse insertions written out as prose, he employed a capital letter sporadically to indicate where a new line was to begin; and that omission to do this frequently caused mislineation in the printing. The best clue to his graphic habits is, however, the evidence of his colloquial contractions and commoner grammatical forms. Taken with the orthographical factors, these may prove decisive in confirming or rejecting the bibliographical evidence which has already advanced Shakespearian textual criticism.

## NOTES

1. *Orthoepia Anglicana*, ed. M. Rösler and R. Brotanek (Halle, 1908), p. 75, ll. 5–12.

2. See Sir Philip Sidney's remarks on English Grammar in 'An Apology for Poetry', *Elizabethan Critical Essays*, ed. Gregory Smith, vol. II, p. 204, ll. 9–14.

3. *The Library*, IV (September 1923), 102–18.

4. *Shakespeare, Man and Artist*, I, 379–85.

5. The late Middle English scribal practice of substituting *o* for *u* in spellings before and after *m, n, v, w* was continued optionally in the New English period, where the pronunciation is obviously *u*.

6. See my *Accidence of Ben Jonson's Plays, Masques and Entertainments* (Cambridge, 1953), § 12.

7. I have counted less than a dozen exclamation marks in the whole of the 1601 Quarto of *Every Man in His Humour*, and less than three times that number in the earliest Quarto of *Every Man out of His Humour* (1600), published by the Malone Society in 1921. The latter play is much longer than the Second Quarto of *Hamlet*, and has many exclamations; but the appropriate mark appears mainly after the interjection O, though inconsistently.

8. *Op. cit.* 'Certaine peculiar Rules of Orthography', p. 76.

9. See *The Poems of Shakespeare*, pp. 223 and 262.

10. E.g. *Richard II* (Quarto 1), II, iii, 24, "I *had* thought my Lord *to* haue learn*ed* his health of you". Here *had* and *to* required half-syncope of the actor, and the ending of *learned* full syncope.

# THE NEW WAY WITH SHAKESPEARE'S TEXTS:
## AN INTRODUCTION FOR LAY READERS
## I. THE FOUNDATIONS[1]

BY

## J. DOVER WILSON

A well-known member of Shakespeare's profession, who is also a regular reader of *Shakespeare Survey*, said to me the other day, "I wish one of you fellows would give us a Textual Introduction to Shakespeare without Tears. We can see that there is a great deal of important work going on and that the scholars are enjoying themselves no end over it. But what it all means is very hard for the layman to understand. What for instance is the exact difference between a folio and a quarto? You are always talking about them, but you never explain what they are."

In the following article I shall try to provide my friend and others like him with what he asks, and I thought I might make it more interesting if I threw it into a quasi-autobiographical form. For the new way of dealing with Shakespeare's text is the result of a number of related discoveries and theories which have been made or formulated during the last forty-five years, i.e. during my adult life, while the authors of most of them were men whom I knew personally.

They were, or are, librarians for the most part or those closely associated with them and what I owe to librarians I cannot even begin to estimate. I well remember, for instance, the day when Charles Sayle, an assistant at the Cambridge University Library, taught me, as a young man, the meaning of folio and quarto. In the eyes of a printer, he explained, the units of a book are not its pages but its sheets, which are of course printed on both sides, and must after printing be arranged in their proper order before being bound up, or stitched up, into book form. The foot of each sheet is accordingly marked on the side on which its first page occurs with a serial number or letter, called the 'signature'. Open any book and you will find these numbers or letters at intervals, the intervals being determined by the total number of pages to the sheet, while that total should tell you what kind, or 'format', of book it is in the printer's category. For, by printers, he explained further, books are classified according not to their contents but to the way their sheets are folded. Thus when the sheets are folded once, so as to form two leaves (or four pages), a printer calls the book a folio or more exactly 'in folio', from the Latin *folium*, a leaf; when they are folded twice, so as to form four leaves (or eight pages), he calls it a quarto; when they are folded once more, so as to form eight leaves (or sixteen pages), he calls it an octavo: and so on to 12mo, 16mo and 32 mo; the book of course growing smaller at every fresh folding. In Shakespeare's day sheets of paper were oblongs of more or less the same size, so that books in folio were tall volumes of fairly uniform height, specially suitable for the printing of large quantities of material. The quarto, on the other hand, being half the height of a folio, was a 'format' more often used when less material was printed. It was natural, then, if not inevitable, that the first collected edition of Shakespeare's plays, published in 1623, should be in folio—the First Folio we call it to distinguish it from its sequels, the Second Folio of 1632, the Third of

1663, and the Fourth of 1685; and that individual plays of his which appeared at intervals from 1594 onwards should be printed in quarto. Such was my first lesson in bibliography and I learnt in later lessons to distinguish between the 'formes' of a sheet, i.e. its two sides when printed,[2] to understand the order in which the printed pages appear on either forme, to speak of the two sides of a leaf as 'recto' and 'verso', and more particularly to concentrate upon the methods of compositors, that is to realize how they went to work in reading their manuscripts or 'copy', and in 'setting up' the words therein as lines of type, first in their 'stick' and later in the 'forme'. Finally, I managed to watch a hand-press in operation and got a general idea of the way the ink was applied to the face of the type, how the sheets were 'laid on' and then 'struck off'. All this was very elementary and easily picked up; and I have never since had time to go much deeper.[3] Yet the knowledge, such as it is, has proved useful, and not only for the editing of Shakespeare. Indeed, I acquired it originally for a very different purpose, viz. in order to track the cross-country movements of a secret Puritan printing press which was bombarding the Elizabethan bishops with ridicule in the Marprelate Tracts, during the years 1588 and 1589. This and subsequent detective work connected with Puritan printing at that period led to articles in a bibliographical journal called *The Library* and to papers for the Bibliographical Society. The editor of that journal and the secretary of that society was Alfred Pollard, who accepted my first article in 1907. Ten years later, as I shall relate in my second article, we were joint detectives in pursuit of a much bigger quarry than a Puritan pamphleteer.

Bibliography is a term often used to denote a list of books, or more strictly a list of books accompanied by a description of their make-up to enable its reader to distinguish one edition or issue from another. But inasmuch as such descriptions to be reliable must be based upon a knowledge of printing and publishing, bibliography has acquired the wider and deeper meaning of a study of the whole mechanics of book-production.[4] This study began to take organized shape towards the end of the nineteenth century, at the hands of a number of librarians and other persons interested in old books and fine books. In 1892 a London Bibliographical Society was founded, and during the next ten years it collected and printed a considerable amount of information about early printed books: their bindings, types and printer's ornaments; the methods of their publishers, press-men and compositors; the water-marks in their papers, and what not. As printing was invented in the fifteenth century, bibliographers at first concerned themselves mainly with fifteenth-century books or 'incunables' (=cradle-books) as they were called. But their researches laid an indispensable foundation for the study of sixteenth- and seventeenth-century books that came later. And it was the application of the knowledge and the methods thus gained which brought about the revolution in Shakespearian textual criticism of our time.

The chief moving spirit behind these developments from the beginning had been Alfred Pollard, at that time in charge of the antiquarian side of the Department of Printed Books at the British Museum[6] and from 1893 to 1934 Honorary Secretary of the Bibliographical Society. But about 1900 he found stalwart allies in two young Cambridge men, Ronald B. McKerrow, who was twelve years, and Walter W. Greg, who was fifteen years, his junior; names that were to become two of the most illustrious in the roll of English scholarship. They had been undergraduate friends at Trinity College, Cambridge, the Vice-Master of which in their time was Aldis Wright, the best of the nineteenth-century editors of Shakespeare, and the library of which contained one of the finest collections of Shakespearian quartos in the world, deposited there by Edward Capell the famous eighteenth-century editor, to say nothing of its wealth of other books belonging to the same period. It was not unnatural therefore that McKerrow and Greg should be fired with an ambition to try the newly shaped bibliographical tools upon Elizabethan and Jacobean texts. And we may guess that they marked down Shakespeare as their chief objective quite early. But both, with Scottish blood in their veins, were cannily aware that much preparatory work needed doing first. So far, for example, no reliable editions existed of any Elizabethan texts, least of all in the field of the drama; the surviving contemporary dramatic documents, which were far more numerous than was generally realized, had not yet been made accessible to scholars in trustworthy reprints or facsimiles; and there was not even a decent history of the Elizabethan theatre.

Greg opened the campaign in 1900 by issuing through the Bibliographical Society a little pamphlet of 158 pages containing *A List of English Plays written before 1643 and printed before 1700*, after which he set to work on an edition of *Henslowe's Diary* and other *Henslowe Papers*, the most important documents, apart from dramatic texts, that have come down to us about the Elizabethan theatre. Henslowe was owner of the Rose theatre and father-in-law of Edward Alleyn, Burbage's chief rival; and his papers (including the 'diary', a kind of account book), which Alleyn bequeathed to the Dulwich Hospital, are full of intimate details concerning the plays, dramatists and finances of the rival theatre and company to Shakespeare's. Greg's great edition, a starting-point for all later exploration into the theatrical conditions of the day, was completed between the years 1904 and 1908. Meanwhile E. K. Chambers, an official at the Board of Education, published two epoch-making volumes on *The Medieval Stage* in 1903; and was already following it up, in frequent consultation with Greg, by writing a still more monumental work on *The Elizabethan Stage*, completed in four volumes in 1923, and ultimately continued and rounded off in his *William Shakespeare* (1930). These eight masterly volumes, stuffed with information and illuminated on every page with common sense and a healthy scepticism, transformed our whole conception of the life and work of the player, dramatist and 'sharer' in the Chamberlain's company whom the world unites to honour. Though now over twenty years old, the full significance of this great encyclopaedic work has not yet I think dawned upon the generality of Shakespeare's readers and actors. It completely superseded much of Sidney Lee's *Life*, hitherto supposed "complete and trustworthy", while by the sheer weight of the documentary evidence, which it has now placed within the reach of all, it left Baconians and other 'anti-Stratfordians' nothing but their own inanity to fall back upon. And, the year after Chambers published his *William Shakespeare*, Greg followed it up in his turn by furnishing magnificent full-scale facsimiles of the remaining theatrical papers left by Alleyn at Dulwich, together with a detailed account of forty-five extant sixteenth- and seventeenth-century plays that have survived in manuscript. But I am running ahead and shall be saying more of these books later.

One further development of a preparatory character must be noticed, the erection and maintenance of a rigid standard of exact scholarship in the editing of printed texts of any kind. "It is high time", Greg wrote in 1906, "that it should be understood that so long as we entrust our old authors to arm-chair editors who are content with second-hand knowledge of textual sources, so long will English scholarship in English afford undesirable amusement to the learned world." And he then proceeded to make mincemeat of an edition of Robert Greene by Churton Collins in a review[7] which put the fear of God into all future editors and is still at once entertaining and salutary to read. And while Greg was thus constituting himself the watchdog of English scholarship, McKerrow was setting up the new model in his palmary edition of Thomas Nashe (1904–10), which placed England once more in the forefront of Elizabethan studies. Closely connected with all this was the founding at Pollard's suggestion in 1906 of the Malone Society for the exact reprinting, in typographical facsimile, of Elizabethan plays, some ninety of which have been issued since that date. In the formation of this society, Greg tells us in his memoir of McKerrow,[8] "one of our early dreams came to fruition", while F. P. Wilson speaks of Pollard, Greg and McKerrow as "a happy band of brothers", whose presence from 1900 onwards "in the British Museum, from necessity or choice or both, made that library and its neighbouring restaurants...the best centre for Elizabethan studies in the world".[9] One may guess that another of the "early dreams" of the two younger men was that McKerrow should follow up his Nashe by producing an old-spelling edition of Shakespeare. Anyhow he was seriously contemplating such an edition in 1910 when his Nashe was finished, though he was not able to begin working at it until 1929; and when, to the irreparable loss of English scholarship, he died in 1940 he had published nothing of it but a *Prolegomena*, 1939. Thus the definitive edition of Shakespeare on the lines of modern scholarship has still to come; and the time for it is probably not ripe even yet. Nevertheless, to quote Greg's memoir again, those "few pages in which" McKerrow "discussed the grounds of his practice as an editor remain the most important he ever penned and should prove the most helpful guide to English critics whose concern is with printed texts".

Down to the beginning of the present century, the steps of most editors of Shakespeare had been dogged by a profound pessimism concerning the texts they were working upon. The plays, as already noted, came to us in two forms: (i) the great collected edition, known as the First Folio, in which thirty-six, i.e. all but *Pericles*, were published in 1623, seven years after Shakespeare's death, under the aegis of Heminge and Condell, the author's friends and fellows; and (ii) eighteen of these which had earlier appeared separately in quarto form at various dates between 1594 and 1623—and with those must be classed *Pericles*, since it is also a quarto, published first in 1609. It takes no great scholarship to see that the texts in this second group vary very much in quality, some of them closely corresponding with the texts of the same plays in the Folio, others departing so widely from these as to be clearly abridged and corrupt, and others again seemingly occupying a rather middle position between the two extremes. And the problems of authenticity thus raised were complicated by problems of chronology. For the quartos issued before 1623 include publications of the same play at different dates, some of them obviously successive reprints of the same text, which gathered fresh misprints with each reprint, others like the First and Second Quarto of *Romeo and Juliet* and of *Hamlet* as obviously giving us different versions of the same play, while there were a few which, bearing the same date, had never been placed in their correct sequence. Editors' practice had usually been to take the Folio as their basis in the preparation of any given text but to help themselves to any readings in any of the quartos, if quartos existed, that appealed to them as likely to be Shakespeare's. The ideal of this type of editing was a complete collation of all previous editions, and Aldis Wright accordingly printed such a collation in notes at the foot of his pages in the old Cambridge Shakespeare, 1863

(2nd edition 1891). But working almost entirely in the dark as to the nature and origin of the manuscripts from which these folio or quarto texts had originally been printed, editors had little confidence in their results. Indeed, they held both types of text under extreme suspicion. Listen to Dr Johnson:

> Most writers, by publishing their own works, prevent all various readings, and preclude all conjectural criticism.... But of the works of Shakespeare the condition has been far different: he sold them, not to be printed, but to be played. They were immediately copied for the actors, and multiplied by transcript after transcript, vitiated by the blunders of the penman, or changed by the affectation of the player; perhaps enlarged to introduce a jest, or mutilated to shorten the representation; and printed at last without the concurrence of the author, without the consent of the proprietor, from compilations made by chance or by stealth out of the separate parts written for the theatre: and thus thrust into the world surreptitiously and hastily, they suffered another depravation from the ignorance and negligence of the printers, as every man who knows the state of the press in that age will readily conceive.[10]

Seldom has fine rhetoric lent colour to a falser thesis. For most of these charges against those responsible for the transmission of Shakespeare's texts, there is, as Pollard pointed out in 1915, "not one shred of evidence...nothing but an imaginative pessimism convinced that this is what must have happened".[11] Yet Johnson's pessimism was shared by most of his successors until Pollard's day.

It is even doubtful whether Pollard himself or his fellow bibliographers Greg and McKerrow realized how false the old editorial principles were until their eyes were opened by researches in which they found themselves involved by events which took place in 1902. In that year the Oxford University Press published a collotype facsimile of the First Folio, with an Introduction by Sidney Lee. Political revolutions are often precipitated by extreme conservatives. The revolution in English textual criticism was, we shall see, directly provoked by Lee's unfortunate essay, which will go down to history as the last, and not the least dogmatic, statement of the traditional views about Shakespeare's text. And in this same year 1902 "a charming little fat volume" in calf was put into Pollard's hands by a German who brought it to the Museum hoping to find a purchaser. Containing nine plays in quarto, all claiming on their title-pages to be Shakespeare's, though two of them were not his and another two were garbled versions of *Henry V* and *The Merry Wives*, it was an attractive book. Pollard, however, was unable to induce his department to buy it, and it crossed the Atlantic. But he kept notes of it, and when a second little fat volume, containing the same nine plays with identical titles, turned up in similar circumstances about three years later, he felt sure the coincidence was no accident, and his suspicions thus roused led him on with Greg's assistance to a succession of discoveries which taken together constitute one of the finest examples of bibliographical detective work in our time. For the thrilling story—how Pollard first proved the previous existence of three other similar volumes, one of which must have belonged to Garrick, since its nine component parts were found among the books of the Garrick collection on the British Museum shelves; how with the help of these last he was able to identify the type and printer's ornaments with those in books produced by Jaggard, who printed the First Folio in 1623; how Greg then came forward and showed from the evidence of watermarks, the similarity of imprints, and the common use of certain large numerals, that all nine quartos must have been printed together by Jaggard in 1619, the latest date on their titles—for all this I must refer you to Pollard's own account in the book he published in 1909, which I shall describe presently. Note first, however, that the final and irrefutable proof was supplied in 1910 by W. Neidig, an American scholar, who demonstrated by composite photography that the same typographical setting had been used for seven out of the nine title-pages. The whole series forms a classical instance of bibliographical demonstration, every step in the argument being deduced from the mechanics of the printer's craft and therefore independent of all literary considerations, which decide nothing but merely lead to wrangles among the critics.

Moreover, its bearing on textual criticism in general and our knowledge of Shakespeare's texts in particular was momentous. First of all, for the reason just given, it established critical bibliography for good and all as a valuable aid to literary scholarship and especially to editors of printed texts. Secondly, it threw an interesting and not altogether favourable light upon Jaggard's eagerness for Shakespeare's copy before he undertook the printing of the First Folio, an eagerness which he was already displaying twenty years earlier when he published under Shakespeare's name *The Passionate Pilgrim*, a book containing a score of poems, only five of which were actually his. Thirdly, it determined the chronological order of certain quartos bearing the same date which had long been a standing puzzle to scholars: now that the Jaggard quartos of *A Midsummer Night's Dream*, *The Merchant of Venice* and *King Lear* are known to have been printed in 1619 and not 1600 and 1608 as they are dated in his faked imprints, editors can regard the *Dream* "Imprinted at London by Thomas Fisher, 1600", *The Merchant* "Printed by I.R. for Thomas Heyes, 1600" and *King Lear* "Printed for Nathaniel Butter...at the signe of the Pide Bull, 1608" as first editions and proceed accordingly. Finally, it made a beginning of that sorting-out and classification of Shakespeare's texts which is one of the more important achievements of the new textual scholarship.

The full detective story, except for Neidig's crowning evidence, was, I have said, told by Pollard in a book published in 1909. This was his magnum opus, *Shakespeare Folios and Quartos*, in which the bibliographical study of Shakespeare took its first great step. The Jaggard quartos formed the subject of Chapter IV only; the rest of the volume, commissioned by Methuen's as an Introduction to facsimiles of the four Folios published by them in 1904–9, was written in reply to the Introduction Lee had contributed to the Oxford facsimile of 1902. The pessimism of scholars in general and of Lee in particular as to the origins and character of the early Shakespearian texts had sprung from two sources: their ignorance of the conditions governing the production and marketing of books in Shakespeare's day, and their misunderstanding of a phrase in Heminge and Condell's preface to the First Folio. This phrase occurs in a passage which, as the title-deed to our greatest national possession, cannot be quoted too often. Commending their volume "to the great variety of readers" they write (spelling and punctuation modernized):

It had been a thing, we confess, worthy to have been wished that the author himself had lived to have set forth and overseen [= read the proofs of] his own writings. But since it hath been ordained otherwise, and he by death departed from that right, we pray you do not envy his friends the office of their care and pain to have collected and published them; and so to have published them as where before you were abused with divers stolen and surreptitious copies, maimed and deformed by the frauds and stealths of injurious impostors that exposed them, even those are now offered to your view cured and perfect of their limbs; and all the rest absolute in their numbers as he conceived them. Who, as he was a happy imitator of nature, was a most gentle expresser of it. His mind and hand went together; and what he thought, he uttered with that easiness that we have scarce received from him a blot in his papers.

I shall recall some of these words later. For the moment I am concerned with the reference to the "variety of readers" having been formerly "abused" with "divers stolen and surreptitious copies". By this they obviously mean certain quartos published before 1623; and, until Pollard wrote, editors and scholars with very few exceptions assumed that they meant *all* of them. Yet if this be so, condemnation of "injurious impostors" recoils with deadly effect upon Heminge and Condell's own heads. For it is certain, and has long been known, that a number of plays in the Folio they vouch for were printed, not from Shakespeare's manuscripts, or indeed any manuscripts, but from those very quartos they seem to characterize as "maimed and deformed". In other words they were convicted out of their own mouths of being themselves fraudulent impostors, and no confidence could be placed in the texts they claimed as "perfect in their limbs". Pollard rid the world of this editorial nightmare by pointing out a very obvious fact, viz. that the quartos fall into two classes quite distinct from each other. Five of them he labelled 'bad' because they furnished texts indisputably corrupt or, to use the players' phrase, "maimed and deformed", and because, as he showed, they were printed and published in circumstances highly suspicious to anyone familiar with the book trade of that age. And the rest he labelled 'good' because they furnished presentable texts and seemed thoroughly respectable as products of the publisher and printer. Further, he pointed out, this simple distinction not only made honest books of most of the quartos, but restored the credit of the Folio as well. For when Heminge and Condell spoke of "stolen and surreptitious copies" it was now clear they meant the handful of 'bad' quartos; and when they handed on to Jaggard some of the 'good' quartos to print from, they were making a perfectly legitimate use of books which they knew had formerly been printed from "true original copies". As for these "originals", the manuscripts from which the 'good' quartos and, as he believed, most of the rest of the Folio texts were printed, they came and could only have come from the playhouse, and the presumption—he felt the strong presumption—was that some at least of them were in Shakespeare's own hand-writing; while if others were prompt-copies that had been used in performance they were in all probability transcripts from Shakespeare's drafts, and were in any case much closer to his autograph manuscripts than any editor had hitherto dared to hope. To sum up: Pollard showed, on the one hand, that we have no reason to doubt the good faith of Heminge and Condell when they speak of "their care and pain" in the preparation of the copy for the Folio or to suppose the subsequent operations of printers and publishers were anything but creditable to all concerned. That Jaggard had twice on previous occasions attempted to palm off other writers' productions as Shakespeare's simply indicates his confidence in the market value of Shakespeare's name, and helps to explain his readiness to undertake what was probably thought a heavy risk, the printing of a large book like the Folio which would lock up much money for many months before any returns could be looked for. In any case, with an official publication of the King's Company everything went to show that it was the players and not the printer who were responsible for selecting the copy.

Pollard's reinterpretation of the textual situation won its way to the general acceptance of scholars with remarkably rapidity; and it rendered obsolete the principles which had governed editorial theory and practice for a couple of centuries. It was necessary to begin afresh from the beginning. This does not imply anything so arrogant or so foolish as a claim that all previous editions are worthless. Try to read Shakespeare in the Oxford or Methuen or Booth [12] facsimile of the First Folio, and you will be held up in almost every other line by misprints, or unintelligible punctuation, or mislining of the verse, or missing stage-directions, to say nothing of the old spelling and a dozen other puzzling features. It took two and a half centuries of editing to convert that mass of perplexities into the familiar 'Globe Shakespeare' of today; and we cannot be too grateful to the editors of the past not only for making the text of the plays readable but for ridding it of a very large amount of corruption. There can be no doubt at all that our current Shakespeares are a great deal nearer to what Shakespeare wrote than the original printed editions. Nevertheless, I repeat, we must begin re-editing them all over again, since despite everything that editors from Rowe to Aldis Wright and Wright's successors have effected in detail, they were wrong in principle, and, being so, the text they gave us was sometimes very wrong indeed. How wrong may be illustrated by an extreme example which has only recently become realized.

In 1951 an up-to-date scholarly edition of Shakespeare in one volume was published by Peter Alexander of Glasgow, the only complete text to appear in this country since Pollard wrote in 1909, except M. R. Ridley's 'New Temple Shakespeare' which is an interesting attempt but too early to have availed itself of our present knowledge. In the light of that knowledge the text of *Richard III* was found to be so different from that printed in the old 'Cambridge Shakespeare' or the 'Globe' that Alexander actually departed from them in some 1500 readings. Nor do I think even he went far enough, since in an edition of the play now in the press I have ventured with the help of others by emendation to add over sixty more new readings. Though, as I say, a rather extreme instance, this serves to indicate at once the seriousness of the textual revolution and the fact that it still has some way to go before we can hope for a settled and generally accepted text, enjoying a prestige comparable with that enjoyed since the middle of the nineteenth century by Aldis Wright's. It is not that we lack the right principles for the preparation of such an edition: those are already fairly well recognized, at least in general terms. What is still required is further research leading to more precise knowledge: knowledge of the kind of copy used in the printing of the individual texts; of the way this copy had been or may have been influenced by the 'prompter', the censor, or the 'editor' charged with the task of preparing it for the printer; of the competence or incompetence of the compositors who set it up in type; and so on. Full or sufficient knowledge of such matters is not yet in sight. But our progress in that direction has been so considerable during the last forty years that we have reason to feel optimistic. I shall attempt to tell the story of that progress in my second article.

## NOTES

1. The best and most comprehensive survey of the subject of these articles is F. P. Wilson's 'Shakespeare and the New Bibliography' (Chapter v of *The Bibliographical Society, 1892–1942: Studies in Retrospect*, 1945), which I am much indebted to, and shall refer to as *Retrospect* in what follows.

2. A 'forme' is literally the body of type, set up by a compositor and secured in a frame called the 'chase', from which one side of a sheet is printed.

3. Those who wish to do so should consult Ronald B. McKerrow, *An Introduction to Bibliography for Literary Students* (Oxford, 1927). I may add that an understanding (or partial understanding) of the way old books were

produced is a very different thing from mastery of the printer's craft oneself. Some years ago I attended a meeting at the Bodleian Library of a class for professors and lecturers in the elements of printing conducted by an expert from the Clarendon Press, who allowed me to try and set up a sonnet of Drayton's in type. I keep the proof which was sent after me and look at it with shame and humility whenever I feel inclined to write contemptuously about Shakespearian compositors.

4. Strictly speaking bibliography embraces a study of the production not only of printed books but of manuscript books also.

5. The classical monograph on watermarks is by a Frenchman, C. M. Briquet, who published, in 1907, *Les Filigranes: dictionnaire historique des marques du papier*, which contains reproductions of over 16,000 marks.

6. He learnt much then, it should however be remembered, from a young colleague, Robert Proctor, a bibliographical genius, who was killed in the Alps in 1903.

7. *Modern Language Review*, I (1905), 238 ff. Those who, like the present writer, have been recently enjoying the little memoir of Edmund Gosse in Osbert Sitwell's *Noble Essences* will guess with what satisfaction Gosse must have contemplated the emulsification at Greg's hands of this hostile critic of his own scholarship.

8. 'Ronald Brunlees McKerrow, 1872–1940', *Proceedings of the British Academy*, XXVI (1940).

9. *Retrospect*, p. 76.

10. *Proposals for printing the dramatick works of William Shakespeare*, 1756; cited from pp. 1–2 of Walter Raleigh's *Johnson on Shakespeare* (1908).

11. *Shakespeare's Fight with the Pirates* (2nd edition, Cambridge, 1920), pp. 96–7.

12. This is a small typographical facsimile, published in 1862, and only purchasable second-hand. It is not photographic like the Oxford and Methuen reproductions; but it is remarkably reliable and very handy, being in quarto format, and issued in three separate volumes, tragedies, histories and comedies.

PLATE I

1

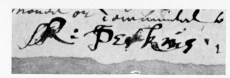

2

3

4

5

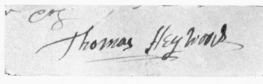

6

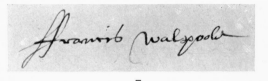

7

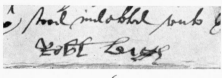

8

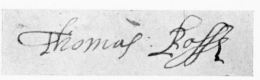

9

## Signatures of the Red Bull Company (1)

1. *Richard Perkins* (1623)  5. *Thomas Heywood* (1623)
2. *Richard Perkins* (1623)  6. *Robert Leigh* (1623)
3. *Christopher Beeston* (1623)  7. *Francis Walpole* (1623)
4. *Thomas Heywood* (1623)  8. *Ellis Worth* (1654)

9. *Thomas Basse* (1623)

PLATE II

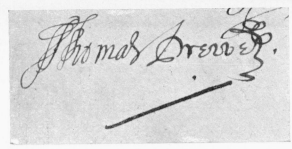

10

11

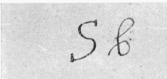

12

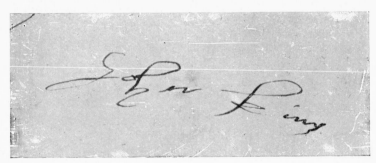

13

14

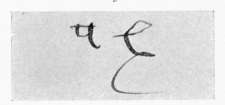

15

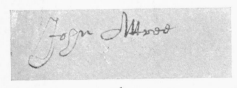

16

17

## Signatures of the Red Bull Company (2)

10. *Thomas Drewe* (1623)
11. *Richard Baxter* (1665)
12. *Richard Baxter* (1623)
13. *John King* (1623)

14. *Roger Clarke* (1623)
15. *Susan Baskervile* (1618)
16. *John Attree* (1614)
17. *Aaron Holland* (1623)

# THE RED BULL COMPANY AND THE
# IMPORTUNATE WIDOW

BY

## CHARLES J. SISSON

We would gladly give a wilderness of monkeys today, with many a turquoise into the bargain, for a sight of Burbage's notes upon his parts of Richard III or Hamlet, or for a record of his discussions with Shakespeare and his fellows when the poet brought a new play and the business of shaping it for the stage began. We may well wonder how far the actors in Shakespeare's day thought of themselves as above all the interpreters of the work of their dramatists. Despite modern experience, we may yet find it difficult to conceive that they may on the contrary have looked upon dramatists as the purveyors of vehicles for their own art. There is, certainly, the First Folio, a monument erected to Shakespeare the poet after his death by his fellow-actors Heminge and Condell, with their famous tribute to introduce it. But we hear little about plays in stage-history except in reference to the accidents of the actors' trade. The performance of *Sampson* at the Red Lion in Whitechapel in 1567 was important chiefly as evidence of the satisfactory completion of carpenters' work done at this theatre. *Eastward Ho!* in 1605 landed two famous dramatists into jail. "Chambers" fired off during a performance of *Henry VIII* in 1613 set the theatre ablaze. But we know nothing of the actors as literary critics. We do not know what Burbage thought of the Hamlet he played, or whether it was in his view a landmark in his career.

We know what Webster thought of Richard Perkins's performance in his great play *The White Devil* at the Red Bull, in his very handsome comment appended to the printed Quarto of 1612. One might have hoped that Perkins cherished the memory of his triumph in this play as eventful even in the stormy history of the Red Bull, and thought no less handsomely of its author. The discovery of two lengthy depositions by Perkins in Chancery, in a suit concerned with the history of the Red Bull and of Queen Anne's Men, might well lead us to look in them for some reflexion of the actor's outlook upon the plays which formed part of that history. When Perkins, for example, refers to the period of his membership of the company, to the years of his joining or leaving the Red Bull, or to the ebb and flow of the prosperity of the theatre, one might think it possible for him, as a modern actor well might, to date an event as in the year when they acted *The White Devil*. It would be pleasing to be able to date the play on the authority of Perkins. Detailed and intimate as are the whole set of depositions of which Perkins's evidence forms part, however, there is nothing in them for the purely literary historian. But there is much for the historian of the stage, for the biographer of actors, and for the student of human nature.

The records of certain suits bearing upon the Red Bull and Queen Anne's Men have long been known in part to historians of the stage, since Greenstreet's discovery of the Chancery suit of Worth *v.* Baskervile, which was reported in *The Athenaeum* and the *Transactions of the New Shakespeare Society* between 1885 and 1895.[1] We are concerned here with the further discovery and study of the depositions in this suit,[2] and of subsidiary and allied documents bearing upon the history of the suit and of the company and its theatres. The depositions are naturally of exceptional interest, inasmuch as the witnesses are almost all the actors themselves, from whom we gain a first-hand account of their own connexion with the Red Bull as members of the company. They include the great ones, the sharers, of the company in its heyday, Christopher Beeston, Richard Perkins, Thomas Heywood, Robert Walpole, Thomas Basse, Thomas Drewe, Robert Leigh. Three 'hired men' appear, Richard Baxter, Roger Clarke, John King. There are, finally, two men of business, William Roberts and William Keble, responsible for engrossing certain deeds in debate, and a friend of Susan Baskervile, Mrs Gertrude Browne, wife of Richard Browne. The three plaintiffs in the suit, naturally, are missing from among the actors appearing. Ellis Worth, John Blaney and John Cumber[3] had had their say in their Bill of Complaint. Another of the company, William Browne, was also a party to the suit, co-defendant with his mother Susan Baskervile, and they had made their Answer to the Bill.

Depositions were taken on behalf of Worth and Blaney[4] from 12 July to 14 October 1623, and on behalf of Mrs Baskervile and William Browne[5] from 13 August to 15 October and again, after a series of orders[6] from the Court extending her time to produce further witnesses, on 18 November, when Thomas Drewe, Robert Leigh, and Mrs Browne were examined on her behalf. It is evident that the Court was bent on giving her full opportunity to complete her case, despite efforts made by Worth's lawyers to have depositions 'published', i.e. communicated upon termination. It might be well to list the witnesses on either side in tabular form, for such a list is instructive:

| C24/500/9 | | C24/500/103 | |
|---|---|---|---|
| (a) FOR BASKERVILE | | (b) FOR WORTH | |
| 14 August | William Roberts | 29 June | John King |
| 10 September | Thomas Basse | 17 July | William Keble |
| 3 October | Thomas Heywood | 8 August | Richard Baxter |
| 13 October | Richard Perkins | 10 September | Thomas Basse |
| 15 October | Christopher Beeston | 17 September | Francis Walpole |
| 18 November | Gertrude Browne | 3 October | Thomas Heywood |
| 18 November | Robert Leigh | 14 October | Roger Clarke |
| 18 November | Thomas Drewe | 14 October | Richard Perkins |

These witnesses are described as follows:[7]

1. William Roberts, now of chancerie Lane gentleman attendent vpon the worshipful Captein Henrie Woodhowse, aged 30. yeares or thereabouts

2. (a) Thomas Basse of the parishe of St James Clarkenwell in the county of Middlesex gentleman aged 37. yeares, or therabouts

(b) Thomas Basse of the parrish of St James Clerkenwell in the County of Middlesex gentleman of the age of 36. yeares or thereabouts

3. (a) Thomas Haywoode of the parishe of St James Clarkenwell in the county of Middlesex gentleman aged 50 yeares, or neare vpon

(b) Thomas Haywood of the parrish of St James Clerkenwell in the Countye of Middlesex gentleman of the age of 49 or thereabouts

4. (a) Richard Parkins of the parishe of St James Clarkenwell in the county of Middlesex neare the city of London gentleman aged 44 yeares, or therabouts

(b) Richard Parkins of the parrish of St James Clerkenwell in the County of Middlesex gentleman of the age of 44 yeares or thereabouts

5. Christofer Hutchinson alias Beeston of the parishe of St Giles in the feilds in the county of Middlesex gentleman aged 43 yeares, or therabouts

6. Gartrude Browne wief of Richard Browne of the parishe of St James Clerkenwell in the county of Middlesex Cowper aged 60. yeares or therabouts

7. Robert Leigh of the parishe of St James Clarkenwell in the county of Middlesex gentleman aged 54 yeares, or thereabouts

8. Thomas Drewe of the parishe of all Hallowes Barking in or near Towerstreete London free of the Company of ffishmongers, aged 37 years, or therabouts

9. John Kinge of the parrish of St Sepulchre london gentleman aged 48 yeares or thereabouts

10. William Keble of the parishe of St Sepulchres london goldsmith aged 55 yeres or thereabouts

11. Richard Baxter of St James Clerkenwell in the County of Middlesex gentleman of the age of 30. yeares or thereabouts

12. Roger Clarke dwelling in Golding Lane in the parrish of St Giles without Creeplegat [London] in the County of Middlesex gentleman of the age of 24 yeares or thereabouts

These particulars, of course, are given by the witnesses themselves, upon their examination. It is valuable to have such firm clues to the birth dates of so many persons of interest in stage history, not least the actors themselves. We do not know, for example, when Richard Burbage, Heminge, or Condell were born, despite much diligent search of parish registers. Heywood, actor and dramatist, is kind enough to fix the date of his birth for us almost exactly. On 3 October 1623 he is 49 years of age, or alternatively "near upon" 50. We may conclude, on his own authority, and with reasonable certainty, that he was born soon after 3 October 1573. It appears consequently that his first plays were written at a much younger age than we could have anticipated. And we may well be inclined to revise our ideas of the probable age of Shakespeare at his beginnings as a dramatist. It is well to remember that Heywood was writing plays for Henslowe before he was 21, when we are given 1592 as a possible date for the beginning of Shakespeare's play-writing, for he was then 28 years of age. And it is interesting to know that Richard Perkins, at the peak of his career, when he gave his great performance in *The White Devil* at the Red Bull, was barely 30 years of age. A professional actor of that age would probably have had 14 years of experience on the public boards.[8]

I think it well to add three further similar descriptions of interest, from other new sources, to complete the picture of this group at the Red Bull Theatre.

(1 February 1654) Ellis Worth of White Cross Streete St Giles Cripplegate, gentleman, of the age of 67 yeares or thereabouts[9]

(31 May 1665) Richard Baxter of St Leonard's Shoreditch Middlesex gentleman, of the age of 72 or thereabouts[10]

(17 April 1618) Susan Baskervile of St James Clerkenwell aged 40 yeares and above[11]

(3 February 1623) Aaron Holland of St James Clerkenwell, gentleman, of the age of 67 or thereabouts[12]

The immediate value of a signature appended to a deposition appears in the identity of the signature of Richard Baxter in 1623 with his signature in 1665, which resolves G. E. Bentley's question concerning a Richard Baxter acting at the Restoration.[13] But there is significance in the very quality and manner of these signatures. They are indeed a kind of portrait-gallery to the seeing and trained eye. We may conclude little from the illiteracy of Mrs Baskervile, who can achieve only the initials which were hers upon her first marriage as upon her third. But the signatures of these men are in some instances graphic evidence of temperament as well as of literacy, or of comparative illiteracy as with Clarke and King, two of the hired men. The signature of Richard Perkins is not only elaborate and complicated: it is dashing, dramatic, and also capricious in detail, as may be seen from the two examples reproduced here. Walpole's, on the contrary, though individual and unmistakable, is trim, symmetrical and steady. Perkins's signature may indeed seem to bear out, and to interpret, this great actor's portrait at Dulwich College. However uncertain the ground here, it can hardly be denied that signatures are, not least with Elizabethans, an act of self-expression, or that Clarke and King seem likely to have been 'slow studies'. These signatures are biographical data. Incidentally, one of these sets of signatures suggests caution in arriving at conclusions concerning changes in handwriting due to the passage of years. The two signatures of Baxter were written at an interval of 42 years, at the ages of 30 and 72 respectively. And at 46 Ellis Worth's signature[14] was hardly to be distinguished from that reproduced here, at the age of 67. Both of these actors would seem to have been men of sturdy timber.[15] And it is evident enough that the conditions of their calling with Queen Anne's Men at the Red Bull made great demands upon a man's toughness of fibre.

It is difficult to conceive a more stormy history for even an Elizabethan theatre and its company of actors than that of this theatre and this company. I have already given some account of the more spectacular disturbances which accompanied their previous occupation of the Boar's Head Theatre in Whitechapel, when they were still under the patronage of the Earl of Worcester, as also of the building and structure of this considerable theatre.[16] Robert Browne was then their manager, and financial debates at law sprang up among this actor-lessee of the theatre and two speculator-landlords, Oliver Woodliffe and Francis Langley, who took the law into their own hands. Their hired bullies raided the theatre during a play and marched off with the gatherings, or occupied the stage and denied it to the actors. In 1600 Langley enforced a payment of £3 a week for the use of the theatre. There can be little doubt that the company found their situation impossible, and sought a new permanent theatre. The building of the Red Bull by Aaron Holland was the consequence, designed for occupation by this company and under a bargain with them. A leading member of the company, Thomas Swinnerton, was indeed a founder-sharer in the house as to one-eighteenth part, almost certainly in return for a contribution to the building costs and for the assurance of the occupation of the theatre by the company.[17]

One further incident remains to be narrated briefly to complete these preliminaries. In Michaelmas 1600 the sharers in the company, numbering six and led by John Duke and Thomas Heywood, exhibited a Bill in Chancery against Browne, who was suing them for the breach of their bonds to play only at the Boar's Head Theatre.[18] Their suit was dismissed finally on 28 June 1601, as "no meet matter for this Court", and they were ordered to pay 26s. 8d. costs to Browne, whose Answer was found "sufficient". The company, in fact, had moved from Browne and the Boar's Head to Henslowe and the Rose, vacant upon the building of the new Fortune

Theatre. Langley's rent and other demands upon the company's purse had made playing at the Boar's Head unprofitable. To Langley's £3 a week, we learn, had to be added 15s. a week to the Master of the Revels, 5s. a week to the poor of the parish, and "much money" for constant suits at Court to defeat attempts by the City to close the theatre. For the Boar's Head was in a vulnerable locality. The full story makes it lamentably clear why Robert Browne of the Boar's Head died "very pore", as Joan Alleyn reports to her husband in a letter of October 1603 preserved at Dulwich College.

The Company made a fresh and promising start at the new Red Bull Theatre, under the high patronage of Queen Anne since 1603. With Thomas Greene as their leader, they seem to have prospered there. The Mrs Susan Browne they had known at the Boar's Head was with them still, for she had married Greene, probably in 1604, bringing with her five young children, two of whom, Robert and William, became actors, William as an apprentice, then hired man, with the company. Greene's death in August 1612 was a watershed in the affairs of the company, which from then on moved again into discontent with the conditions under which they pursued their calling, under the renewed pressure of private taxation upon the communal purse. The hitherto agreeable presence of Mrs Susan Greene, still a young woman of 35 or so, became a menace by virtue of her claims under Greene's will. The Red Bull became as inhospitable as the Boar's Head, in their eyes, as the situation developed. The story is told in retrospect in the Chancery suit of Worth v. Baskervile eleven years later, and in the depositions we have the comments of the actors themselves on the points at issue.

Susan had inherited under Greene's will his full share in the profits of the company, and a claim upon them for money expended by Greene on their behalf. Her son William Browne had a claim for wages as hired man, upon which they had fallen into arrears. She had, moreover, married again, and James Baskervile, her third husband,[19] had invested money in the company in return for a daily payment from the company's receipts. A series of five agreements had been entered into by the company acknowledging their commitments to Susan, to Baskervile, to Francis Baskervile, the child of Susan and Baskervile, and to Browne, as follows:[20]

1. 1612–13. To Susan, to pay her the income of a half-share as instalments of £137 due. This was entered into after an appeal by Susan to the Earl of Leicester, Chamberlain to the Queen, and instructions from him to satisfy her.

2. 7 July 1615. To Susan and Baskervile or the survivor, to pay 1s. 8d. on each acting day in return for £57 more invested by them in the company. Agreement 1. continued in force. Engrossed by Roberts.

3. June 1616.[21] To Susan, Baskervile, and Francis Baskervile, to pay 3s. 8d. a day, being 1s. 8d. in respect of Agreement 2. and 2s. in respect of the half-share[22] and of £38 further invested.

4. 3 June 1617.[23] In trust to William Jordan, for Susan and Browne, to pay 3s. 8d. a day. This agreement was preceded by a suit moved at Common Law by Jordan for Susan, by a consequent appeal by the company to Bacon in the Court of Requests, and a reference of the case to Sir Charles Caesar, a master in Chancery.[24] Engrossed by Keble.

5. Christmas 1618. To Susan for 2s. 6d. a day for one year only up to the Feast of St Thomas the Apostle (21 December) 1619.[25] This was a verbal agreement by which Susan sought to meet temporary difficulties of the company. It was in force up to Whitsuntide 1623, when Susan had taken action under Common Law and the rump of the company appealed to the Court of Chancery.

E*

The merits of Chancery records, and in particular of Chancery depositions, from the point of view of the modern world inquiring into the Elizabethan world, are their catholic interest in all conceivable detail affecting the issues of the case. This may well be exemplified here by evidence bearing upon Baskervile's claims upon the company, and evidence which resolves doubts concerning the *état civil* of Francis Browne or Baskervile.

Mrs Gertrude Browne deposes to Baskervile's entry into the affairs of the Queen's Men at the Red Bull:

upon a tyme about 5 or 6 yeares agone[26] in Summer last, as I remember the tyme. It was my chance after the end of a Play at the Red Bull to be in Company with Worthe, James Baskervile, the defendants Susan and William Browne hir sonne, drinking a cup of Wyne togither, at a Taverne on Clarkenwell Greene and at the same tyme, amongst other words that then passed amongst them, I heard Worthe say vnto James Baskervile, Father Baskervile, why doe you not buy something amongest us, I pray you buy something amongest vs, And I will see that you shall haue your Right, and afterwards by reporte there was some Pension of twenty pence by the day, bought by Mr Baskervile of the then Company, or some other Pension, which was afterwards payd by the Company.

This reference to "Father Baskervile" by Ellis Worth helps to dispose of the suggestion that Francis was the son of Susan by Robert Browne.[27] Baskervile was, one gathers, a proud father, and a recent father. (He was certainly not a venerable elder.) Greene's will, which refers to Susan's five children by Browne, knows no Francis. The depositions cite the boy throughout as Francis Baskervile. And Thomas Drewe relates in evidence how the daily draft of 3s. 8d. upon the company's takings was made, which he remembers

Bycause Francis Baskervile vsually came for yt, with a grote in his hand, and would pay the Company the grote, and carry away foure shillings from them.

We are manifestly dealing with a small child here. Francis could have been born by February 1614, and by June 1616 he could well have carried out this childish transaction, probably accompanied by a nurse, to the delight of fond parents and even of Susan's older friends among the company. It is a pleasing picture. The daily blow was softened, no doubt, by the innocence of the little tax-gatherer. But the blow had cumulative force, especially as takings diminished, and broke up the company.

Before long, Thomas Drewe tells us, the company was grieved,

for that their Gettings were but small. . . . And would have put downe the Flag, being weary of the payment,

had not Susan consented to the reduced pension of 2s. 6d. According to Basse the company

did refuse to play any longer att the red Bull vnles Susan would abate of the 3s 8d a daye,

and Perkins' version is that

they were determined to have played at another house. . .for if they had left that house then Susanna should have lost a greater profite by the benefite she made of the said house.

The company was clearly in a state of disintegration, from which it was saved by the verbal agreement for a reduced payment which came into force upon its re-formation, to quote Perkins,

ever since their last Joyning togither which was about Xristmas 1618.

The history and validity of these various agreements is obviously the principal issue upon which evidence was taken. But the distribution of the witnesses called is dependent upon minor issues also, as well as upon their personal relations with Susan and Worth, and with each other. The value of a share in the company as a form of property is one such issue of importance to Susan as claiming by inheritance from Greene his full share, valued at £80. Evidence is given on both sides by leading actor-sharers in the company.[28] It is plain that Robert Leigh and in a minor degree Thomas Drewe were Susan's mainstay on this issue, which was vital to the question of consideration for the agreements, along with that of other debts and payments in cash by Greene, Susan, and Baskervile, to which Mrs Browne testified. These three witnesses appeared last, on 18 November, after an interval of a month and despite attempts by Worth to close depositions. None of them, it is to be observed, was called by the other side, whose case they were not likely to assist.

Leigh, we may note, had known Susan for 28–29 years,[29] since she was about 17 years of age, probably since her marriage to Robert Browne, his leader in the old Boar's Head days of the company, and a widower since the plague of 1593. This marriage may be dated late in 1594 or early in 1595 with some certainty. (Their first child, Robert, was baptized on 19 October 1595.) Leigh had known William Browne from his infancy. He was obviously a friend of the family, to be depended on in Court, and his evidence gave full support to Susan at all points.

Three of the actors, Baxter, King and Clarke, were called by Worth to give what might be called expert evidence upon the claim for arrears of wages to Browne, like themselves a 'hired man' in the company, and their evidence was devastating upon this issue. Clarke's deposition is perhaps the most revealing, though all three tell the same sad tale:

I myself have bene for the space of these twoe yeares ⌜or thereabouts⌝ an hyred servant in the Company of players at the Red bull. . . . When they hyred me they agreed to give vnto me six shillings a weeke so long as I should continue their hired servant and they did so sett downe in their booke and when good store of Company came to the playes that the gettings would beare it, I was truly payed my vjs a week but when company fayled I was payed after the rate of their gettings which sometymes fell not out for my part ijs vjd a week ⌜nor sometymes xijd a weeke⌝ neither had I any more payed me then the gettings would beare, although they agreed with me to paye me six shillings a weeke and the Company and all other companyes of players in and about London, whatsoever they agreed to give vnto any that they hyre to be their servants ⌜or men⌝ they doe vsually paye them no more then it will fall out to their Shares as Company doe come in to playes and if Company doe come in so fast and so many as that the gettings will beare it then the said servants as hyred men have the full of that was agreed they should have or ells not.

Clarke was a young man and fairly new to the company. But Baxter was older and experienced, and seems to have been with them for 13–14 years, the period of his acquaintance with Worth, Blaney, and Susan.[30] His "wages certain" agreed upon were ten shillings a week, but they were as uncertain as Clarke's, and descended to so little as nothing in bad times. He kept account of such arrears, but to no purpose, for he could not make claim upon any individual. The company, apparently, was a vague entity which could not be sued on a merely verbal agreement. As for King, a veteran of 48, who

for the space of these 30 yeares past and uppwards hath beene a hyred servant vnto the companie of Sharers of the players of the redd Bull,[31]

his arrears are estimated ruefully at over £100 over this period, the more ruefully because he acknowledges that his agreement for wages with the players was conditioned by a normal proviso:

if att any tyme it should happen the gettings of the Companie to bee but small and to decrease, that then I should not have my whole wages agreed to be paide vnto me but to beare my part of the losse thereof aswell as the company and to have a part proportionablie only to those gettings.

It does not seem to occur to any of these men to remark on the absence of any proviso concerning a possible "part proportionably" in unusually high "gettings". 'Heads we win, tails you lose', was the sharers' position in relation to their hired men. Yet Heywood tells us how, even after the palmy days of Greene's leadership, when Beeston managed their affairs,

there hath bin eight or nyne pownds in a day received at the dores and Galeries.

King must have known of this, and been able to compare it with the four pounds cited as the day's takings at the Boar's Head on 24 December 1599.

Beeston is the remaining witness appearing for one side only, for Susan and not for Worth. His departure from the company had been accompanied by grave quarrels reported in the Requests suit Smith *v.* Beeston.[32] He was suspected not only of leaving the rump of the company to bear the burden of its agreements with Susan, but of having feathered his own nest. Leigh retorts upon Beeston a charge to this effect that Perkins cast even at the "well-beloved" Greene.[33] And Heywood reports similarly that

the complainants and the rest of their then Company, both before and synce the decesse of Thomas Greene did repose their mayne Trust and Confidence in Hutchinson alias Beeston, for and concerning the Managing of their Affayres, he havinge a kynde of powerfull Comaunde over the complainants and their then fellow Actors in that behalfe [insomuch as at one tyme they trusted him three yeares together ⌐or thereabouts¬ with their moneys gotten by their labours and paynes in Acting or Playing, without any accompt thereof made vnto the complainants or Company to my knowledge.][34]

Perkins, on the contrary, has nothing but praise for Beeston. There is much support for the belief that the fourth agreement was obtained in effect by bribery of the principal actors, especially Beeston. Basse reports Susan's statement to him that she "worked underhand" with Beeston, giving him various sums of money, including one of twenty shillings, and elsewhere reports the total as £20. Beeston himself told Basse that she gave him twenty nobles.[35] Drewe's account of it is that

Beeston ⌐and others of the Company have¬ received gratuityes of her, in money, Beaver hatts, and silke stockins, to drawe the Rest of the Company to allow of her demands.

Perkins reports that he himself, Beeston, and Worth each had twenty nobles of her in this way. And Beeston adds Leigh, Basse, "and others" to the list of beneficiaries, with the explanation that these were mere gratuities, freely given by Susan. Everything points to a desperate endeavour by Susan to have her claims fortified by validation by the company upon its break-up and the departure of most of its leading members to the new Cockpit Theatre, in the belief that their successors at the Red Bull would be liable under it. Perkins, it is plain, believed that a change of theatre freed them from all obligations.[36] And Beeston expressed his plain view, concerning her claims under Greene's share, that

every man's share ends, whensoever the Company dissolveth,

a view which implies validity until that event, and freedom from such claims upon dissolution for the seceding members. This dissolution, it appears from Beeston's own evidence, took place as far as he was concerned at some date between 3 June 1617 and Christmas 1618, when he left the company.

It is impossible to pursue here the many clues given by the actors in their evidence to the dates of their joining and leaving the company. They require close scrutiny and interpretation, and are plainly of importance to the historian of the company and the biographer of the actors. The explanation of one small puzzle, however, in the story of the meteoric intrusion and disappearance of James Baskervile, may serve as a further instance of the wealth of detail contained in these depositions.

Thomas Basse, the oddity of whose character emerges in his evidence, in June 1617 was "then but newly come in to the Companye" and gravely suspicious of all that he found going on. He would have nothing to do with the agreements

whereof I was alwayes so warie; As that I would never seale therevnto, Nor be acquainted therewith.

But he was less wary than his fellows in his references to Baskervile. It may be that his loyalty to Greene—he was at Greene's bedside when he died in August 1612—made him resentful of Baskervile succeeding him less than a year later. His first reference to Baskervile is as Susan's "supposed husband", and this fling is explained when he comments upon the departure for Ireland. This comment is best given in two versions apparent in the recorded deposition, first as originally made:

James Baskervile having taken vp diuerse commodityes in and about London vpon creditt, and being taxed for having two wieves lyving both at one tyme did about vij yeares agone fly into Ireland where he yet liveth. But the cause or reason of his flying I certeinly know not

then as amended:

James Baskervile about vij yeares agone did goe into Ireland as I have heard where he yet liveth. But the cause or reason of his going thither I certeinly know not.

The original is plainly Basse's real thought, and the revision is innocuous and non-committal. The original is probably the truth.

It is Basse again who furnishes us with the interesting information that one of the witnesses to the deed of 1617, drawn up by Keble, was a certain George Wilkins. Keble assures the Court that all the witnesses to the deed were dead by 1623. We may reasonably identify this George Wilkins with the dramatist and novelist who has by so many been credited with the part-authorship of Shakespeare's *Pericles*. If so, this Wilkins must have died before 1623.

Finally, a further new document points the moral of all such elaborate scholarly research concerning the Elizabethan theatre and drama. On 25 May 1626, one Francis Smyth went on behalf of the Court of Chancery to Sir Henry Herbert, Master of the Revels, to inquire of him concerning his study of the whole case, remitted to him by the Court on 27 January. Herbert's interests were bound up with the actors, who laboured indefatigably to fill his pockets. But Herbert found it all too much for him. He told Smyth on 24 May how

by reason of great sicknesses whereof he still languisheth he could not heare yt (the suit) nor appointe any tyme and that nowe yt did noe more concerne him but the Courte to take order in yt which he desiered and said he would rather gyue 20li then be troubled anie further in yt.[37]

The company had now exhausted the energies of three Lords Chamberlain[38] and a Master of the Revels. Sir Thomas Coventry, the third Lord Chancellor to deal with it, heard this bitter lamentation from Herbert read in Court on 9 June. Without more ado, he dismissed the actors' bill and removed the stay upon Susan's suit at Common Law, leaving her free to get what she could out of them on their agreements and bonds. This order was confirmed on 23 June, on a suit

which this Court conceaved to bee vnfitt to bee releeved or Countenanced in a Courte of equitie,

even as the Court had judged 26 years before when Heywood and Duke brought their suit against Robert Browne of the Boar's Head. It would perhaps come as a shock to some of these great folk to be told how eagerly men seek today to know more about the despised players and their affairs, how intelligent people read the tale of their doings, people to whom Herbert is interesting only because he was connected with the players, their theatres, and the plays they wrote and acted. They were the servants of a Queen, a Prince, or some great lord, and they paid heavy tribute to Herbert. But they were also the servants of something greater than any of these, of a great art, at the time when that art had attained its highest perfection, and through their mouths that art reached the world and made the world desire to have it made immortal in print and upon the stage to come.

When we think of what is sordid, self-seeking, or petty or cunning, in these people, we should not forget that in the very year in which the actors and Susan joined battle in Chancery, in 1623, the great First Folio of the works of Shakespeare was published.

[*This article has been prepared with the assistance of a Research Grant from the University of London for the provision of photostats of documents.*]

## NOTES

1. The documents were again printed by Fleay in 1890, in his *Chronicle History of the London Stage*.

2. P.R.O. C24/500/9 and 103.

3. Cumber died in the interim between the entering of the Bill and the taking of depositions, at Whitsuntide 1623.

4. C24/500/9.

5. C24/500/103.

6. C33/1623 B/f. 82a; *ibid.* f. 109a; *ibid.* f. 177a; *ibid.* f. 228b.

7. Quotations are given throughout with abbreviations extended. Words enclosed in [ ] are deleted in the documents. The sign ⌐ ¬ indicates interlineation. For the most part, depositions are slightly modified to give the actual words of the witness, omitting legal expletives added by the recording clerk.

8. John Wright, of Prince Charles' Men, for example, says he was apprenticed to Du Caine at the age of 15, and acted throughout his apprenticeship. (C24/785/55).

9. C24/785/55.

10. C24/907/43.

11. C24/446/156. Mrs Baskervile, widow in turn of Robert Browne and Thomas Greene, two leaders of the Earl of Worcesters-Queen Anne's Men, then wife of James Baskervile, who deserted her in 1617, was buried on 1 February 1648. (Parish Registers, St James Clerkenwell.)

12. C24/497/Bingham *v.* Bonham. He kept an inn in Gray's Inn Lane in 1589, and in the Savoy in 1598, and appears in a number of suits. He was born at Bletchington in Oxfordshire.

13. *Jacobean and Caroline Stage*, II, 361.

14. St. Ch. 8. 31/16. Reproduced in *Lost Plays of Shakespeare's Age*, Plate 1, which also reproduces Aaron Holland's signature.

15. Ellis Worth married his second wife, Katherine, after 1654, when he was over 67 years of age (his son Ellis celebrated his own second marriage in 1652) and had two daughters by her, Katherine and Blandina, before he died in 1661, at the age of 74.

16. 'Mr and Mrs Browne of the Boar's Head', in *Life and Letters Today*, Winter, 1936–7. A full account of the Chancery suits, together with material in Star Chamber, from which this information is derived, must await another opportunity. The theatre, a converted inn, was built in 1595, and rebuilt on a larger scale in 1599, when Browne became lessee of both inn and theatre. It is specifically described as a "winter house".

17. C3/390/47, Woodford *v.* Holland, October–November 1623, a continuation of an earlier suit in Requests. This may explain, and possibly date, the reference in an undated draft licence to any playhouse "by Thomas Greene hereafter to be built". (E. K. Chambers, *The Elizabethan Stage*, II, 230.)

18. I have so far found only Decrees in this suit, from which, however, the facts emerge. C33/1601 A/ff. 573, 611, 643, 648, 735, 798.

19. The marriage took place in June 1613.

20. The depositions furnish further material for this account.

21. In August Beeston took a lease of the Cockpit in Drury Lane, and began preparing it for use as a theatre.

22. So Beeston explains it.

23. On 13 September 1616 Francis Baskervile was buried. In Lent 1617 Baskervile disappeared into Ireland. Before 4 March 1617 the Cockpit Theatre was in use, and on 4 March it was attacked and damaged by rioters.

24. So Beeston deposes.

25. Leigh describes his leading part in promoting this agreement, and introduces a new figure in the history of the theatre, John Attree, part owner of the playhouse in 1618 and dead before 1623, who helped Leigh to complete the agreement. Leigh had just rejoined the company.

26. Mrs Browne's memory was at fault by a couple of years. It was the summer of 1615.

27. Chambers, II, 237; Bentley, I, 159; II, 391.

28. I have treated this question, as also that of the wages of hired men, in a previous article, with brief notes on the results of other unpublished research, 'Notes on Early Stuart Stage History', in *M.L.R.* XXXVII (January 1942).

These notes were, however, put together under difficult war-conditions and after the destruction of my library and other material. The article contains errors which are, I hope, corrected here. In particular, for "C24/500 and 501" read "C24/500/9 and 103" throughout.

29. It is worth noting that the actors giving evidence had known Susan and Worth respectively as follows: Leigh, 28–29 and 18 years; Heywood, 25 and 16; Perkins, 27 and 20; Walpole, 12 and 16–17; Drewe, over 12 and 12; Basse, many years both; Beeston, "divers years" both and Cumber "many years"; King, 30 and since childhood; Baxter, 13–14 both; Clarke, 12 both.

30. His phrase is "entertayned of the Company of Players at the Red Bull as an hired man".

31. This takes us back to before 1593, before the days of the Red Bull or of the adaptation of the Boar's Head, when the company is thought to have played only in the provinces. There is no question that in King's mind the company was a continuous entity. It may be concluded that he served it under Robert Browne for some time before he came to know Susan 30 years ago, in 1593, the great plague-year, when he was 18 years of age.

32. Cf. C. W. Wallace, *Three London Theatres*.

33. Beeston's phrase.

34. Deleted by Heywood on reading over before signing, perhaps as irrelevant, or as risky for Heywood, to whom Beeston was useful.

35. £6. 13s. 4d.

36. I think it extremely likely that the riot at the Cockpit, which damaged it upon its opening, was a gesture of resentment by Clerkenwell for the desertion of the Red Bull and the injustice done to Susan in a matter of local notoriety.

Agreement 2 (of 1615), so Roberts deposes, contained a clause providing for playing at "the red Bull or elswhere within two myles of London". But according to Keble Agreement 4 (of 1617) was limited to playing at the Red Bull by the company or any three or four of them.

37. Affidavit by Smyth: *Affidavit Register*, 25 May.

38. Leicester, Pembroke, and Carey, Lords Chamberlain to Queen Anne, the King, and Prince Charles respectively.

# VAULTING THE RAILS

## BY

## J. W. SAUNDERS

### I

In Thomas Middleton's *Black Book*, Lucifer, "as Prologue to his own Play",

> ...vaulted up so high
> Above the stage-rails of this earthen globe,

to ascend "this dusty theatre of the world".[1] Remembering the 'vaulting' Herods and Lucifers of Miracle tradition, readers of Elizabethan drama must have often wondered whether in Shakespeare's time players ever stepped beyond the confines of their platform stages, or whether the stage-rails constituted a frail but sure barrier between the demesnes of actor and audience, a sacrosanct frontier between two inviolable territories, like the line of footlights on the modern 'picture' stage.

A clear case can, I think, be made out for some continuity of tradition and convention between the Miracle and Elizabethan theatres in these matters: gesture, delivery, contemporary costuming, sound and light effects, machinery, affection for gruesome properties, spectacles, music, songs and dancing, soliloquies and asides, 'simultaneous' setting, trapwork, unlocalized settings, attitude to the Unities, fusion of the Tragic and Comic, and other aspects of production. It is clear too that the two theatres shared the same basic tradition of intimacy between actor and audience. This being so, there is a *prima facie* probability that the Elizabethan attitude to the barrier of the stage-rails developed from the medieval. All the precedents indicate 'traffic' in both directions, between platform and yard. The Coventry Herod, when he heard that the Wise Men had escaped his messengers, stormed up and down:

> I rent! I rawe! and now run I wode!
> A! thatt these velen trayturs hath mard this my mode!
> The schalbe hangid yf I ma cum them to...
> (Here Erode ragis in the pagond and in the strete also)[2]

The Devil in the York Play of the *Temptation of Jesus* ascended the stage from the street, declaring:

> Make rome be-lyve, and late me gang,
> Who makis here all this thrang?
> High you hense! high myght you hang right with a roppe.[3]

The spectators provided the throng, because the scene was Wilderness, and there were only three other players, silent upon the pageant, Jesus, Primus Angelus and Secundus Angelus. In the Towneley Play of the *Judgement*, the Devils sometimes marched off to Hell-Mouth with victims selected from the audience! This tradition was known to the author of the *English Wagner Book*, who describes an aerial vision of the Tragedy of Doctor Faustus in which "Faustus...leapt down headlong of the stage" and "the people verily thinking that they would have fallen uppon them ran all away".[4] When players were on horseback the street or yard was a normal part of the 'stage': when the Coventry Herod, for instance, received the news that the Holy family had escaped to Egypt, he called for his horse and made an impressive exit, riding away through the assembled spectators as if in hot pursuit.

The audience showed no more respect for the confines of the Miracle stage than the players. In the early years of liturgical drama the *plataea* extended, in fact, over the whole body of the pewless church, while the *domus* were cleared, and perhaps raised, areas or platforms situated at different points round the nave and choir. Congregations were accustomed to throng around and *between* the various acting areas. In later years, the producers of Miracle Plays on the 'simultaneous' setting of the stationary stage must have been quite prepared for the invasion of the *plataea*, and even of the *domus*, by inquisitive spectators. The text of the *Castle of Perseverance* discloses the details of a stage-manager's 'defence-plan' against the audience: "lete no men sytte ther [i.e. the tower *domus*] for lettynge of syt, for ther schal be the best of all.... This is the watyr a bowte the place, if any dyche may be mad ther it schal be pleyed; or ellys that it be stronglye barryd al a bowte: & lete nowth ower many styttelerys be withinne the plase".[5] The Guilds employed guards to protect the pageants from similar interference in the streets of York.

When drama was transferred from the streets to the innyards and tiled courtyards, players must still have been compelled to make some of their entrances from the 'auditorium'. The same scaffold stage had only two regular entrances, the trapdoor from Hell, and the curtained recess at the rear traditional in the *théâtre de foire*.[6] The building against which the scaffold was erected provided doors at yard-, not stage-, level. Elizabethan audiences must, therefore, have been accustomed to the spectacle of actors playing their parts not only on the platform and in galleries above, but from the floor of the yard itself. We know that the public and private stages were not entirely forbidden territory to the audience. In some theatres gallants were allowed to sit on the stage. A citizen, his wife and his apprentice climb from the yard to the stage in Beaumont's *Knight of the Burning Pestle*. On one occasion, as we learn from Gayton's *Pleasant Notes on Don Quixot* (1654), a butcher vaulted the rails to go to the rescue of a Hector assailed by Myrmidons. Leslie Hotson has recently suggested that officers known as stage-keepers, who were on the stage throughout performances, kept the peace across the rails, tying offenders like pickpockets to the stage-posts while the play was in progress.[7] Many dramatists and players exploited the inter-connexion between stage and auditorium, not only by way of extempore pleasantries,[8] by simulating the presence of multitudes and treating the groundlings as an extension of the stage-crowd in scenes describing battles, armies and mobs,[9] but also by more direct reference.

Shakespeare provides a good instance in *Henry VIII*, v, iv. John Cranford Adams has noted the reference to the stage-rails at the close of this scene, when the Porter calls out:

> You i' the camlet, get up o' the rail;
> I'll peck you o'er the pales else. (93–4)

But he assumed that "a crowd of citizens congregated about one of the stage doors" was being threatened at this point.[10] No such crowd, not even a symbolic two or three, is present on the stage, empty throughout but for the Porter, his Man, and later the Lord Chamberlain, and the doors are kept closed. If the man "i' the camlet" were one of a stage-crowd, he and the rails and the pales must have been offstage. Yet it becomes increasingly clear during the scene that the remarks in the dialogue are prompted by the spectacle of a real London crowd. In fact, gibing at the crowd makes up the whole content of the scene.

You'll leave your noise anon, ye rascals: do you take the court for Paris-garden? ye rude slaves, leave your gaping.                                                    (v, iv, 1–3)

Who gapes in the Porter's sight?

do you look for ale and cakes here, you rude rascals?...Is this Moorfields to muster in?...These are the youths that thunder at a playhouse, and fight for bitten apples; that no audience, but the tribulation of Tower-hill, or the limbs of Limehouse, their dear brothers, are able to endure.
                                                                   (10–11, 33–4, 63–7)

What Paris-garden, Moorfields, playhouse crowd can he be looking at?

Mercy o' me, what a multitude are here!...There's a trim rabble let in....We shall have Great store of room, no doubt, left for the ladies, When they pass back from the christening.      (71, 75, 76–8)

What multitude or rabble confines the Lord Chamberlain? These references, in intention and in practice, must have been aimed at the *Globe audience* itself. The trumpets would indeed have been needed to bring an end to this boisterous and tumultuous scene!

Ultimately, the Lord Chamberlain directs the Porter

> Go, break among the press, and find a way out
> To let the troop pass fairly;                                    (88–9)

It is at this point that the Porter and his Man go to leave the stage. The Porter cries "Make way there for the princess", and then threatens the man "i' the camlet". The Man selects his victim and shouts "You great fellow, Stand close up, or I'll make your head ache". Not until then do they "exeunt". The two members of the crowd singled out for attention (the identifying details could apply to virtually any two groundlings at any performance) must have been spectators in the auditorium. The implications are exciting. Did the Porter make a Herod's leap into the yard? Was a path cleared in the yard 'alley' by making the groundlings "stand close up"? And did the great procession of v, v approach the stage as through a street, along the alley and up steps to the platform?[11]

Before this suggestion could be accepted, we need to have more evidence about the 'traffic' between the yard and the platform. Such evidence cannot be expected from stage-directions. There are no directions to vault the rails. Why should there be? It was not Elizabethan usage to mark the movements of players between adjacent stages, like the study and the platform, or the chamber and the window-stages.[12] It was not even considered necessary to mark the passage of a player from the platform to the study via the stage-doors.[13] We must look elsewhere.[14]

## II

The staging of the monument-scenes in *Antony and Cleopatra* has been interpreted in an infinite variety of reconstructions, none of them, to my mind, wholly satisfactory. Scholars have only been agreed on one point—that the 'monument' was represented by an acting area elevated above another area, and accessible from two opposite sides. Adams guessed that V, ii was an inner-stage scene, requiring the chamber and the window-stages (into one of which the Roman soldiers climb while Proculeius engages Cleopatra's attention at the other).[15] Hodges has expressed what many of us feel about the modern tendency, which Adams shares, of trying "seemingly in very spite of our better knowledge, to find some sort of a proscenium somewhere upon the Elizabethan stage; to open up an inner-stage, no matter how questionable the evidence for its existence, and to thrust back into it a greater and greater proportion of the action of the Elizabethan plays...leaving the great stage before it empty and unattended".[16] Watkins, who accepts the main lines of the Adams blue-print, has joined in protest against "our tendency...to exaggerate the importance of the curtained inset over that of what we incurably think of as an annexe".[17] This monument-scene, as read by Adams, is a case in point. Unlike its predecessor, IV, xv, there are no stage-directions to indicate staging 'above', or to suggest that action takes place on more than one level. Moreover, it was written at a time when Shakespeare was making little dramatic use of the window-stages.[18] The soldiers, it is true, appear to scale the walls of the monument in order to unbar the doors and capture the Queen, but this feat can be represented without abandoning platform staging. Bernard Jenkin has provided one ingenious solution,[19] not less acceptable than the Adams hypothesis that the rope which hauled Antony aloft in IV, xv was left dangling from a window for the soldiers to climb in V, ii![20] Yet with only one dubious justification—continuity of staging between the two scenes—Adams would have us accept that Shakespeare wanted this last great climax of the play staged on the relatively remote and tiny upper stage, while the platform before the audience remained uninhabited. It is inconceivable that the dramatist would have brought "High order in this great solemnity" (V, ii, 369) by crowding, for the final scene, thirteen players, of whom three sink to the ground in death, into the narrow confines of the chamber, a stage of which so many spectators (the gentlemen in their rooms or on the rushes, the groundlings in the yard, and the important patrons in the ground-floor gallery) would have had an imperfect view or no view at all.[21]

Many other chamber-scenes are similarly suspect. *Othello*, V, ii, was staged there, according to Adams, with Desdemona's bed, in which she 'enters', pushed to the rear hangings, to allow more space.[22] But again it is inconceivable that this tragedy should have come to an end "in the middle air" above an empty platform, while twelve players (including three, dead after violence, on the bed, and Cassio in his chair) crowded into the chamber.[23] I do not wish to insist, as W. J. Lawrence once did,[24] that *no* bedchamber-scenes were enacted on the upper-stage, or that *no* scenes involving swift action could have been played there, but merely to suggest that scenes requiring a large number of players, *especially at the end of a play*, and *also* portraying violent action, would inevitably and naturally have been staged on the platform. *Romeo and Juliet*, III, v, played in the chamber (after Romeo's descent from the window-stage), never requires more than four players on stage at once, so that Capulet has the freedom of the whole of the upper-stage for the representation of his anger. There is a world of difference between this scene and those we have been discussing. The overwhelming probability, then, is that *Antony and Cleopatra*, v, ii, was mounted on the platform.

With the other monument scene, ɪv, xv, Adams is on stronger ground. Stage-directions like "Enter Cleopatra, and her maids aloft" and "They heave Anthony aloft to Cleopatra" imply two-level staging. The two sides of the monument were, to Adams, simply the opposite bay-windows of the tiring-house façade; Antony was raised aloft by means of a rope secured to his great shield and operated by windlass from the huts above.[25] The drawback about this interpretation is not the mechanical device itself, despite the fact that there is no proved example of this usage, in serious Elizabethan drama, except for theophanies and similar fantasies. Jesus in the Mysteries was raised to the pinnacle by means of block and tackle, and doubtless the Elizabethan audience would have accepted the same machinery for Antony. I remember Sir Godfrey Tearle, playing Antony in a modern production, achieving dignity and tragic decorum while he was hoisted aloft. The problem is rather this: *Where was the top of the two-sided monument on which Antony was finally deposited?*

Adams, advocating the window-stages, suggests that the hero was manœuvred by Cleopatra's attendants "feet first through the window to the point where his head and shoulders come within reach of Cleopatra's embrace".[26] What a feat of balancing this implies! The attendants struggled to keep him level, while the dying man ensured that the anguished raptures of the Queen did not tip him over the windowsill, while the audience made what they could of two heads protruding out of a casement. This is a desperate theory, not to be endorsed unless there is no other alternative. Needless to say, the Tearle-Antony had no such problem: once aloft, he lay on the *terra firma* of a property monument. Antony needs the decorum of firm ground underneath him. Where was there any that was suitable? Certainly not *inside* a window-stage, since nothing would have been seen of the lovers behind the solid walls of the bay. Could it have been the tarras?

We must, however, gravely doubt whether there was a tarras at the Globe at all.[27] All that appears certain is that between the stage-windows was a curtained recess, windowed or balustraded. If this recess (let us call it a balcony, to be neutral) had anything like a wall or solid fence on the audience side, then it is out of the question for the monument—the lovers would not have been seen. If it were balustraded, how far apart were the balusters? Adams argues "5 or 6 feet apart",[28] but without conclusive evidence.[29] The scraps of fact that exist—the *Roxana* and *Messalina* vignettes, Henslowe's purchases for the Rose—suggest that when Elizabethan carpenters erected balusters the normal spacing was twelve inches or less. The likelihood, then, is that there was a wall, either of palings or of closely spaced balusters, on the audience side of the balcony. This wall would not always be disadvantageous: in *Romeo and Juliet*, ɪɪɪ, v, for instance, Juliet is only on her knees for a few moments and is not therefore significantly obscured; in any case, the audience's attention is concentrated not upon the heroine but upon Capulet as he storms up and down. In the monument-scene, however, every eye in the audience is fixed upon the two lovers, and playing the scene on the floor behind a wall or line of balusters would have been ridiculous. There have been suggestions that either the balustrade was hinged to swing open, like a level-crossing gate, or that the tarras was rail-free. These hypotheses at least face the central problem squarely; but, of course, there is no evidence to support them, and there surely would be some reference somewhere to matters of such delightful convenience to dramatist and stage-manager.

F

Over and above these objections to the balcony, there is the further difficulty of representing *two* sides to the monument (hence Adams's preference for the window-stages). W. J. Lawrence proposed that Diomedes' side of the monument was at the rear of the chamber, while the other was the tiring-house front.[30] But this obliges Diomedes to appear to ascend the monument, and there is no other indication that he ever proceeds 'aloft'. Jenkin's alternative suggestion that the rear of the monument was the 'wall' of the chamber *and* study, out of sight of the audience, on the tiring-room side, implies an ingenuity of staging of which, I feel, not even the Elizabethans were capable.

No part, then, of the upper stage seems to afford a thoroughly satisfactory setting for the scene of Antony's death.

How else could two-level staging be arranged, the stage-directions vindicated, and a two-sided monument provided? There is no practicable way of employing the traps. A property monument, a feasible solution otherwise, must be ruled out on the grounds of its enormous size. It would have been, necessarily, much larger than any other known property; it would have to be removed at the end of IV, xv, and replaced at the beginning of V, ii. Would the players have taken all that trouble? There is still one other practicable alternative: the platform itself, as was proper and desirable, could have served as the main stage, the top of the monument, and the lower level could have been represented—why not?—by the yard. On this hypothesis, Diomedes entered the yard on one side of the platform, the alley between it and the gallery palings, and urged Cleopatra to "look out o'the other side" (IV, xv, 8), that is to say, into the opposite alley, into which Antony was borne by the Guard. Whatever the height of the platform, four and a half feet, five feet, six feet, the Attendants and Guard could have raised Antony 'aloft' without tackle or machinery, and the lovers would have had all the prominence and spaciousness of the front of the platform, visible (if they placed themselves away from the stage-rails) to the entire auditorium. Similarly, if we insist upon two-level staging for V, ii, Proculeius could have distracted Cleopatra's attention on one side of the platform, while his soldiers in the opposite alley went through the motions of assaulting the monument by vaulting the rails, and, in truth, "you see how easily she may be surprised" (V, ii, 35).

Such a solution, completely satisfying in itself, would not have offended Elizabethan conventions, even if it does take liberties with the yard. We need to be sure, however, that players had access to the yard alleys from the tiring-house rear.

It must be emphasized that no reconstruction of the Globe, no matter how persuasive or convincing, is as yet finally authoritative. Particularly, we do not know the exact disposition of that part of the theatre that bounds the junction of the tiring-house façade, the platform, and the ground-floor gallery, the area in fact at the head of the yard alleys on each side of the platform. Adams has placed the 'gentlemen's rooms' at a point where raucous groundlings in the yard alleys would have interrupted the view of the forestage from the boxes, and at an angle which must have prevented box patrons from seeing anything at all of the action proceeding on the inner-stage, or on that area of the stage at the rear of the platform, adjacent to the nearest stage-door. These twelvepenny customers, thirty of them to a box,[31] a financially important part of the audience, would have required better things of the "best roome in a playhouse". Something is wrong with the reconstruction. I should prefer to locate these rooms in the tiring-house front itself, and at a sharper angle; if this were so, another problem would be solved, for the 'bulk' so fashioned would have provided the 'hedge corner' (mentioned in scenes where one player, approaching the platform via a stage-door, is ambushed by others lying in wait). Adams suggests that this place of concealment was represented by the door-posts.[32] While one man might conceivably have secreted himself in such a place, as did, for instance, Roderigo, waiting for Cassio in *Othello*, v, i, a couple of pillars on a straight wall could hardly have served, symbolically or otherwise, for a larger ambush (as many as six or seven players ambush Parolles in *All's Well that Ends Well*, IV, i). Where, too, was the 'Tarras' which Sogliardo, Carlo, Fastidius Brisk and Cinedo "stand by, close" in *Every Man Out of his Humour*, II, i, where they would have been invisible to Puntarvolo on the platform *and* to the Ladies at the window, but visible to the audience *and* to the Grex (wherever these 'presenters' might be sitting)? Adams assumes that they hid under the penthouse of the stage-tarras.[33] But, quite apart from the difficulty that such a position would be visible to Puntarvolo and invisible to the Grex (if they were 'aloft'), this hypothesis is apparently contradicted by the direction "Sordido and Fungoso withdraw at the other part of the stage". These two players apparently moved to an *opposite* place of concealment without meeting the other four. The tarras, clearly, cannot fulfil these requirements, and Adams's reconstruction allows for no such opposite 'hedge corners' except the door-posts (and these here provide no solution, since one door was always within the Ladies' view and the other within Puntarvolo's). It would appear that there were two angles in the wings of the tiring-house front not allowed for by Adams.

One of the intriguing problems left by the (presumable) inaccuracies of the De Witt picture of the Swan is the question whether in fact the entire *mimorum aedes* protruded forwards so that at the wings of the scenic wall adjoining the galleries there may have been angled bulks, imitated in later theatres. The existence of the 'angles' is corroborated, for what it is worth, by the *Messalina* vignette. In these angles (formed possibly by the walls of the boxes, if these were part of the tiring-house front), accessible from the platform, a dozen players could have concealed themselves, hidden from all parts of the stage except the very front of the platform, yet visible to the whole audience; and the penthouse, if this is needed, would have been provided by the "juttey forwards" of either the upper boxes or some other part of the second storey. And if this were so, there would have been room too (either behind the boxes, or between them and the scenic wall) for additional doors leading to the tiring-rooms backstage.

Perhaps the *ingressus* depicted in the De Witt sketch next to the *orchestra* (the Gentlemen's rooms) represent these doors backstage? These are very inconveniently situated, as Adams has pointed out,[34] if they represent entrances to the galleries, since during performances they would have been continuously obstructed by groundlings. But entries at these points certainly existed. R. C. Bald, on the evidence of the Hollar sketch, has suggested that they led to the two external entrances to the Globe (lying north-east and south-east).[35] They may, if that were so, have served a dual purpose. Hodges, in his reconstruction, accepts that there were indeed passages, behind the Gentlemen's rooms, leading from these entries backstage.[36] Every early reconstruction, before Adams, allows for a door or some kind of passage between the alleys of the yard and the tiring-rooms.[37]

But, even if it could be clearly demonstrated that no such passage existed, there would still be another means of access to the yard alleys from backstage. In early theatres like the Swan, or that described in the *English Wagner Book*, where 'Hell' was completely open to the view of the audience, or in theatres like the Globe, where the cellarage was screened only by curtains,[38] and the platform was not "paled in belowe with good stronge and sufficyent newe oken bourdes" (as at the Fortune), players could have passed freely into the yard *from the cellar*. It is quite certain, then, that there was freedom of access into the yard from backstage. The last difficulty is removed: nothing really disqualifies the use of the yard in the monument-scenes. Are there any other instances of yard-staging?

There certainly are. One swallow does not make a summer. The sceptic will expect further examples.

### III

Crowd scenes, battle scenes, panoramic scenes of complex geography, scenes requiring raised locations—these provide, if we analyse the logical necessities of staging, evidence of the use of the yard access. There is one instance in *Pericles*, v, i—the problem of the barge. The stage-directions of the 1609 Quarto are extremely scanty, but Malone has obliged with a description of the scene with which internal evidence has not the slightest quarrel: "On board Pericles' ship off Mytilene. A pavilion on deck with a curtain before it; Pericles within it, reclining on a couch. A barge lying beside the Tyrian vessel." It has been suggested that the pavilion was represented by the chamber, the deck by the tarras and the barge by the platform; an external rope ladder, from the barge to the ship, would have made it unnecessary for the Sailors and Gentlemen to pass through the chamber, disturbing the sleeping Prince. The objections to this setting are manifold. *Was* there a tarras to use? Why waste the platform on the barge, which is the location of none of the action? Why distract the attention of the audience from events on the upper-stage by a constant stream of visitors crossing the platform from the stage-doors to the ladder to arrive in time for their cue aloft? Why crowd this climax of the play, its gravity and tenderness, and twelve to fourteen players, into the chamber? Why set Pericles, in his four-poster bed, in a position whence he would be invisible to half the audience? Yet we must have two-level staging. It seems unnecessary to moor, as Hodges has proposed, a practicable boat alongside the platform, following the precedent of the Noah's Arks of the Cycles or the ships of Miracles like *Mary Magdalen* ("Here xall entyre a shyp with a mery song"). We do not need a *property*, only a *location*. The simple solution, to my mind, is to represent the pavilion by the study, the deck, the scene of the main action, very properly by the platform, and the barge by the yard alley. This interpretation is endorsed by the allusions to a similar barge in *Antony and Cleopatra*, ii, vii, a scene in which, to judge from remarks like "Come, down into the boat" and "Take heed you fall not", departing guests were handed down over the stage-rails into the yard. When Octavius says "Good Antony, your hand" or Antony "give's your hand", they and Pompey are not shaking hands in farewell, because all three players are supposedly going ashore together. They need each other's hands, we must assume, to steady their drunken wits as they feel for the steps down to the barge.

A monument, a barge, and next an orchard wall (*Romeo and Juliet*, ii, i). The problem of the wall evidently worried Chambers: "Romeo pretty clearly comes in with his friends in some public place of the city, and then leaps a wall into an orchard, where he is lost to their sight, and finds himself under Juliet's window. He must have a wall to leap".[39] Benvolio clearly says: "He ran this way, and leap'd this orchard wall" (ii, i, 5). It is also evident that Juliet is at a window-stage, that Romeo, *after* vaulting the wall, is among the trees of the platform orchard, and that Benvolio and Mercutio do not enter the orchard but call and peer into it from outside. Any property wall on the platform would have unnecessarily obstructed the view of spectators on the ground-level. This scene could only have been staged in one way: the wall was provided by the sides of the platform and the stage-rails, and Benvolio and Mercutio remained in the yard alley whence Romeo had vaulted on to the platform.

With more than a thousand square feet of platform stage at his disposal, added to the areas afforded by the study and the upper-stage, it is unlikely that the Elizabethan producer would often have required any extension of the action beyond the stage-rails, but the 'ditches' of the yard-alleys must sometimes have been useful. Chambers has argued that the Orleans scenes of *1 Henry VI*, "with the leaping over the walls, and the rapid succession of action in the market-place within the town and in the field without", demanded "walls standing across the main stage from back to front".[40] Such walls, of course, would have been monstrously unnecessary obstructions. The extra space and the second city-wall afforded by the yard alleys and stage-rails would have removed any necessity for a property wall to supplement the balcony, and the action could still have occupied the platform at all times. It would have been just as realistic to assault the rails as to scale the 'tarras'. *Coriolanus*, I, iv, is another instance. This play is full of mammoth conflicts requiring the presence on stage of twenty or more contestants; moreover, it is graced with unusually full stage-directions to describe the staging of the battles, especially the siege of Corioli, in which "the Army of the Volces" defends the city against "Martius, Titus Lartius, with Drumme and Colours, with Captaines and Souldiers". At one point "the Romans are beat back to their trenches". Thus unusual specification of exact location (the phrase comes from North's *Plutarch*) replaces any 'exeunt' stage-direction, but, immediately afterwards there is a new direction "Enter Martius Cursing", and, although no mention is made of any re-entry by his troops, he proceeds to harangue them:

> ...come on;
> If you'll stand fast, we'll beat them to their wives,
> As they us to our trenches followed. (I, iv, 40–2)

After a further alarum, other directions indicate that Marcius follows the Volsces inside their city-gates. The Roman forces are clearly still on stage, even if Marcius is cut off from them, for at this point two soldiers discuss their leader's foolhardiness. When Marcius reappears "bleeding, assaulted by the Enemy", the Romans rally, "they fight, and all enter the City". We can reconstruct nearly the whole of this action: the 'tarras' provided the city-walls and the study-doors the city-gates, the focal point about which the battle ebbs and flows. But where were the *trenches*? They were not out of sight of the audience; they must have been represented by the extreme edge of the platform, that is to say, the stage-rails and yard alleys. In that event, the absence of 'exeunt' and 're-enter' directions is explained. The direction "Enter Martius Cursing" is similar to those illogically entered in other plays, when a player has not left the stage but has moved between two different visible areas.[41] Thus, the panorama of the battle royal would have had the whole platform from the rails to the study-doors, at its majestic disposal.

The neo-classic theatres based upon Vitruvius had, besides the *porta regia* and *portae minores* of the scenic wall (the equivalent of the study-doors and stage-doors), *viae ad forum* in the *versurae*.

'Ways to the Yard' at the wings of the platform would have immensely improved the accessibility of the Elizabethan stage. Whenever the study was *closed*, by virtue of the location it represented or for any other reason, there were only two routes on and off the stage, via the stage-doors, if there were no possibility of entrances from the yard. *The Merry Devil of Edmonton*, IV, ii, is a case in point. Here, the study-curtains are closed, to conceal the tree properties used in the previous forest-scene. One stage-door represents the church porch at Enfield, in the gloom of which sits Banks the Miller, "wet with climing ouer into an orchard for to steale some filberts", awaiting the return of his fellow-poachers, and mistaken for a ghost, in turn, by the Sexton, the Priest, and Host Blague. The other stage-door represents the road to the village, whence comes the respectable Sexton to ring curfew. The other characters all enter the stage from *other* directions, for they have each "shifted for themselues" and taken separate routes back from their poaching expedition. I envisage them scrambling, furtively and hastily, over the rails on to the platform from every point of the compass. It is significant that the Host asks "Did you not see a spirit all in white, crosse you at the stile?" There was indeed a stile: the stage-rails.

Another stile is mentioned in the *Merry Wives of Windsor*, III, i, when Simple, having looked "the pittie-ward, the park-ward, every way; old Windsor way, and every way but the town-way", is urged by Sir Hugh Evans to look that way too, and at last espies the approach of a party "from Frogmore, over the stile, this way". In scenes like these, 'distant' or 'country' entrances seem to have been assigned, perhaps by convention, to the yard access. When Hamlet enters "a farre off" (v, i, 63) to the Gravediggers in the study, or in similar instances, the yard route to the stage is more accurately described than any other. When stage-directions specify "Enter at one end...at the other end" or "Enter...on the one side...in the other part" or "At one corner of the stage", the ends, corners and parts to which they refer are not just loose terms for the stage-doors but attempted descriptions of something which was not easy to define exactly—specifically different points of access to the platform from the yard.[42]

It is not expected, in an argument like this, that every instance quoted will have had equal persuasive weight. But most of them will give the sceptic pause, and, taken all in all, the case for the yard access is formidable enough. Many types of scene remain undiscussed. Scenes of ceremonial and procession would have been the more impressive with entrances from the yard. In the many riverside scenes, the rails would have provided an ideal bridge or bank, and the yard alley an excellent river, useful for instance in staging the *Devil's Charter*, III, v, where Caesar Borgia hurls into the Tiber first the Duke of Candie, and then Frescobaldi.[43] The alley steps and the railed sides of the platform may well have been employed in scaffold or tilt-yard scenes, to obviate the use of large properties.[44] The yard alleys would have been first-class ditches and hollows, close walks and closets, much to be preferred to the traps.[45] Were 'plays within the play' *always* enacted in the study, so that the stage-spectators had to sit with their faces away from the audience, or was the forestage the setting for such performances with the stage-spectators in the study or on the rear platform or in the chamber, and the yard access available to the actor-players?

Only the fringe of the subject has been touched upon. We have been concerned only with the entrances and exits made possible by the yard access, and action in the yard alleys in these scenes has been restricted, at the most, to forty lines or so of introductory conversation. We need to know whether or not the yard was ever used for prolonged action; whether, as the public theatre outgrew its innyard origins, the use of the yard became obsolescent; whether differences existed in the use of the yard in theatres with fixed stages, like the Globe or Fortune, and theatres with removable stages, like the Hope or Swan.

The emphasis given in this paper to the platform and the yard rather than the inner stage is surely healthy. It helps to concentrate attention upon the best asset of the Elizabethan stage, the intimacy of the audience and the actors, an intimacy achieved not by the silence and the darkness of the modern little theatre, but in broad daylight by a complete communion and familiarity one with the other. To the Elizabethan the play was more than a performance on a stage divided from the auditorium; it was an exciting experience in which good listening and good watching were rewarded by a sense of feeling part of the performance. There was no terrain alien to the spectator; the whole theatre shared the stage, and, conversely, the actors' personalities extended to every corner of the "wooden O". Great drama in this intimate theatre must have been all the more urgent and tangible, because it did not shrink from, but was rather based upon, the physical and contemporary setting of the "scaffoldage", the "thronged round", these "stories of men and women, mix'd together.... So close that all of heads the room seems made". Any theory that advances the action of the play further into the midst of this audience must, in the last analysis, contribute towards, and not divert attention from, a better understanding of the heart of Elizabethan drama.

## NOTES

1. *Works*, ed. A. H. Bullen, VIII (1886), pp. 7–8.
2. *Two Coventry Corpus Christi Plays*, ed. H. Craig, Early English Text Society (1902), p. 27.
3. *York Plays*, ed. L. T. Smith (1885), p. 178,
4. Chambers, *Elizabethan Stage*, III, p. 72.
5. Chambers, *Mediaeval Stage*, II, p. 437.
6. C. Walter Hodges, 'Unworthy Scaffolds', *Shakespeare Survey*, 3 (1950), p. 94.
7. *Times Literary Supplement*, 16 May 1952, p. 336.
8. *Vide* L. Wright, *Anglia*, LII (1928), p. 53 and G. L. Taylor, *J. Q. Adams Memorial Studies* (1948), pp. 21 ff.
9. Ronald Watkins, *On Producing Shakespeare* (1950), pp. 144–6, 193.
10. *The Globe Playhouse* (1943), p. 100.
11. It is interesting to note that in a recent Stratford production of *Henry VIII*, although there were four doors to the stage, it was decided, as an experiment, to arrange ceremonial entrances from the orchestra pit (see the account given by Muriel St Clare Byrne in *Shakespeare Survey*, 3 (1950)).
12. Adams, *op. cit.* p. 274.
13. *Ibid.* pp. 206 ff.
14. I shall restrict myself to plays performed at the Globe between 1599 and 1613, hoping thus to avoid confusion. But I have added to Chambers's list (*Elizabethan Stage*, III, p. 105) early plays by Shakespeare, which we may reasonably assume to have formed part of his company's repertoire at the Globe.
15. *Op. cit.* pp. 176, 349–50.
16. *Op. cit.* p. 83. In a recent article (*Shakespeare Quarterly*, II (January 1951), 3–11), Adams estimated that "in the plays written between 1599 and 1610 Shakespeare mounts 43% of all his scenes on the outer-stage alone. If one adds those other scenes in which the outer-stage is used in combination with another stage, the total mounts close to 55%. These figures attest the importance of the platform in the greatest period of English drama." I find this very peculiar testimony indeed. What he is saying is that 45% of these scenes did not use the platform at all! That the great stage should be left empty for nearly half of the action in Shakespeare's plays of this period I find so

incredible that the figures must be wrong. It ought to be said that direct evidence, textual or otherwise, helps to locate only at most one-third of these scenes. The vast majority are determined by the estimator's analogies, pre-suppositions and guesses. I once estimated myself that, of 819 scenes in 39 plays produced at the Globe between 1599 and 1613, at least 60% could be played on the platform alone, and that, at the outside, less than 10% did not require the platform at all. 716 scenes did not require an upper-stage. It is obvious the scientific value of such figures is not high.

17. *Op. cit.* p. 101.

18. Adams, *Shakespeare Quarterly*, II (January 1951), 10.

19. *Review of English Studies*, XXI (January 1945), 1–14.

20. For a simpler solution, see H. Granville-Barker, *Prefaces to Shakespeare*, II (1930), p. 164.

21. G. F. Reynolds (*Shakespeare Quarterly*, I (January 1950), 13) has drawn attention to the difficulty of visibility in most of the commonly accepted reconstructed models of the Globe. Adams himself notes the necessity to "minimize stage business conducted near the floor or in the lower portion of the rear alcove" (*Globe Playhouse*, p. 296). Elsewhere (*J. Q. Adams Memorial Studies*, p. 320) he has also insisted that "in chamber scenes as in study scenes the number of actors present rarely exceeds ten".

22. *Globe Playhouse*, pp. 176 and 284.

23. Chambers denied the validity of chamber-staging for this scene (*Elizabethan Stage*, III, p. 112). Cf. the similar problem of *A Maid's Tragedy*, v, ii.

24. *Times Literary Supplement*, 30 May 1936, 460.

25. *Globe Playhouse*, pp. 263–4, 346–9.

26. *Ibid.* p. 347n.

27. *Vide* G. F. Reynolds, *Shakespeare Survey*, 4 (1951), pp. 97 ff.

28. *Op. cit.* p. 256n.

29. Henslowe bought 48 "turned ballyesters" for the Rose (*Henslowe's Diary*, ed. W. W. Greg, 1 (1904), pp. 8–9, two entries). If all these were used on the balcony, the spacing would have been at most six inches. The item seems too expensive for interior staircases; the galleries, paled with "elmebordes", did not need balusters; the price (2¼d. each in one lot, 1d. each in the other) seems rather high for stage-rails. Even if only twenty-four of them were used on the balcony, the spacing would have been at most twelve inches, far closer than Adams suggests.

30. *The Physical Conditions of the Elizabethan Public Playhouse* (1927), pp. 119–20.

31. *Globe Playhouse*, pp. 53, 88.

32. *Ibid.* pp. 165–6.

33. *Ibid.* p. 249.

34. *Ibid.* pp. 49–50.

35. *Shakespeare Quarterly*, III (January 1952), 17–20.

36. *Shakespeare and the Players* (1948), pp. 62–3.

37. In W. H. Godfrey's diagram (*A Companion to Shakespeare Studies* (1934), p. 24), there are doors situated at the end of the yard alleys in the very position I have postulated, but Godfrey intended them to represent entries to the galleries. William Archer, who superintended Godfrey's plan, accepts the existence of the 'angles' in the sketch reproduced by W. J. Lawrence in *The Physical Conditions of the Elizabethan Public Playhouse* (1927), facing p. 22.

38. C. Walter Hodges, *Shakespeare Survey*, 3 (1950), pp. 92–3.

39. *Elizabethan Stage*, III, p. 98. To the best of my knowledge, most of the scenes I am now discussing have not been publicly mentioned by Adams.

40. The problem scenes are I, iv, v and vi, and II, i and ii, especially perhaps the first of these with its walls *and* turrets.

41. E.g. *Julius Caesar*, v, iii. Pindarus is summoned to report on the battle from "above". There is no 'exit' marked for him, but, after his report, comes the direction "Enter Pindarus". I do not believe that Pindarus went out of sight of the audience. His ascent of the "hill" is complete in 2½ lines, and his descent in 2. There is no time for him to reach the tarras by the stairs backstage. Adams has insisted (*Times Literary Supplement*, 15 February 1936, p. 139) that such a journey would require a *minimum* of six lines of covering verse. Pindarus must either climb a visible rope ladder to the upper-stage or mount a property. In either event, he would never disappear from view. The "hill", of course, must be identified with the "Pulpit" or "public chair" in III, ii, in which scene stage-directions

are again deficient (except for "Brutus...goes into the Pulpit", and this appears to be in the wrong place). Here too there was no time to climb to the tarras via the backstairs: Brutus's ascent takes only 2½ lines and his descent 3, and Antony's ascent 5 lines and descent only 1½.

42. Chambers has a list of such directions. See *Elizabethan Stage*, III, 74.

43. Adams suggests (*Globe Playhouse*, p. 210) for this bridge the use of the study-trap with a property balustrade. Chambers (*Elizabethan Stage*, III, p. 107) was not able to envisage it at all.

44. Or for the spectacle of warriors passing in procession: e.g. *Troilus and Cressida*, I, ii; *Pericles*, II, ii.

45. E.g. *Merry Devil of Edmonton*, IV, i, where Millicent is hidden in a "brake of ferne" in the "bottome" of the platform, while Clare and Ierningham take refuge in the study-wood.

# SHAKESPEARE AND THE ACTING OF EDWARD ALLEYN

## BY

## WILLIAM A. ARMSTRONG

In 1763, the *Theatrical Review* (No. 2) published a letter forged by George Steevens but supposed to have been written by George Peele to Christopher Marlowe. Showing a carefree disregard for chronological possibilities, the letter informed Marlowe that Shakespeare had based the speech about the "excellencie of acting" in *Hamlet* upon "opiniones gyven by Alleyn touchyng that subjecte".[1] Sir Sidney Lee has amply demonstrated the wide currency attained by this amiable fiction during the following hundred years.[2] Its wide acceptance during the nineteenth century is of some interest because its exaltation of Alleyn into an authority on acting fit to instruct Shakespeare offers so diametrical a contrast to modern theories of the relationship between these two men. Alleyn's reputation as an actor has certainly declined during the present century. "Somewhat over-heavy"[3] and "an exaggerated style of acting"[4] are recent and typical pronouncements on his histrionic art. Two reasons explain the rather patronizing tone of many modern assessments of Alleyn's quality. First, it is assumed that when Burbage took the role of Hamlet and delivered his advice to the players at the Globe in 1602, he was indirectly criticizing the technique of Alleyn, the leading actor of the rival company at the Fortune playhouse. Thus Hamlet's remarks about good and bad acting, far from having been originally expounded by Alleyn, are now widely believed to have been directed against him. Secondly, the discovery in *2 Henry IV* of parodies of passages in plays acted by Alleyn's men at the Rose has encouraged at least one critic to assume that Shakespeare was gibing at Alleyn's style of acting even before he wrote *Hamlet*. It is the purpose of this article to assess the validity of these interpretations of passages in *Hamlet* and *2 Henry IV* by relating them to sixteenth- and seventeenth-century references to the acting of Edward Alleyn.

During the past fifty years, several items of the advice given by Hamlet to the players have been annotated as strictures on Alleyn's methods. In 1904, for instance, Karl Mantzius asserted that when Hamlet decries "the robustious periwig-pated fellow" who tears a passion to tatters and declares, "I would have such a fellow whipped for o'erdoing Termagant, it out-herods Herod, pray you avoid it", he is alluding to "the exaggerated acting of Alleyn and his school".[5] This assertion rests rather precariously on the belief that "Termagant" can be identified with *Tamar Cam*, a lost play in which Alleyn acted, and that "Herod" refers to Alleyn's having acted in *Herod and Antipater*, even though that play is first mentioned as having been acted at the Red Bull in 1622,[6] long after Alleyn had retired. It is obviously simpler and certainly more plausible to assume that Hamlet referred to Termagant and Herod, not as parts played by Alleyn, but as prototypes of a bombastic tradition of acting deriving from the tyrants of the miracle-plays, which, incidentally, were still being performed in certain parts of England during Shakespeare's lifetime.[7]

In the notes to his edition of *Hamlet*, first published in 1934, J. Dover Wilson makes it clear that he, too, regards Hamlet's first speech to the players in III, ii, as "a criticism of the acting of the Admiral's Men".[8] He suspects that the "robustious periwig-pated fellow" denounced by Hamlet was Alleyn,[9] has "strong suspicions" that the First Player was deliberately "made up" as Alleyn,[10] and believes that when the First Player took the part of Lucianus in the play within the play he committed all the faults condemned by Hamlet in his first speech in this scene.[11] Against these hypotheses, it may be observed that in II, ii we are clearly given the impression that Hamlet admired the players, that they had enjoyed high repute when he last saw them, that they are friends of his, and that in the past he took particular pleasure in the First Player's acting. Rosencrantz describes the players to Hamlet as "those you were wont to take such delight in" (II, ii, 341): Hamlet asks whether they "hold the same estimation they did when I was in the city" (II, ii, 348–9): he greets them as "good friends" (II, ii, 441): he requests the First Player to recite "a passionate speech" which he himself "chiefly loved" even though "'twas caviare to the general" (II, ii, 452–68). These details can hardly have been calculated to prepare an audience for a display of bad acting by the First Player or for an attack by Hamlet upon the leading member of a rival company as represented by the First Player. Moreover, if Shakespeare's own company "made up" the First Player as Alleyn, they themselves would have acted contrary to Hamlet's advice by providing a distraction when "some necessary question of the play" was to be considered.

The critic who has done most to bring Alleyn's reputation down to its present level is, however, G. B. Harrison. In his essay on 'Shakespeare's Actors',[12] for instance, he interprets Hamlet's remarks on acting as a deliberate contrast between an older and cruder style practised by Alleyn and a more refined one developed by Burbage. In this connexion, he discerns a special pertinence in Hamlet's remark, "O there be players that I have seen play, and heard others praise, and that highly, not to speak it profanely, that, neither having the accent of Christians, nor the gait of Christian, pagan, nor man, have so strutted and bellowed that I have thought some of nature's journeymen had made men and not made them well, they imitated humanity so abominably" (III, ii, 32–9), for, he states, "Alleyn's chief humour was for a tyrant, or a part to tear a cat in. He was Orlando in Greene's *Orlando Furioso*, he was Faustus, Barabas in *The Jew of Malta*; above all he was Tamburlaine and Jeronimo in *The Spanish Tragedy*. All these parts were made for 'strutting and bellowing'....".[13] The last remark seems to belittle Marlowe's art as well as Alleyn's. To be sure, an actor in the role of Barabas will bellow from the cauldron at the close, and in the role of Tamburlaine will cultivate an heroic stride which might be described as "strutting", but the characters of Tamburlaine and Barabas, to say nothing of Faustus, demand much more than "strutting and bellowing" on the part of an actor; in particular, an ability to dominate the stage, to recite lyrical and oratorical blank verse, and to interpret climactic soliloquies both passionately and intelligently. And in the opinion of at least one judicious contemporary, the actor-playwright Thomas Heywood, Alleyn's interpretation of Tamburlaine and Barabas satisfied these demands. In his Prologue to *The Jew of Malta*, Heywood praises Alleyn as "best of actors" and states that he won "the attribute of peerless" for his rendering of Tamburlaine and Barabas.[14] Thomas Nashe, moreover, gives us reason to believe that when Alleyn had to take part in a poor play his acting was so distinguished that he made it seem better than it was. In his pamphlet, *Strange News*, Nashe specifies a character as one whose "very name (as the name of *Ned Allen* on the common stage) was able to make an ill matter good".[15]

According to Harrison, however, Alleyn's reputation as an actor had been waning for several years before *Hamlet* was performed at the Globe. In *Elizabethan Plays and Actors* (1940), he bases arguments to this effect upon certain passages in Shakespeare's *2 Henry IV* which appear to be parodies of passages in plays by Marlowe, Greene and Chapman which were part of the repertory of the Admiral's Men at the Rose. "Pistol's whole vocabulary", he declares, "was made up of play scraps; misquotations from *Tamburlaine*, from *The Blind Beggar*, from Greene's *Alphonsus* and other Rose plays. *He was a kind of walking parody of Alleyn and the ranting style, which hitherto had been so popular at the Rose, but was now beginning to appear as ridiculous to the younger generation of playgoers as the stiff artificialities of Lyly's Euphues*".[16] One may justly comment that a parody of certain phrases is not necessarily a parody of the style of the actor who may have delivered them. Alleyn's style may have appeared ridiculous to "the younger generation of playgoers" when *2 Henry IV* was performed in 1597 and 1598, but, so far as I know, no contemporary opinions to this effect are extant. His style certainly did not seem ridiculous to Queen Elizabeth in 1600, since he resumed acting in that year at her request.[17]

The thesis that Shakespeare wrote Hamlet's strictures on strutting, bellowing, and extravagant gestures with Alleyn's acting in mind necessarily implies that Burbage practised the type of acting of which Hamlet approved. Shakespeare would not require Burbage to preach what he could not practise. Hence one might justifiably expect contemporary references to the acting of Alleyn and Burbage to fall into the pattern of a sharp contrast between a turgid, blustering technique on the one hand, and a discriminating and finely modulated style on the other. Such is not the case. Sixteenth- and seventeenth-century appraisals of the acting of Alleyn and Burbage display a remarkable similarity in the warmth of their praise and in the terms in which it is expressed. Ben Jonson's praise was never lightly won, but the acting of both Alleyn and Burbage had it in full measure, as his eulogistic epigram to Alleyn (1616) and his equation of the terms "Burbage" and "best actor" in *Bartholomew Fair*[18] (1614) attest. Both Alleyn and Burbage were compared to Roscius, the celebrated Roman actor, by other contemporaries who assessed their abilities. According to Nashe, "Not Roscius...could euer performe more in action than famous Ned Allen".[19] Correspondingly, the anonymous author of *A Funeral Elegy on the Death of the famous Actor, Richard Burbadge* honoured Burbage with the title "England's great Roscius".[20] Other admirers credited Alleyn and Burbage respectively with a Protean capacity for adapting their personalities to the needs of different roles. Thomas Heywood[21] describes Alleyn as a

> Proteus for shapes, and Roscius for a tongue,
> So could he speak, so vary,

and Thomas Fuller, speaking from hearsay, praises him for "so acting to the life that he made any part (especially a majestic one) to become him".[22] In the same strain, Richard Flecknoe characterizes Burbage as "a delightful Proteus, so wholly transforming himself into his part, and putting off himself with his cloathes, as he never (not so much as in the Tyring-house) assum'd himself again until the play was done...".[23] It is thus not surprising to find that both Alleyn and Burbage were exalted far above other players of their time by Sir Richard Baker, who refers to them in *A Chronicle of the Kings of England* (1643) as "two such actors that no age must look to see the like".[24]

In the quality of their acting and in the range of their interpretations, contemporary judges obviously found little to choose between Alleyn and Burbage. To conclude this series of significant parallels, it may be observed that both Alleyn and Burbage were able orators and were accorded some measure of civic recognition of their eminence as actors. Alleyn was chosen to appear as the 'Genius of the City' in the coronation procession of 1604, when, according to Thomas Dekker, he delivered a "gratulatory speach" to King James "with excellent action, and a well tun'de audible voyce".[25] Six years later, Burbage was employed by the City to take the part of the "Genius of Wales" and deliver a complimentary speech to Prince Henry at a water-pageant on the Thames.[26]

Certain similarities between Burbage's art as an actor and the art of an orator, as his contemporaries understood the latter, were emphasized by Flecknoe when he praised Burbage as having "all the parts of an excellent orator (animating his words with speaking, and speech with action)....".[27] Moreover, when Dekker referred to the excellence of Alleyn's "action" and "voyce" in his delivery of the speech to the king in 1604, he was using these two words in the technical sense which they had acquired in contemporary treatises on oratory and rhetoric. Rhetoric was one of the most important subjects of study in the grammar schools and universities of the Elizabethan period, and one of its most important branches was known as "pronunciation", a term which comprehended the art of graceful gesture as well as the art of speaking sonorously and expressively, or, as Dekker phrases it in his description of Alleyn, the capacity for speaking "with excellent action, and well tun'de audible voyce'. Quintilian and his Renaissance disciples counselled dignity and discretion in the use of these arts, which, as B. L. Joseph has impressively demonstrated in his book on *Elizabethan Acting*, were practised according to their precepts in the plays acted at schools and universities.[28] Moreover, Hamlet's advice to the players has affinities with contemporary teachings concerning the arts of pronunciation. He requests the First Player to deliver a speech as he himself has "pronounced" (significant word!) it to him. He warns the First Player against mouthing his words like a town-crier, and, like Quintilian and his followers, he counsels his pupil not to "saw the air too much" with his hand. "Temperance" and "discretion" are likewise the watchwords of his advice concerning voice and "action". Indeed, Hamlet's praise of the actor who suits "the action to the word, the word to the action" is the same as Flecknoe's praise of the orator who animates "his words with speaking, and speech with action". Joseph has effectively illustrated other parallels between Hamlet's recommendations and those provided by treatises on oratory.[29] It is sufficient for our present purposes to suggest that if Alleyn possessed the oratorical discipline and grace of voice and gesture with which Dekker credited him, his technique was not, as his detractors have maintained, antithetical to Hamlet's ideals of discretion and restraint.

Though the records of Alleyn's career as an actor extend from 1583 to 1604, it is an unfortunate fact that only seven of his roles can be specified with absolute certainty. Alleyn took the parts of Tamburlaine, Barabas, Faustus, Muly Mahamet (in *The Battle of Alcazar*), Tamar Cam (in *1 Tamar Cam*), Sebastian (in *Frederick and Basilea*), and Cutlack in a play of the same name.[30] The last three plays mentioned are not extant, so that only four of Alleyn's roles are accessible as texts. He may have played Orlando in Greene's *Orlando Furioso* since the actor's copy of that part preserved in Dulwich College has corrections which seem to be in Alleyn's handwriting. Some critics claim that he played Hieronimo in *The Spanish Tragedy*, which is probable, but

I have seen no contemporary evidence which puts this claim beyond the realms of conjecture. In omitting this role from Alleyn's known repertoire, I appear to be in agreement with W. W. Greg,[31] Sir Edmund Chambers[32] and E. Nungezer,[33] none of whom includes it in his list of the parts played by Alleyn. Inevitably, perhaps, Alleyn's technique has been identified with a narrow range of parts, and, in particular, with the most lurid and bombastic scenes in Marlowe's plays. Some commentators, indeed, seem to assume that Alleyn treated every role as though it were that of Tamburlaine in his most tyrannical mood. Yet versatility and even a capacity for comedy can hardly be denied to one who was "bred a stage player"[34] in the repertory system of Elizabethan times and was praised as a "Proteus for shapes" by so knowledgeable a man of the theatre as Thomas Heywood.

Ben Jonson's epigram to Alleyn merits close scrutiny, for it may be a tribute to his versatility as well as to his eminence as an actor. Besides, its estimate of Alleyn's quality must necessarily give pause to those who would dismiss him as the exponent of a "ranting style" which soon became outmoded. Jonson was evidently an able producer as well as a playwright. John Aubrey, for instance, remarks, "Now B. Johnson was never a good actor but an excellent instructor",[35] and Flecknoe likewise praises Jonson as an "instructor" of players.[36] As an "instructor", Jonson was certainly inimical to a "ranting style". For example, in his Induction to *The Staple of News*, he censures the actor who "*doe's ouer-act prodigiously in beaten satten, and, hauing got the tricke on't, will be* monstrous *still, in despight of* Counsell".[37] This is very like the charge that Shakespeare is assumed to have levelled against Alleyn. Yet Jonson obviously had a great admiration for Alleyn's acting. In the epigram which he addressed to Alleyn in 1616, Jonson first refers[38] to the glories which "skilfull ROSCIVS, and graue ÆSOPE" brought to the Roman stage, and then tells Alleyn that he is one

> Who both their graces in thy selfe hast more
> Out-stript, then they did all that went before.

Though Elizabethan panegyrists often apply the name "Roscius" indiscriminately to any actor of outstanding merit, it is worth remarking that in ancient Rome Roscius was famous as a *comic* actor whereas Aesopus was famous as a tragic actor, and that Jonson, whose scholarship was exact, may have been paying tribute to the comic as well as the tragic felicities of Alleyn's acting when he exalted him above both the "graces" of Roscius and Aesopus.[39] Of the plays in which he acted, *The Jew of Malta* has been cogently interpreted by T. S. Eliot as a savage comedy.[40] Alleyn's interpretation of Barabas certainly had its comic moments since part of his make-up was a false nose, to which Ithamore alludes sarcastically more than once.[41]

One of the few comparative descriptions of Elizabethan players written by a contemporary is elaborated in the Prologue and Epilogue which Thomas Heywood wrote for a production of *The Jew of Malta* staged at the Cockpit in 1632 or 1633. His comparison relates the acting of Alleyn to that of Richard Perkins. Richard Perkins did not begin his professional career until 1602, i.e. two years before Alleyn retired from the stage, and records of his acting continue until 1641. During this period Perkins was acknowledged to have been one of the ablest actors in the troupes known as the Queen's Men, the Players of the Revels, and Queen Henrietta's Men. During the last fifteen years of his career, he performed mainly at the private theatres known as the Cockpit and Salisbury Court.[42] Much earlier, John Webster was so impressed by Perkins's acting in *The White Devil* that he appended the following note to his edition of the play in 1612:[43]

For the action of the play, twas generally well, and I dare affirme, with the Joint testimony of some of their owne quality, (for the true imitation of life, without striving to make nature a monster) the best that ever became them: whereof as I make a generall acknowledgement, so in particular I must remember the well approved industry of my freind *Maister Perkins*, and confesse the worth of his action did Crowne both the beginning and end.

Webster's standard of good acting, "the true imitation of life, without striving to make nature a monster", reminds one of Hamlet's warning against overstepping "the modesty of nature" and of his recommendation that the player should hold "as 'twere, the mirror up to nature" (III, ii, 22–6).[44] Hamlet's denunciation of strutting, sawing the air, and tearing a passion to tatters, and his approval of the actor who suits "the action to the word, the word to the action" (III, ii, 36, 5, 11, 20–1) likewise have much in common with the criteria of good and bad acting outlined by Thomas Heywood in the following passage from his *Apology for Actors* (1612):[45]

And this is the action behoovefull in any that profess this quality, not to vse any impudent or forced motion in any part of the body, no rough, or other violent gesture, nor on the contrary, to stand like a stiffe starcht man, but to qualify everything according to the nature of the person personated: for in oueracting trickes, and toyling too much in the anticke habit of humors, men of the ripest desert, greatest opinions, and best reputations, may breake into the most violent absurdities.

As Webster, Shakespeare, and Heywood thus seem to have had certain ideas in common about the best kind of acting, Heywood's comparison of Alleyn and Perkins is especially significant.[46] In his Prologue to *The Jew of Malta*, after making the remark that Alleyn, "best of actors", won "the attribute of peerless"[47] for his interpretation of Barabas and other roles, Heywood frankly states that Perkins does not hope to emulate his illustrious predecessor:[48]

> nor is it his ambition
> To exceed or equal, being of condition
> More modest.

Heywood's Epilogue is even more apologetic; no sculptor could compete with Pygmalion, no painter could compete with Apelles, nor has Perkins attempted the hopeless task of challenging comparison with Alleyn:[49]

> our actor did not so,
> He only aim'd to go, but not out-go.

Praise of this kind, recited from the stage nearly thirty years after Alleyn's last recorded appearance, was surely the greatest compliment ever paid to his acting. It proves that Alleyn's acting, far from seeming crude or outmoded in style to the discriminating patrons of a private theatre in the early 1630's, could be confidently cited to them as a paragon of histrionic excellence.

It is no exaggeration of the evidence which has been quoted and discussed above to claim that in the opinion of such well-qualified contemporary critics as Nashe, Jonson and Heywood, Edward Alleyn was an actor of genius. The testimonies of Jonson and Heywood are especially relevant to the theme of this article because they were men of Shakespeare's generation, because they very probably saw Alleyn act, and because their standards of judgement were as high as those professed by Hamlet. Both Heywood and Jonson were skilful and experienced men of the theatre and both condemned over-acting as roundly as Hamlet does. Heywood's opinions are particularly important since it may be inferred from them that Alleyn's technique as an actor was not essentially different from that of Burbage, for Heywood's ideals, as expounded in some detail in his *Apology for Actors*, are substantially the same as Hamlet's. If Shakespeare was indirectly attacking Alleyn's acting in the first two speeches delivered by Hamlet in III, ii of *Hamlet*, his opinion of it was certainly a minority one, and should not be accepted, as it has been, without question. But as the 'judicious' of Shakespeare's time assessed Alleyn's abilities so highly, it seems unlikely that he would have capriciously run counter to the ideals that he shared with them by stigmatizing Alleyn as a strutting, bellowing, robustious, periwig-pated fellow, whose imitation of humanity was abominable. A savage attack of this kind upon the most celebrated tragic actor of the day would certainly have vitiated the contribution which Shakespeare made to the cause of the adult actors in the War of the Theatres in his shrewd but not unkindly references to the boy actors in II, ii of *Hamlet*. Hamlet's speeches about the art of acting do not fall flat if they are interpreted without continuous reference to personalities. On the contrary, they are exquisitely in character. They express the ideals of an enthusiastic amateur who has but lately left his university. And Hamlet, the perfectionist who demands perfect proof of his perfect father's murder and a perfect revenge on his uncle, inevitably demands perfect acting, too, even though it is impossible.

## NOTES

1. Steevens's forgery is reprinted in J. Bakeless's *The Tragicall History of Christopher Marlowe* (Cambridge, Mass., 1942), II, 295.

2. *A Life of William Shakespeare* (1915), pp. 646–7.

3. D. Brook, *A Pageant of English Actors* (1950), p. 35.

4. G. Freedley and G. A. Reeves, *A History of the Theatre* (New York, 1941), p. 102.

5. *A History of Theatrical Art* (1904), p. 197.

6. See Sir Edmund Chambers, *The Elizabethan Stage* (Oxford, 1923), III, 417.

7. At Chester, York, Perranzabulo, and possibly Newcastle. See Sir Edmund Chambers, *The Medieval Stage* (Oxford, 1903), II, 353, 404, 390 and 385.

8. *Hamlet* (Cambridge, 1941), p. 195.

9. *Ibid.* p. 195.

10. *Ibid.* p. 181.

11. *Ibid.* p. 195.

12. In the Shakespeare Association's *Shakespeare and the Theatre* (1927).

13. *Shakespeare and the Theatre*, p. 83.

14. *The Jew of Malta and The Massacre at Paris*, ed. H. S. Bennett (1931), p. 28.

15. *The Works of Thomas Nashe*, ed. R. B. McKerrow (1904–10), I, 296.

16. *Elizabethan Plays and Players* (1940), p. 173. The italics are mine.

17. See Sir E. Chambers, *The Elizabethan Stage*, II, 273, 297.

18. *Ben Jonson*, ed. C. H. Herford and P. and E. Simpson (Oxford, 1925–52), VI, 119–20.

19. From *Pierce Pennilesse: The Works of Thomas Nashe*, I, 215.

20. See M. M. Stopes, *Burbage and Shakespeare's Stage* (1913), p. 119.

21. See Marlowe's *The Jew of Malta and The Massacre at Paris*, p. 28.

22. *A History of the Worthies of England*, ed. J. Nichols (1811), II, 84.

23. *A Short Discourse of the English Stage* (1664), sig. G4ʳ.

24. *A Chronicle of the Kings of England* (1643), p. 120.

25. *The Magnificent Entertainment* (1604), sig. C1ʳ.

26. See Sir E. K. Chambers, *The Elizabethan Stage*, I, 134, ii, 309–10.

27. *A Short Discourse of the English Stage*, sig. G4ʳ.

28. *Elizabethan Acting* (Oxford, 1951), pp. 13–16.

29. *Ibid.* pp. 146–9.

30. The evidence is conveniently summarized and documented by E. Nungezer, *A Dictionary of Actors* (New Haven, 1929), p. 8.

31. See his essay on Alleyn in the Shakespeare Association's *Shakespeare and the Theatre* (1927).

32. See his biography of Alleyn, *The Elizabethan Stage*, II, 296–8.

33. See his entry in *A Dictionary of Actors*, pp. 4–11.

34. The phrase is Fuller's. *A History of the Worthies of England*, II, 84.

35. *Brief Lives*, ed. A. Clark (Oxford, 1898), II, 226.

36. *A Short Discourse of the English Stage*, sig. G4ʳ.

37. *Ben Jonson*, ed. C. H. Herford and P. and E. Simpson, VI, 280.

38. *Ibid.* VIII, 56–7.

39. The adjectives applied by Jonson to Roscius and Aesopus respectively prove that his knowledge of them derived from contemporary Roman sources. His phrase "skillful Roscivs and graue Æsope" derives from Horace's *Epistle to Augustus*: "Quae *gravis* Aesopus, quae *doctus* Roscius egit".

40. In his essay 'Christopher Marlowe'. See *Selected Essays* (1946), p. 123.

41. *The Jew of Malta and The Massacre at Paris*, p. 88, l. 174; p. 104, l. 10; p. 120, l. 24. Moreover, in his pamphlet, *The Search for Money* (1609), William Rowley describes a character as having "his visage (or vizard) like the artificiall Jewe of Maltae's nose...". See the Percy Society Reprint (1890), p. 19.

42. There is a useful summary of Perkins's career in E. Nungezer's *A Dictionary of Actors*, pp. 274–8.

43. *The Complete Works of John Webster*, ed. F. L. Lucas (1927), I, 192.

44. The criteria suggested by Shakespeare and Webster may derive from the same classical source. J. E. Spingarn has pointed out that Cicero, according to Donatus, said that comedy was "imitatio vitae, speculum consuetudinis, imago veritatis", and has remarked that this phrase "runs through all the dramatic discussions of the Renaissance, and finds its echo in a famous passage in *Hamlet*". (*Literary Criticism in the Renaissance* (New York, 1925), p. 104.) Webster, too, seems to hark back to the same classical authority.

45. *An Apology for Actors*, ed. R. H. Perkinson (New York, 1941), sig. C3ᵛ.

46. The marginal references to "Allin" and "Perkins", which accompany Heywood's Prologue in the 1633 Quarto of *The Jew of Malta*, make his comparison explicit.

47. *The Jew of Malta and The Massacre at Paris*, p. 28, ll. 4, 8.

48. *Ibid.* p. 28, ll. 13–15.

49. *Ibid.* p. 30, ll. 3–4.

G

# THE BIRMINGHAM SHAKESPEARE
# MEMORIAL LIBRARY

BY

## F. J. PATRICK

I want to see founded in Birmingham a Shakespeare Library which should contain (as far as practicable) every edition and every translation of Shakespeare; all the commentators, good, bad, and indifferent; in short, every book connected with the life or works of our great poet. I would add portraits of Shakespeare, and all the pictures, &c., illustrative of his works.

So, in the columns of *Aris's Birmingham Gazette*, wrote George Dawson, the celebrated Birmingham preacher, lecturer and politician, in the year 1861. He was writing in his capacity of President of the local Shakespeare Club and in furtherance of an idea first publicly mooted by another prominent citizen, Samuel Timmins, in 1858. The year 1863 saw the formation of a committee to pursue the project and collect donations. On 23 April 1864, the tercentenary of Shakespeare's birth, the then Mayor of Birmingham, William Holliday, gave a public breakfast at a local hotel, when a number of volumes were presented and an address and deed of gift were received and accepted by the Mayor on behalf of the town. In accordance with the deed of gift, a room was set apart in the Central Public Library, and, on 23 April 1868, the Shakespeare Memorial Library was opened to the public.

The foundation collection included many generous gifts comprising, *inter alia*, more than a hundred volumes used by Charles Knight in the preparation of his various editions of Shakespeare; a copy of the Fourth Folio (1685); and an original quarto *Henry V* (1608). Purchases by the Committee of Subscribers included the Second (1632) and Third (1663) Folios and J. O. Halliwell's edition of 1853–65 in sixteen folio volumes.

The energy displayed by the Free Libraries Committee and their staff in endeavouring to implement the ambition of George Dawson is sufficiently indicated by the appended table showing the numbers of volumes in the Shakespeare Memorial Library at 31 December in each of the following years:

| Year | Volumes | Year | Volumes |
|------|---------|------|---------|
| 1868 | 1239 | 1873 | 5332 |
| 1869 | 2249 | 1874 | 5663 |
| 1870 | 3463 | 1875 | 6198 |
| 1871 | 4012 | 1876 | 6450 |
| 1872 | 4713 | 1877 | 6739 |

On Saturday, 11 January 1879, the whole of the Central Library, and with it the Shakespeare Memorial Library, was destroyed by a disastrous fire. The loss, including, as it did, much irreplaceable material in the general Reference Library, was staggering, but the Free Libraries Committee immediately set to work to replace, with the aid of insurance monies, public subscriptions and the town rate fund, the lost libraries (Reference, Lending and Shakespeare) by new ones. Gifts of books, as well as money, poured in. By the end of 1882, and following the opening of the rebuilt Central Library on 1 June of that year, no less than 4,390 volumes had been acquired for the new Shakespeare Memorial Library and by the end of 1884 it possessed a stock (6,734 volumes) almost exactly equivalent to the figure at the end of 1877, the last year for which statistics were recorded prior to the fire. No further disaster has since befallen the Library, and, through the steady pursuance of the aims of its founders, its holdings have grown to such an extent that they now number approximately 35,000 books and pamphlets in no less than sixty-five different languages.

Apart from the normal intake of new editions and general Shakespeariana, there have been some outstanding acquisitions. The cornerstone of a Shakespeare Library is, of course, a copy of the First Folio. The Birmingham copy is in good condition, but has the letterpress of the title and the last leaf in facsimile. There is an excellent copy of the Second Folio, the two Third Folios, dated 1663 and 1664, and a Fourth Folio.

Of the Quarto editions of the separate plays, including Restoration adaptions and alterations, the Library possesses over seventy published before 1709, many of them extremely rare. It is fortunate in having three of the Quarto editions printed in 1619 for Thomas Pavier, but with the title-pages undated, or falsely dated to make them appear to have been printed earlier. They are *The Chronicle History of Henry the fift*, 1608, *The excellent History of the Merchant of Venice*, 1600, and *The Whole Contention betweene the two Famous Houses, Lancaster and Yorke*, undated.

Perhaps, however, the greatest richness of the Shakespeare Memorial Library is in its collection of early eighteenth-century editions. An examination of the relevant sections of Jaggard's *Bibliography* and Ford's *Shakespeare 1700–1740* will show that there is little that it lacks.

The three copies which the Library possesses of Nicholas Rowe's first illustrated edition of *The Works*, as they now came to be called in 1709, are all, unfortunately, of the second issue. It is an edition in six volumes, handsomely printed by the great Jacob Tonson. A seventh volume containing the poems appeared the next year, and the prefatory material to the whole set includes the first Life of Shakespeare. A few copies were printed on large paper, and Birmingham has two of these.

For those interested in the lively quarrel which arose between the two booksellers Jacob Tonson and Robert Walker there is much of interest in the Library. It has the two separate editions printed between 1734 and 1736 by Tonson and by Walker, and many of the separate plays issued by Walker later, under the imprint 'Printed in the Year'. There are also parallel copies of the three early eighteenth-century editions of *Hamlet*, 1723, *Othello*, 1724, and *Macbeth*, 1729, which Giles Dawson has recently demonstrated to be piracies.

A valuable and unique possession is the more complete of only two known copies of Theobald's first Dublin edition, published in 1739. The other copy is in the Folger Library.

The fierce battles of the eighteenth-century editors in their efforts to 'restore' and reshape the text of Shakespeare can be readily surveyed here, for there are not only all the well-known editions, but all the commentators on the editions. These make good reading.

The nineteenth-century editions of Shakespeare are legion. The Library has over 800 English editions of the Complete Works.

Particularly interesting to students of this period are the engravings and illustrations to Shakespeare, of which there are many thousands. These hold the mirror up to nature in a new way, and one cannot but be amazed at the society which enjoyed some of these spectacles upon the stage. Here is Miss Ellen Bateman as Richard III and Miss Kate Bateman as Richmond looking as fierce as is possible in a tiny skirt and Victorian curls; a buxom, middle-aged Ariel in ballet dress and angels' wings; and Romeo and Juliet played by the sisters Charlotte and Susan Cushman. The Library has a copy of *Studies of Shakespeare*, 1847, by George Fletcher, which has manuscript notes by Ellen Terry. Referring to the Cushman venture the author says "There is little cause to fear that so unnatural an outrage...as that recently perpetrated at the Haymarket Theatre will ever more be tolerated on the London stage". "No," writes Miss Terry "but I was asked to play Juliet to Miss Leighton's Romeo in Manchester a few years ago, June 1900."

Among this illustrative material which richly covers all periods from 1709 to the present day the great collection made by H. R. Forrest of Manchester is, perhaps, the most remarkable. He took Kenny Meadows's, Charles Knight's, Staunton's and Cassell's illustrated editions of Shakespeare and added to these all known illustrations by Boydell, Fuseli, Howard, Smirke, Chodowicki, Retzsch and Ruhl. Every other illustration that he could procure, whether historical, descriptive or artistic, was included, together with portraits of actors, both English and foreign, who had made their mark on the Shakespearian stage. The whole of this vast collection was sorted, mounted and bound into seventy-six folio volumes, each of which was provided with an index.

The Library possesses, altogether, over 200 scrap-books containing illustrations, photographs, and newspaper cuttings, and there are fifty-two volumes of playbills. All newspaper cuttings are sorted and mounted into volumes. Since all this scrapbook material is indexed, it is readily available for consultation. The usefulness of such material, which is often in inverse ratio to its intrinsic value, needs no emphasis. A considerable body of the Shakespeariana recorded in the catalogue is not in the Shakespeare Memorial Library itself, but in general works and periodicals in the great Reference Library of which the Shakespeare Memorial Library forms a part. All books and periodicals added to the Reference Library are systematically scanned for essays and articles on Shakespearian topics, all of which are duly noted under author and subject in the Shakespeare Memorial Library catalogue.

In the search for other material, help has been sought and obtained from theatrical producers in many parts of the world, and foreign visitors to the Library are frequently asked for information about Shakespearian publications in their respective countries. Foreign Office and British Council representatives abroad have also been most helpful. At home, the British Broadcasting Corporation have presented scripts of the plays by and relating to Shakespeare which have been broadcast from time to time.

An important function of the Library is the systematic collection of photographs of modern productions of the plays. An attempt is made to secure copies of all current Shakespearian news and comment, however fugitive, and to record news of productions from near and far. Programmes and photographs of these are preserved when obtainable. Most theatres in this country and many theatres abroad now send photographs and programmes of their Shakespearian productions. This material, gathered together where it is readily available for consultation, will become immensely valuable to historians of the future, and a national record of all that has been achieved.

The aim of George Dawson—completeness—he qualified himself by his parenthetical "as far as practicable", and it is worth while to examine how far practice has progressed in its effort to reach his admittedly unattainable objective. On 31 March 1953, the Shakespeare Memorial Library contained 1,258 English editions and selections of the works comprising 6,135 volumes, together with 5,284 editions of separate plays and poems and no less than 13,444 items of Shakespeariana—a grand total of 24,863 books and pamphlets in English, inclusive of those emanating from the United States of America. In German, there were 184 editions in 1,303 volumes, 911 separate plays and 2,525 items of Shakespeariana making a total of 4,739, nearly one-fifth of the total in English. French publications came next in total, numbering 77 editions in 331 volumes, 502 separate plays and 519 Shakespeariana items, together making 1,352. For the rest, there were publications in sixty-two other languages ranging from Afrikaans to Yoruba, but reaching three-figure totals in only Italian (613), Spanish (351), Danish (331), Dutch (341), Japanese (279), Swedish (239), Russian (219), Hungarian (209) and Polish (105). Surely, if cold statistical evidence of Shakespeare's universal appeal is needed, here it is.

There is no need to stress the vital need for an adequate catalogue to enable a special collection such as the Shakespeare Memorial Library to be fully exploited for research purposes. A printed catalogue of the pre-fire library appeared in 1872, but surviving copies are merely mournful reminders of the loss that the fire caused. The only other printed catalogue appeared in parts between the years 1900 and 1903, and, since the stock of the Library in the latter year was less than one-third of its present magnitude, is of little relevance today. It is a matter of great regret that present economic conditions preclude the printing of the completely up-to-date catalogues which are available at the Library for the use of readers. They consist of a typescript catalogue in four folio volumes recording the acquisitions of the Library up to 1932 and a card catalogue listing additions from 1933 to date, both catalogues being arranged, of course, on the same plan. Subdivision is first by language, English, German and French leading in that order and being followed by the sixty-two other represented languages in alphabetical order. Each language is further subdivided to give complete editions of the works in order of dates of publication, smaller collections of the works and selections therefrom in alphabetical order of editors' names, editions of separate plays arranged first in alphabetical order of titles, and secondly in chronological order of dates of publication under each title, collected editions of plays ascribed to Shakespeare and separate editions of such plays, collected editions of the poems, selections therefrom and editions of separate poems, editions of the songs and sonnets, and, finally, Shakespeariana.

Shakespeariana are exhaustively catalogued under authors, editors, illustrators, subjects and forms, and are, therefore, of the greatest value to scholars pursuing specific lines of research. Individual plays and characters each have their subject-headings under which are listed books and articles relating to them. Noted Shakespearian actors and actresses are treated in the same way and editions of the works containing portraits of them are noted. Shakespearian music, newspaper cuttings and playbills are listed, general collections coming first, followed by those relating to particular plays. In addition, a wide range of Shakespearian topics is displayed under some four hundred subject-headings ranging from archery to Yorkshire and displaying an astonishing diversity of subjects. No more effective tribute to the catholicity of the works could be paid than is evident from this formidable list of topics which are either treated in such masterly fashion in the plays themselves, or judged by all sorts and conditions of men to be relevant to some of the ideas which the plays express. Equally impressive are the fifty odd 'form' headings under which are listed a variety of illustrative material from "allusion books" to "tributes to Shakespeare".

The foregoing outline of the content and arrangement of the catalogue gives some idea of the scope of a collection which, founded on the lines of George Dawson's original conception of completeness, has been systematically and industriously developed ever since. He probably gave little, if any, thought himself to the techniques which would be developed in the process of amassing the collection and exploiting it by means of detailed cataloguing and indexing. He did not envisage the appointment of a librarian whose sole duty would consist of fostering the collection and assisting all comers to use it. So conscientiously, however, has the Birmingham Public Libraries Committee pursued the founders' intentions over the seventy-four years which have elapsed since the fire, that the Shakespeare Memorial Library has now become a collection of such importance in both comprehensiveness and organization that no worker in the field of Shakespearian research can afford to neglect it. Since the potential users of a specialized library of this kind are scattered all over the world, it is perhaps worth while to state that postal requests for information on Shakespearian topics may be addressed to the City Librarian, Birmingham 1, and will be given expert attention by the Librarian of the Shakespeare Memorial Library.

It remains to be added that the Library is maintained by the Corporation of the City of Birmingham as part of its general public library service, such maintenance involving the acquisition of all new Shakespearian publications as they appear and old ones which come into the market if the Library does not already possess them. Many thousands are received as gifts, while the Corporation, in its efforts to purchase the remainder, receives valuable assistance from a small local committee of subscribers.

# SHAKESPEARE'S ITALY

BY

## MARIO PRAZ

It has been remarked that the audience of an Elizabethan theatre must have been not very different from a modern cinema audience: they cared chiefly for the spectacular and the sensational. The influence of Senecan tragedy is responsible for the way in which the Elizabethan taste for thrillers developed, but assimilation takes place only when there exists an affinity: Seneca supplied the Elizabethan dramatists with a justification for horrors for which there was certainly a spontaneous taste. Plays like *The Yorkshire Tragedy* and *Arden of Feversham*, though posterior to *The Spanish Tragedy* which is clearly indebted to Seneca, cannot be traced to a foreign or classical influence, but are the direct outcome of a native interest in the police-court horrors of the time. Such interest is perhaps nowhere better witnessed than in Nashe's *Unfortunate Traveller*, with its sensationalism continually overreaching itself in the display of horrors piled upon horrors, and its iterated showman's cries: "Prepare your eares and your teares, for neuer tyll thys thrust I anie tragecall matter vpon you."

The English translators of Seneca's *Tenne Tragedies* were enabled to enlarge on Seneca's horrors by an inborn taste for loathsome details; but had not already the foremost of the Italian imitators of Seneca, Giraldi Cinthio, interpreted as *orrore* the φόβος Aristotle required for tragedy, had he not given to the Thyestean banquet that widespread popularity we find recorded not only in the very plays, but also in such descriptions of their effect on the audience as Cinthio's in his *Discorso intorno al comporre delle commedie e delle tragedie*? The effects Senecan tragedy was expected to produce on the audience were, according to Cinthio, astonishment and "a thrill which puts the spectator beside himself" (*un certo raccapriccio che fa uscire chi l'ha veduto come di sè*). What then about Vernon Lee's theory (in her somehow charmingly antiquated essay in *Euphorion*) that the Renaissance Italians "rarely or never paint horror or death or abomination", that "the whole tragic meaning was unknown to the light and cheerful contemporaries of Ariosto"; do not we know now that the taste for horrors was first indulged in by the Italian Senecans? Do not we know from the Italian chronicles utilized by Stendhal how fond were the crowds of capital executions? The Italian dramatists, however, chose to dramatize the story of some unfortunate Armenian or Persian couple of lovers, rather than the pathetic, but too familiar story of the Duchess of Malfy; the English found in the story of the Duchess of Malfy or Bianca Cappello that exotic thrill which the domestic police-court horrors lacked. The favourite background of the Elizabethan dramatists became, to use Vernon Lee's picturesque description, "the darkened Italian palace, with its wrought-iron bars preventing escape; its embroidered carpets muffling the footsteps; its hidden, suddenly yawning trap-doors; its arras-hangings concealing masked ruffians; its garlands of poisoned flowers". Italy made very good copy, being considered the academy of manslaughter, the sporting place of murder, the apothecary shop of all nations. The Elizabethan dramatist who made the most of the lurid exotic appeal of Italy is admittedly Webster. He exploits the two sides of the Italian appeal: the splendour of its princely courts, and the practice of poisoning. The taste for processions, jousts, investitures, in a word, gorgeous display of every description, was inborn in the crowds of the Renaissance; see how many shows Webster contrives to cram into his Italian plays! Webster is the supreme exponent of a school of Italianate horrors which begins with Kyd's *Spanish Tragedy* and Marlowe's *Jew of Malta*, and blossoms in such productions as Massinger's *Unnatural Combat* (which is about the famous Cenci trial), Marston's *Antonio and Mellida* and *Insatiate Countess*, Tourneur's *Revenger's Tragedy* and *Atheist's Tragedy*, Middleton's *Women Beware Women* and *The Changeling*.

It is a matter of no little surprise, then, when we turn to Shakespeare, to see how his Italian plays are comparatively free from the usual horrors and thrills. Horrible murders and treasons occur indeed on the Shakespearian stage, but, oddly enough, not as a rule in the plays whose action takes place in Italy. Was it because Shakespeare disdained the cheap appeal of Italian criminality? Or because the broadness of his vision made him keep in the background the abject and horrible side of human nature, and stress the pure and noble one? Or because the acquaintance he had of Italian things enabled him to take a more sober view of Italian society than the current one circulated by religious or conservative fanatics and cherished by the thriller-seeking crowd?

From one among the first of his plays, the *Two Gentlemen of Verona*, to the one which is his last finished work, *The Tempest*, Shakespeare frequently brought Italian characters on the stage, and yet the majority of them are exempt from those moral monstrosities on which other dramatists used to gloat. Rather, Shakespeare's Italy is so near to the idyllic Italy which we can picture from Ariosto's and Castiglione's works that some have ventured to suggest that Shakespeare travelled there: how could he otherwise be able to draw such a true-to-life image, when everybody round him in England was spellbound by the myth of Italian wickedness? Every now and then, in Shakespearian criticism, we come across such statements as: "We marvel at his intimate description of Italian life, explicable apparently only on the supposition that he was an eye-witness of the scenes he describes" (Boecker). Some have found "a pure Paduan atmosphere" hanging about *The Taming of the Shrew* (Charles Knight), others, that the first act of *Othello* is thoroughly Venetian in spirit. One critic observes that as in *The Merchant of Venice* Portia is the type of the brilliant, playful, sprightly Venetian lady, so in *Othello* Desdemona personifies the gentle, loving, submissive, patient type so dear to the Italians; the same critic (Horatio F. Brown) declares Shylock to be more Venetian, in many respects, than Jewish. George Brandes believed Shakespeare's knowledge of Italy to have been "closer than could have been gained from oral descriptions and from books". William Bliss, in his playful 'Counterblast to Commentators', *The Real Shakespeare* (1947), actually makes him travel round the world with Drake, and, for the second period in which we have no record of his whereabouts (from 1586 to 1592), maintains as a paradox that he was shipwrecked on the Illyrian coast, and went to Venice where he would have known the Earl of Southampton who would have succoured him and remained his patron afterwards. Bliss wanted to demonstrate for fun that anything can be plausibly argued about Shakespeare; but there is not the slightest suggestion of leg-pulling in G. Lambin's articles 'Sur la trace d'un Shakespeare inconnu' which appeared in *Les Langues modernes* in 1951-2. For Lambin there is no doubt that the author of the plays which go under the name of Shakespeare visited Italy, particularly Florence and Milan. The "Saint Jaques le Grand" to which Helena is supposed to betake herself on a pilgrimage in *All's Well*, would not be the well-known sanctuary in Spain, but San Giacomo d'Altopascio not far from Florence, and the palmers' hostel "at the S. Francis here beside the port" (III, v, 37) would stand for the oratory of San Francesco dei Vanchetoni in the neighbourhood of Porta al Prato in Florence. This "unknown Shakespeare", according to Lambin, writes passages of *All's Well* in the style of the French *pasquils* about the League, with whose workings he is shown to be intimately acquainted,[1] and *The Tempest* as a panegyric for Maria de' Medici. For Maria de' Medici, Lambin is convinced, is Miranda, and her father Prospero is Francis I, Grand Duke of Tuscany, Sycorax is Bianca Cappello, and Caliban Francesco's spurious son by her, Antonio. The key to this hidden meaning of *The Tempest* has been supplied to Lambin by an article on the Grand Duke he has found in the *Dictionnaire général de biographie et d'histoire* by Charles Dezorry and Th. Bachelet, in which he has read about Francesco's chemical laboratory, the *studiolo* in Palazzo Vecchio. He goes even so far as to suggest that Ariel and the famous line "these are pearls that were his eyes" were suggested by the figures of *amoretti* represented in that study as working at precious substances such as coral, crystal, pearls. But there is no knowing how far Lambin is prepared to go, assisted by second-hand historical information, which he naïvely twists to prove his assumptions.[2] There is, in fact, nothing which cannot be manipulated by Lambin into a proof: even the hackneyed Petrarchan metaphor of the *navicella* (little ship) he finds in the madrigals of Francesco (first published, 1894) would have suggested to the author of *The Tempest* the episode of Prospero being abandoned in a "rotten carcass of a boat" adrift on the sea. His is a series of arbitrary equations and far-fetched associations such as we are accustomed to find in the writings of the followers of Freud (for instance in Marie Bonaparte's study of Poe) or in Joyce. His "discoveries" would point in the direction of M. A. Lefranc's *Découverte de Shakespeare* (Paris, 1945 and 1950): Lambin's "unknown Shakespeare" would have utilized personal recollections of his travels in Italy and France and his contacts with people of importance in those countries: he might well be William Stanley, 6th Earl of Derby. But is this new proliferation of the old Baconian heresy in any way warranted by whatever evidence of actual acquaintance of topography of Italian cities we can safely sift from Lambin's and others' straining of the text of the plays? Madame Longworth Chambrun, on whose hypothesis I shall have to speak further on, writes: "What strikes us above all in Shakespeare's work, is to see how the dramatist has succeeded in giving us a true impression of Italian culture whereas, all things considered, one finds in him very little real knowledge. Shakespeare, though having a very slight acquaintance with the Italian language, gives to the spectator or the reader a very strong illusion of local colour". On the same theme F. E. Schelling warns: "Much nonsense has been written about Shakespeare's power of local coloring. This power he undoubtedly possesses in a high degree, but it comes from the suggestions of his sources and only the unimaginative commentator can think it needful to send him to Italy for the coloring of *The Merchant of Venice* and *Othello*, or to Denmark for his *Hamlet*. Shakespeare's personages are seldom foreigners".

Before coming to the actual question about the way in which Shakespeare may have got acquainted with Italian things, let us make a rapid survey of his Italian plays.

The scenes of *The Two Gentlemen of Verona* are Verona and Milan. The names of the chief characters are more or less Italianate, but those of the two servants, Speed and Launce, are English. Several inconsistencies have been noticed. In I, iii, Valentine is said to attend the Emperor in his royal court; but later on we find that the court is actually a duke's court. In II, v, which is supposed to take place in Milan, Speed is heard welcoming Launce "to Padua".

Elsewhere we find Verona where we would expect Milan. These local inaccuracies have led critics to think that Shakespeare had written the whole of the play before he had settled where the scene was to be laid. At any rate the plot structure of *The Two Gentlemen* is modelled on that of a typical Italian *commedia dell'arte*,[3] so that Shakespeare either used as a source a thoroughly Italianate play, such as might have been the lost *Felix and Philiomena*, or he developed with devices derived from the Italian comedy the slender thread of a story such as that in Montemayor's *Diana* which is usually given as his source.[4] The influence of the *commedia dell'arte* is already evident in Shakespeare's first comedy, *Love's Labour's Lost*, where the characters of Armado and Holofernes respectively correspond to the Spanish Captain and the Pedant of the Italian comedy. *Lazzi* and other proceedings familiar to the *commedia dell' arte* are so frequent in Shakespeare that one critic[5] has jumped to the conclusion that most of the prose of the plays must be due to the collaboration of the actors themselves.

Does Shakespeare try to make his Italians speak like Italians? When in *The Two Gentlemen* (I, iii, 6 ff.) we hear Panthino declaring:

> other men, of slender reputation,
> Put forth their sons to seek preferment out:
> Some to the wars, to try their fortune there;
> Some to discover islands far away;

we are led by this last line to think rather of the English oversea adventurers than of the citizens of an inland town like Verona. But was Verona an inland town for Shakespeare? It is perhaps well to settle at once the curious problem of Shakespeare's Italian geography.

In *The Two Gentlemen* Valentine's father "at the road" expects him coming there to see him shipped to Milan. In II, iii, Panthino says to Launce: "Away, ass! you'll lose the tide, if you tarry any longer", to which Launce retorts: "Lose the tide.... Why, man, if the river were dry, I am able to fill it with my tears". Verona, then, is imagined on a river with tides that ebb and flow, connected to Milan by a waterway. In *The Tempest* (I, ii, 144 ff.) Prospero tells how he was put aboard a bark at the gates of Milan, with his little daughter,

> In few, they hurried us aboard a bark,
> Bore us some leagues to sea, where they prepared
> A rotten carcass of a boat, not rigg'd,
> Nor tackle, sail, nor mast...
> ...there they hoist us,
> To cry to the sea that roar'd to us....

Milan, therefore, is imagined in a waterway communicating with the sea. Again, in *The Taming of the Shrew* (I, i, 42), where the scene is Padua, we hear Lucio saying: "If, Biondello, thou wert come ashore", and later on: "Since I have come ashore". Gremio, a citizen of Padua, boasts (II, i, 376) of being the owner of a large merchant vessel, an argosy. Further on (IV, ii, 81) we hear of Mantuan ships which are stayed at Venice, because of a quarrel between the two towns. Finally, we are told of a sail-maker in Bergamo, another inland town.

Sir Edward Sullivan, in an article published in *The Nineteenth Century* (August 1908) was at great pains to show that those seeming inaccuracies, far from revealing Shakespeare's ignorance of Italian geography, show an intimate acquaintance with it, since it can be proved by quotations of Italian writers of, and prior to, the seventeenth century, and with the aid of a map of Lombardy of the time, that the high road from Milan to Venice was by water, and a journey from Verona to Milan could be performed by water. Lambin has recently [6] added some further considerations, particularly an attempt to interpret the "tide" as a sudden and transient flood in a torrential river, since, even supposing that Verona could be reached by the far from conspicuous tide of the Adriatic sea, it would have been dangerous for a ship to try to descend a river against the tide.[7] The navigation of the two gentlemen and their servants is not therefore, concludes Lambin, "an ignorant invention of the playwright. It exactly corresponds to what was taking place in his time. A boat was the only comfortable conveyance from Verona to Milan. But one must have made use of it oneself to be so well informed". As for the other difficulty caused by the passage of *The Tempest* in which Milan is imagined near the sea, Lambin maintains that it is a deliberate absurdity (*une absurdité voulue*), for really, according to Lambin's interpretation of that drama to which we have already referred, Milan stands for Florence, "from which the access to the sea is of the easiest" (*l'accès à la mer est des plus aisés*), at least so it seems to M. Lambin.

Let us admit for a moment that Sir Edward Sullivan's and Lambin's demonstration of the possibility, nay, the advisability of travelling from Verona to Milan by water be quite convincing. So far as Shakespeare is concerned, it seems wide of the mark. There are other allusions in those plays which bear on the matter of local colour, but, while some of those allusions point to Italy, most of them point to England, specifically to London.

In *The Two Gentlemen* we hear of the custom of begging for 'soul-cakes' on Hallowmas (II, i, 24–5), of the pageants held at Whitsuntide (IV, iv, 163): the former allusion points to a Staffordshire custom, the latter to the Chester plays. Speed, in the same scene in which he welcomes Launce to Padua, where he ought to have said Milan, says: "I'll to the alehouse with you presently", and Launce alludes to the custom of going "to the ale"—a rustic festival during which ale was brewed, sold and drunk. Now it might perhaps be shown by some painstaking antiquarian that ale was occasionally brewed in Padua even in the Renaissance (as beer is brewed today), but surely if Shakespeare had ever thought of Italian local colour, he would have spoken of wine, and not of ale. In *The Taming of the Shrew* we hear several beginnings of English ballads sung by Italian characters, we are told of an inn in Genoa called the "Pegasus", which was one of the popular signs of London, and of a sleeve carved like an apple-tart, which is a typical English sweet. In a similar way in *Twelfth Night* the best hotel in the Illyrian town is said to be the "Elephant", which was the name of an inn near the Globe Theatre. In *The Merchant of Venice*, Gobbo says to Launcelot: "thou hast got more hair on thy chin than Dobbin my fill-horse has on his tail". Those who maintain that *The Merchant of Venice* shows a strong Venetian local colour, will not find it easy to reconcile with the town of the canals and gondolas the fact that Gobbo possessed a horse, and a horse which had such an English name as Dobbin. Perhaps an emulator of Sir Edward Sullivan and Lambin will come to tell us that horses could exist somehow in a town so peculiarly unfit for them (actual proofs are not lacking until the late sixteenth century), and that the extremely intricate system of Venetian narrow lanes allowed a horse to journey from one end of the town to the other. But the obvious explanation is that, although Shakespeare speaks of gondolas and the Rialto and the "tranect" or *traghetto*, when he mentions the fill-horse Dobbin he is thinking of England and of his characters as English characters. And so when he speaks of alehouses and of festivals and ballads peculiar not to Italy, but to England. Therefore the only reasonable conclusion we can draw about Shakespeare's conception of the town in which the play takes place as of a town on a river with a tide, connected with the sea, is that he was thinking of London, and using Milan and Verona as mere labels. This is after all what we should expect from an artist of Shakespeare's time, when, for instance, painters would represent the Adoration of the Magi as taking place in a familiar landscape, with figures partly dressed as Orientals, partly as contemporary Europeans. Something approaching a careful study of an historical background can be found only in Ben Jonson.

As for the characters of Shakespeare's Italian plays, none of them is so self-conscious about his supposed Italian characteristics as, for instance, Webster's Italians are in *The Devil's Law-Case*, where we come across utterances like these:

> I have not tane the way,
> Like an Italian, to cut your throat
> By practise—                                   (II, i, 269)

and:

> Me thinks, being an Italian, I trust you
> To come somewhat too neere me—            (*Ibid.* 325)

or such a painstaking explanation of the use of the stiletto as:

> Come forth then,
> My desperate Steeletto, that may be worne
> In a womans haire, and nere discover'd,
> And either would be taken for a Bodkin,
> Or a curling yron at most; why tis an engine,
> That's onely fit to put in execution
> Barmotho Pigs—                              (III, ii, 94 ff.)

words which sound like a commentary intended for the use of the English spectators.

However, the second of Shakespeare's Italian dramas, *Romeo and Juliet*, displays a much stronger local colour than *The Two Gentlemen of Verona*. Romeo's love expresses itself in the metaphors of the school of Serafino Aquilano, that school of sonneteering which anticipated the *concetti* of the seventeenth century. In Romeo's speeches, much more than in Shakespeare's *Sonnets*, we find the influence of the conventional tropes of the flamboyant sonneteers. Such is for instance the passage (I, i, 137 ff.):

> Many a morning hath he there been seen,
> With tears augmenting the fresh morning's dew,
> Adding to clouds more clouds with his deep sighs.

In a sonnet attributed to Serafino, the poet boasts that his tears are able to supply Neptune with new seas, in case he were deprived of his oceans, while his sighs could compensate Aeolus for the loss of his winds. In the third Act Capulet rebukes Juliet for crying:

> How now! a conduit, girl? what, still in tears?
> Evermore showering? In one little body
> Thou counterfeit'st a bark, a sea, a wind;

> For still thy eyes, which I may call the sea,
> Do ebb and flow with tears; the bark thy body is,
> Sailing in this salt flood; the winds, thy sighs,
> Who, raging with thy tears, and they with them,
> Without a sudden calm, will overset
> Thy tempest-tossed body.                    (III, v, 130–8)

Here Capulet is rehearsing a very hackneyed Alexandrian *concetto*,[8] found in a Latin poem of Hercules Strozza (*Unda hic sunt Lachrimae...*), in an Italian sonnet attributed to Serafino, and in one of the poems (the 85th) of Watson's *Passionate Century of Love*, where it runs thus:

> Error was maine saile, each wave a Teare;
> The master, Love him selfe; deep sighes were winde, *etc.*

Another well-known *concetto* of the flamboyant school is heard, improved, from Juliet's mouth (III, ii, 21 ff.):

> Give me my Romeo; and, when he shall die,
> Take him and cut him out in little stars,
> And he will make the face of heaven so fine
> That all the world will be in love with night
> And pay no worship to the garish sun.

Romeo's famous passionate address in Capulet's orchard (II, ii) consists of a string of traditional *concetti*. First: the window is the east and Juliet the sun. Second: Juliet is like the sun and outshines the moon. Third: her eyes are two stars; if Juliet's eyes changed place with the stars

> The brightness of her cheek would shame those stars,
>                 ...her eyes in heaven
> Would through the airy region stream so bright
> That birds would sing and think it were not night.        (19–22)

Fourth: Romeo wishes to be a glove upon Juliet's hand, that he might touch her cheek. Further on Romeo wishes to be Juliet's bird.

For each one of these *concetti* parallels and analogues could be quoted in the Petrarchan sonneteers of the flamboyant school. And the interesting question arises, whether Shakespeare deliberately aimed at portraying a passionate Italian lover on the lines suggested by the sonneteering literature. Such an aim seems almost to be implied in Mercutio's sneering remark: "Now is he for the numbers that Petrarch flowed in: Laura to his lady was but a kitchen-wench."

In fact Shakespeare succeeds so well in imitating the language of the Italian Petrarchists that in two passages his similes coincide with those used by Romeo's counterpart, Latino, in a tragedy by Luigi Groto, the *Adriana* (published 1578), which is also inspired by the story of Juliet and Romeo. Latino, also, waiting in the garden for his beloved to appear at the gate, says:

> ...e par ch'io senta aprir la porta,
> La qual meglio chiamar posso oriente:
> Ecco spunta il mio sol, cinto di nubi
> A mezzanotte! mira come gli astri
> Dan loco al lume suo smarriti in vista.[9]

And Adriana's definition of love is similar to that of Romeo. Romeo says:

> Why then, O brawling love! O loving hate!
> O any thing, of nothing first create!
> O heavy lightness! serious vanity!
> Mis-shapen chaos of well-seeming forms!
> Feather of lead, bright smoke, cold fire, sick health!
> Still-waking sleep, that is not what it is!
> This love feel I, that feel no love in this.

Groto's Adriana had vented a similar litany of Petrarchan oxymora:

> Fu il mio male un piacer senza allegrezza...
> Un ben supremo fonte d'ogni male,
> Un male estremo d'ogni ben radice...
> Un velen grato ch'io bevvi pegli occhi...
> Una febbre che il gelo e il caldo mesce,
> Un fèl più dolce assai che mèle o manna...
> Un giogo insopportabile e leggero,
> Una pena felice, un dolor caro,
> Una morte immortal piena di vita,
> Un inferno che sembra un paradiso.[10]

The resemblance between the passages just quoted, and the mention of the nightingale in the parting scene between the lovers, in both plays, led some critics to conclude that Shakespeare knew Groto's tragedy, though the two plays are as different as they could be in the treatment of the story and in the study of the characters. I am inclined to believe that the resemblances, which bear on commonplaces of the Petrarchan school, are due to a coincidence; and that they prove only that Shakespeare succeeded so well in depicting an Italian lover that the language he puts into his mouth may occasionally appear derived from that extremely artificial poet of the flamboyant school, Luigi Groto. If this is local colouring, and of the most effective, on the other hand when Mercutio inveighs (II, iv) against the ridiculous fashion-mongers, who use Italian fencing terms and French expressions and dresses, he is no more an Italian than the character of *The Merchant of Venice* who speaks of his horse Dobbin is 'genuinely' a Venetian; Mercutio is there a Londoner.

The local colour of *The Merchant of Venice* has been declared well-nigh astonishing. Accurate sailors' expressions are put into the mouths of Salanio and Salerio, mention is made of the "tranect" or *traghetto* which connects Venice to the mainland, and of the correct distance that Portia and Nerissa would have to travel from Belmont, i.e. Montebello, to Padua.[11] Portia has sunny locks, she is, therefore, the true Venetian type with red-gold hair made famous by Titian. To complete Shakespeare's Venetian canvas we have also a Prince of Morocco and his train, just as in the feasts and pageants painted by the Venetian painters there is always some turbaned Oriental or some African wearing "the shadow'd livery of the burnish'd sun". Against the considerable amount of accurate information (Shakespeare knows about 'the liberty of strangers' which formed one of the points of the Venetian constitution; and, in *Othello* (I, i, 183), mentions the "special officers of night", i.e. the *signori di notte*), we may record as mere slips Gobbo's mention of his horse Dobbin, and Launcelot's objection to the conversion of the Jews: "If we grow all to be pork-eaters, we shall not shortly have a rasher on the coals for money", which alludes to that peculiarly English dish, a fried slice of bacon. However, if Launcelot blunders apropos of food, Gobbo seems to be quite aware of the Venetian custom when he brings a dish of pigeons for his son's master. As for the characters themselves, one cannot say that they are more Venetian than anything else. They seem to fit the setting so well because they are humans in the broadest sense of the word; their type is universal, whereas the Italian characters of the picture-palace school of Elizabethan drama are generally caricatures of the seamy side of Italian life. But what about that sinister Italian knave, Iago?

Courthope called Iago "the most thoroughly Machiavellian figure on the English stage". Iago's counterpart, the *alfiero* in Cinthio's seventh *novella* in the third decade of the *Hecatommithi*, is perhaps even more so. Cinthio's ensign cannot justify his behaviour through any provocation or slight he has suffered at the hands of the Moor; he is the ideal knave who, finding obstacles in the way of his perverse will (he had been repulsed by Desdemona with whom he had fallen in love), seeks revenge through deceit and treachery. Iago, an accomplished Machiavellian demon in Cinthio, would become much more human and excusable in Shakespeare, if we could believe that he is actually incensed by the public report that Othello has cuckolded him: if so, Iago's story, as told by Shakespeare, would find parallels in many cases of retaliation instanced by Italian *novelle*. The reality of Iago's jealousy seems indeed to be doubted by some commentators. The lines (IV, i, 46–8):

> Thus credulous fools are caught;
> And many worthy and chaste dames even thus,
> All guiltless, meet reproach.

are commented upon, for instance, by H. C. Hart in the old Arden Shakespeare edition: "These lines show the unreality of Iago's motives with which he formerly pretended to salve his conscience. He finds that he can ruin the happiness of innocent people. He can do it causelessly, and he is triumphant." Those lines, however, would be seen in a different light by anyone who knows that they reproduce almost literally the moral of Cinthio's story:

Aviene talhora che, senza colpa, fedele et amorevole donna, per insidie tesele da animo malvagio, et per leggerezza di chi più crede che non bisognerebbe, da fedel marito riceve morte.[12]

This almost literal translation of Cinthio's moral could be, by the way, one of the proofs that Shakespeare knew Italian. Needless to say, the character of Iago does not imply any acquaintance with Machiavelli's writings. What Machiavellism is displayed in Shakespeare's dramas seems either to be already present in the historical sources (as in the case of *Richard III*), or to be derived from the current popular legend.[13]

In the last of his great plays, *The Tempest*, Shakespeare deals with a theme of Italian political intrigue. But how different his treatment is from the usual practice of the Elizabethans! Instead of the ordinary Elizabethan chain of murder, revenge and wholesale butchery against the background of the darkened Italian palace, we seem to breathe the purified atmosphere after a sea-storm; the grace of heaven with its dews has touched the shores of the island secluded from the world, and that sweet aspersion fallen from heaven consecrates into a kind of holy mystery the human story displayed before our eyes. *The Tempest* could hardly be called a conventional study in Italian criminality; still there can be little doubt about the Italian inspiration of the play, which has been convincingly traced by Ferdinando Neri to a group of scenarios of the *commedia dell'arte*. Even the clowns, who are as a rule portrayed as Elizabethan Londoners in Shakespeare's other plays, here seem to have been borrowed from a Neapolitan farce.

As a result of this rapid survey, the conclusion can hardly be resisted that Shakespeare not only had an acquaintance with Italian things, but that he actually knew Italian. In *Measure for Measure*, for instance, he must have taken the idea of the substitution of the bodies from Cinthio's drama *Epitia*, since that substitution does not occur in the story of the *Hecatommithi* (Deca VIII, Nov. 5), of which *Epitia* is a dramatic version. Neither does it occur in Whetstone's rehandling of Cinthio's story. Since Italian books were widely read in the society in whose midst Shakespeare lived, there is nothing extraordinary in his acquaintance with Italian literature; rather, the contrary would be surprising. That this acquaintance must have been little more than superficial seems shown by the fact that Shakespeare generally has recourse to English translations and imitations; this is chiefly noticeable in the *Sonnets*, whose conventional passages recall English rather than Italian or French sources.

What seems to be more puzzling is Shakespeare's accuracy in certain local allusions. Some of them I have already discussed; and even if Lambin has overstated the case of Shakespeare's knowledge of the topography of Milan, the mention of St Gregory's Well near that town, in *The Two Gentlemen*, seems definite enough; we find moreover Bellario as a Paduan name in *The Merchant of Venice*, which in fact it is, and, in *Romeo and Juliet*, details about Juliet's funeral (found, however, already in Brooke's poem) and about the evening mass in Verona. We have also noticed the inconsistencies which imperil the local colour in Shakespeare's Italian dramas, but most of them occur in the farcical scenes, where the characters are really English clowns; and the practice of the stage—in the old *commedia dell'arte* as well as in to-day's pantomimes and puppet-plays—is always to give a contemporary national character to the comic scenes, irrespective of the time and place in which the serious plot is staged. In short, even when those inconsistencies spoil the effect of Italian atmosphere, the accuracy of the occasional local allusions remains to be accounted for. How did Shakespeare get hold of those local details?

An important fact is that those allusions are confined to a very definite part of Italy: Venice, and the neighbouring towns Verona, Padua, Mantua and Milan. Local allusions to Florence, in *All's Well*, seem only to be the fruit of Lambin's ingenuity; while Messina of *Much Ado* is clearly an imaginary town. There are two possible alternatives: either Shakespeare travelled to the North of Italy, or he got this information from intercourse with some Italian in London.

There is no evidence for the first alternative. As for the second, Shakespeare may have had frequent occasions to meet Italian merchants; the Elephant Inn, which he mentions with praise as being the one where it was "best to lodge" in the unknown Illyrian town of *Twelfth Night* and being, of course, nothing else but the inn called 'The Oliphant' on Bankside, was patronized by Italians.[14]

But whatever his relations may have been with those Italian tradesmen and adventurers (many of whom were Northern Italians, chiefly, as it is natural, from the commercial town of Venice), it is today well established that Shakespeare must have come across, at least, John Florio, the apostle of Italian culture in England.[15]  Both Florio and Shakespeare moved in the same circle; they were fellow-members of Southampton's household.  Florio was a teacher in both the Italian and French languages, and it has been surmised[16] that it may have been William Cecil, Lord Burleigh, who appointed him as tutor to Southampton when he was a minor under his guardianship, possibly to report about a young man destined to be influential in the Essex camp. If Florio had this unenviable role, then it can be understood why Shakespeare would not have hesitated to ridicule him as the pedant Holofernes in *Love's Labour's Lost*.  Florio supplied Ben Jonson with whatever information that dramatist shows about Venice in *Volpone*:[17] a copy of this play in the British Museum has this autograph dedication: "To his louing Father, & worthy Freind Mr. John Florio: The ayde of his Muses. Ben: Jonson seales this testemony of Freindship, & Loue."  It is from Florio's manuals for the study of Italian, entitled *First* and *Second Fruites*, that come the Italian sentences which occur in I, ii, of *The Taming of the Shrew*, a scene, however, which is not entirely ascribed to Shakespeare.[18] The expression found in *The Taming of the Shrew*, I, i, "Lombardy, the pleasant garden of great Italy" is similar to Florio's "La Lombardia è il giardino del mondo" in the *Second Fruites*, and very likely Florio is ultimately responsible for the currency of the phrase "the garden of the world" applied to England.[19]  Florio's vocabulary has a prevailing Lombardo-Venetian character,[20] Venice is for him the foremost Italian town, as can be seen in the eighth chapter of the *First Fruites*; this may help us to understand why the local allusions in Shakespeare's Italian plays are limited to Venice and the neighbouring towns. Florio was a rhetorician whose taste for style sinned on the florid side; some of his sentences, studded with proverbial expressions (he compiled also a collection of proverbs) seem to anticipate Giambattista Basile's Baroque grotesqueness; nevertheless his translation of Montaigne, plethoric as it is with pretended elegances, has become a classic, and a source for Elizabethan dramatists, first of all Shakespeare, who bred his Hamlet on it; his manuals of conversation and his Italian dictionary were responsible for most of the knowledge of Italian of Shakespeare's contemporaries; he was called "the aid of his Muses" by Ben Jonson, and probably would have deserved a similar appellation from Shakespeare; he may have been a sycophant, as he certainly was a pedant, in a word, a tool for greater purposes, a help for travellers to that garden of the world, Italy, and also, strangely enough, for travellers to the eternal garden of Poesy.

## NOTES

1.  M. Lambin displays a perverse ingenuity in trying to identify the names of the captains given by Parolles in *All's Well*, IV, iii, 165 ff., with historical supporters of the French League: thus Gratii is a name which evokes so well "les faveurs et les complaisances" that it must needs be that of a minion of Henry III; and Bentii, that is *le tordu*, bent, is surely Charles Emmanuel, Duke of Savoy; the more obvious explanation, that those two names are peculiar spellings of the Florentine family names Grazzi, Benci, does not cross his mind.  But his solving the riddle of Chitopher is a good sample of his method: Henri, comte de Bouchage, presented himself to Henri III disguised as Jesus Christ: "vêtu de la 'tunique' du Seigneur, celle que vont se partager les soldats: la 'chitôn' du texte grec de l'Evangile (Saint Jean XIX, 23)": he wore a chiton, so he is Chitopher.  Guiltian would be a pun on Guisian: "le rapprochement entre 'Guise' et 'guilt' (crime) [allusion to the St Bartholomew Massacre] n'est pas accidentel".

2.  After reading Mary G. Steegman's book on *Bianca Cappello* (1913), "ouvrage de vulgarisation auquel nous avons emprunté plusieurs renseignements", Lambin draws a lurid picture of the "morts brutales" which had "favorisé Bianca": among them the wife of Francesco, Joan of Habsburg, "se rompant le col à point voulu". If, instead of having recourse to an "ouvrage de vulgarisation" like Mary Steegmann's, Lambin had consulted Gaetano

Pieraccini's *La stirpe de' Medici di Cafaggiolo* (Florence, 1947, second edition), he would have found that the Grand Duchess died of childbirth: "si trovè il putto fuora della matrice et il collo della matrice stracciato" (contemporary report: the child had broken the 'neck' of the womb). He would also have found that, contrary to the legend which he accepts, Francesco and Bianca were not poisoned by Francesco's brother, the Cardinal Ferdinando, but died of malarial fever. He would have found also that Francesco, far from offering a likely model for Prospero, was a bad prince, inclined to lechery, punctilious over petty matters of etiquette, weak-willed and incontinent in eating and drinking: "si è dilettato poco della virtù, non dimostra troppo bell' ingegno" (contemporary Venetian report). Lambin seems to be aware that *The Tempest* "est avant tout une œuvre théâtrale et une magnifique fantaisie, ne l'oublions pas. Ce n'est pas une monographie historique". But whatever part imagination plays in the actual drama, it is nothing in comparison to the boldness of Lambin's own flights. It was daring enough of Shakespeare to write about "the cloud-capped towers, the gorgeous palaces, The solemn temples," etc., but more daring still of Lambin to see there an allusion to the view of Florence which Francesco would have enjoyed from his villas.

3. Cf. Valentina Capocci, *Genio e mestiere, Shakespeare e la commedia dell'arte* (Bari, Laterza, 1950), pp. 56 ff.

4. O. J. Campbell, 'Love's Labour's Lost Re-studied' and 'The Two Gentlemen of Verona and Italian Comedy', in *Studies in Shakespeare, Milton and Donne* by members of the English Department of the University of Michigan (New York, 1925).

5. Valentina Capocci, *op. cit.*, chiefly p. 113.

6. 'Shakespeare à Milan', *Les Langues modernes* (1952), pp. 245 ff.

7. Lambin quotes a passage from *Eastward Ho!* where Sir Petronell (III, iii, 138 ff.) is warned against embarking "against the tyde" in the Thames. However, Sir Petronell wanted to reach Blackwall, where his ship lay, with a small boat, and a storm was expected, so the warning was justified; on the other hand the Thames could be navigated by bigger ships only during the tide.

8. See M. Praz, *Studies in Seventeenth-Century Imagery*, I (1939), p. 102.

9. "I seem to hear open the gate, which I may better call the east: there my sun rises, girt with clouds at midnight! look how the stars, dismayed, make room for its light."

10. "My evil was a pleasure without mirth...a supreme good, source of every evil, an extreme evil, root of every good...a delightful poison I drank through my eyes...a fever mixing iciness and heat, a gall far sweeter than honey or manna...an unbearable and light yoke, a happy pain, a dear sorrow, an immortal death full of life, a heaven-seeming hell."

11. Belmonte is, however, already in the source, the tale in *Il Pecorone*, without a proper location, and there are several places named Montebello, so that the impression of a precise place-reference is possibly deceptive.

12. "It sometimes happens that without guilt on her part, a faithful and loving woman, through a deceit engined by an evil soul, and the folly of some credulous person, is killed by a loyal husband."

13. See my essay on 'Machiavelli and the Elizabethans' in *Proceedings of the British Academy*, XIII (1928), p. 31 of the offprint. Feebler replicas of Iago and Othello are Iachimo, the "false Italian" of *Cymbeline*, and the Sicilian Leontes in *The Winter's Tale*.

14. See G. S. Gàrgano, *Scapigliatura italiana a Londra sotto Elisabetta e Giacomo I* (Florence, 1923), and A. C. Southern, 'The Elephant Inn' (Times Literary Supplement, 12 June 1953, p. 381).

15. Madame Clara Longworth de Chambrun was the first to discuss this connexion in *Giovanni Florio, Un Apôtre de la Renaissance en Angleterre* (Paris, 1921).

16. See Frances A. Yates, *John Florio* (1934), p. 218.

17. See M. Praz, 'L' Italia di Ben Jonson' in the volume *Machiavelli in Inghilterra ed altri saggi* (Rome, 1942).

18. See *The Taming of the Shrew*, ed. J. Dover Wilson, in 'The New Shakespeare' (1928).

19. See letters by J. B. Leishman and others in *The Times Literary Supplement* for 7 and 28 November and 5 December 1952.

20. See my essay on 'L' Italia di Ben Jonson' quoted above, p. 186.

# INTERNATIONAL NOTES

*A selection has here been made from the reports received from our correspondents, those which present material of a particularly interesting kind being printed wholly or largely in their entirety. It should be emphasized that the choice of countries to be thus represented has depended on the nature of the information presented in the reports, not upon either the importance of the countries concerned or upon the character of the reports themselves.*

### International Shakespeare Conference

The Sixth International Conference of Shakespeare Scholars was held at Stratford-upon-Avon in August 1953. Thirty-four delegates representing ten countries attended the Conference, at which papers were read and discussions held on various aspects of the chosen theme, Shakespeare's Comedies. On Friday, 14th August, the Conference began with a paper by Ludwig Borinski of Germany on 'Shakespeare's Comic Prose', after which a public lecture was given by Sir Barry Jackson on 'The Production of Shakespeare's Comedies'. On Saturday 15th August, the private discussion, led by Karl Brunner of Austria, and the public lecture by J. Dover Wilson were devoted to *The Merchant of Venice*. On Monday, 17th August, Clifford Leech's paper on 'The Theme of Ambition in *All's Well that Ends Well*' preceded a public lecture by Georges Bonnard of Switzerland on '*A Midsummer Night's Dream*: a Possible Significance'; on Tuesday, 18th August, Kenneth Muir spoke on *Troilus and Cressida*, and Harold Jenkins gave a public lecture on *As You Like It*; on Wednesday, 19th August, Nevill Coghill opened the private session with a talk on 'Comic Form in *Measure for Measure* and *The Winter's Tale*', and D. C. Allen (U.S.A.) gave the last public lecture on 'The Poetic Miracle and the Last Plays'.

### Australia

The Swan Hill National Theatre group continues its ambitious project of a week-long Shakespeare festival. *The Merchant of Venice* was the play chosen for the 1952 season. The festival week and play represent a major achievement for a country town of 5,000 inhabitants.

In Sydney, The Metropolitan Theatre (which was formally opened in 1948 by Tyrone Guthrie) produced

*Richard II*, "a play which may not have been produced in Australia before", said a programme note. Again, an ambitious undertaking. Unfortunately the production was rather fussy and committed the serious error of playing the lovely garden scene as low comedy.

'The Tin Alley Players' of the University of Melbourne, a graduate group which has little connexion with the University, produced the seldom seen *King John*. Simply set, well lighted, beautifully costumed and above all, well spoken, the production showed some of the best and most careful amateur work to be seen in Australia.

By far the most enterprising production yet undertaken in Australia was that of *Richard III* in Perth. The production was sponsored by the Adult Education Board of Western Australia and formed part of the Festival of Perth, 2 January to 14 March 1953.

Michael Langham, who has produced Shakespeare at Stratford, the Birmingham Repertory Theatre and The Old Vic, was invited to visit Australia for five months. During that time he started from scratch and produced in a theatre with a stage approximating that of an Elizabethan-Jacobean theatre a production in which use of controlled light and recorded music formed the main points of difference from Elizabethan staging.

WAYNE HAYWARD

### Austria

In February 1953 the first volume of Richard Flatter's new German translation was brought on the market. This first volume contains the translations of *Othello*, *Macbeth*, *A Midsummer Night's Dream* and an adaptation of *Henry IV*, in which, by cutting much of the political material and a general shortening of the comic scenes, the two parts have been condensed into one play of the usual length. The translator aims, as is to be expected from the author of *Shakespeare's Producing Hand*, to render the Folio text as accurately into German as possible, paying particular attention to its punctuation. One may wonder whether Flatter's translation will eventually conquer the German stage. It may be that modern actors will be attracted by his terser diction, but tradition stands against him.

Not much can be reported on activities of the Austrian stage. The Vienna Burgtheater played *Othello*, with the cast of last year's Vienna performance, in the new large open-air theatre in Bregenz and gathered an enthusiastic public from Western Austria, Eastern Switzerland and South-West Germany. The Innsbruck Landestheater for some weeks in the autumn of 1952 performed *Romeo and Juliet* in an adequate production, which was, however, on the usual lines.

KARL BRUNNER

### Belgium

The performances of Shakespeare's plays have been rather numerous, both in French and Flemish, and they have been generally successful. Shakespeare has become a regular and important asset in the programmes of all the Belgian theatres.

April 1952: *Romeo and Juliet*, by the Théâtre National de Belgique, in Brussels and in the provinces. French text by Raymond Gérome, who is an actor and a poet. Producer: Jacques Huisman. Costumes and setting designed by Denis Martin. Actors: Pierre Michaël (Romeo) and Jacqueline Huisman (Juliet). The street scenes with broils and fighting were exceptionally animated.

May: The celebrated company of Jean-Louis Barrault and Madeleine Renaud occupied the Théâtre Royal des Galeries (Brussels) and visited other towns with a repertory which included brilliant performances of *Hamlet* in André Gide's version.

May–June: At the Théâtre Royal du Parc (Brussels), *Twelfth Night* in a remarkable French translation by Jacques Copeau and Suzanne Bing. Producer: Oscar Lejeune. Actors: Raoul Demanez (Orsino) and Viviane Chantel (Viola). A beautiful setting designed by Emile Lane.

Summer: Impressive open-air performances of *Hamlet* in the castle of Beersel (near Brussels) and in the castle of Bouillon (on the River Semois). Adaptation in French by Romain Sanvic. Direction by Jean-Pierre Rey. Production by Louis Boxus. Ivan Dominique scored a success in the title-role.

Each year the Flemish Nationaal Toneel van Belgie starts its season with Shakespeare simultaneously in Antwerp and in Ghent. This is a firmly established tradition. The Koninklijke Vlaamse Schouwburg of Brussels follows the same example.

The former, for the beginning of its autumn campaign, chose *The Tempest*, always a popular play. Translator: Martinus Nijhoff. Producer: Ben Royaards. Actors: Jos. Gevers (Prospero) and Jean Cammans (Caliban). The latter opened in September with *A Midsummer Night's Dream*. Translator: Burgersdijk, a Dutch classic. Producer: Gust Maes. Actors: Roger Coorens (Oberon) and Magda Kleyne (Puck).

December 1952–January 1953: The Théâtre National de Belgique played throughout the country *La Mégère Apprivoisée*, a very free adaptation by Henry Grane of *The Taming of the Shrew*. Boisterous production by Georges Vitaly, well known French producer. Actors: Marcel Berteau (Petrucchio) and Irène Lecarte (Katherine).

February: The company called the Rideau de Bruxelles, under the leadership of Claude Etienne, who produced the play and spoke the part of the Chorus, gave *Henry V*, which, to our knowledge, had never been performed in French before, either in France or in Belgium. A gallant venture. The text is by François Victor Hugo. Ivan Dominique played the title-role.

It should be added that a French company, headed by Marie Bell, sociétaire of the Comédie Française, visited several Belgian towns with *Antony and Cleopatra*, in André Gide's version.

ROBERT DE SMET

### Canada

Canadian productions of Shakespeare are never numerous, even if we include all amateur performances, and the occasional visits of touring companies. The professional theatre of Canada is only just coming into being, and usually consists of 'summer stock' with its frothy repertoire. But there are, perhaps, brighter days ahead. One of the two permanent Repertory companies in the country has already shown enough courage to put Shakespeare into its programme. This was the Canadian Repertory Theatre in Ottawa, which produced *Hamlet* in April 1952 and *The Taming of the Shrew* in September 1951. In addition to these two, there was a most spritely performance of *The Merry Wives of Windsor* by the Peterborough Little Theatre in February. The members of this group are all school-teachers in Peterborough but they have in Robertson Davies the advantage of a producer who was for some time with the Old Vic in England, and whose wife was the Old Vic stage-manager. The series of productions done by this team have been excellent and within the limits of a high-school auditorium stage have shown a resourcefulness and energy of presentation wholly commendable in such plays as *The Taming of the Shrew* (1950), *Twelfth Night* (1951), and now *The Merry Wives*. In the summer the Earle Grey Players continued their tradition of giving a series of plays in Trinity College Quadrangle. This year their repertory consisted of *The Merchant of Venice, Julius Caesar* and *The Winter's Tale*.

The difficulties of teaching Shakespeare in a country where it is often impossible for students to see the plays performed were thoroughly discussed at a conference in Toronto of University teachers of English. Many ideas were put forward to compensate for the lack of live theatre, including the use of recordings, of theatre models (especially of the Globe Theatre), and of 'acting out' the plays on a stage as part of class-work. The conference was also aware of how such ideas were limited in their application and the view that Shakespeare was 'enough for us', even only on the page, was firmly held by some members.     A. EDINBOROUGH

## Czechoslovakia

Czechoslovak Shakespearians have found a new platform for their work in the Czech Academy of Sciences and Arts, whose Shakespearian Commission came to life in the spring of 1952. The aim of this Commission, which even in the first half-year of its existence has proved very active, is not only to further the study of Shakespearian influence in Czech and Slovak cultures and of Shakespearian trends in our English studies, but also to be of practical help in new productions of Shakespeare. Though it has existed for such a short time, its members can already point to one or two promising results of their efforts: a long-lost first poetical adaptation of *King Lear* by J. K. Tyl, the father of Czech drama, has been unearthed, and another recent discovery is that of a manuscript containing 1,171 verses of an adaptation of *Romeo and Juliet* made by Alexandre Dumas père: this has come to light in Kynžvart Castle in Bohemia.

In the nation-wide festival 'Theatre Harvest 1951–52' the Olomouc production of *Othello* was among the best of the productions in Czechoslovakia, chiefly due to the sensitive direction of J. Pleskot and the performance of J. Bek (as Othello), who was awarded a Golden Badge for this role. A Silver Badge was awarded to J. Blaho's Leonato in the Žilina production of *Much Ado about*

*Nothing*, which was honourably mentioned in the festival. Other Shakespearian productions (*Hamlet, A Midsummer Night's Dream, Twelfth Night*) did not meet the requirements of the jury.

With several Shakespearian broadcasts (*Twelfth Night*, etc.) and a successful matinée in Prague's *Gramoton*, the interest in Shakespeare and his works is steadily increasing.     BŘETISLAV HODEK

## East Africa

The twentieth anniversary of the East African Shakespeare Festival was celebrated in 1953. The dramatist's birthday was marked by a broadcast of scenes from *King Henry V* linked with a commentary condensing the work and describing its construction. The broadcast was followed by a Shakespeare birthday dinner at a Nairobi hotel, which was attended by the actors and their friends. Plans were made for the 1953 stage production to be presented as a part of the official Coronation Celebrations, with *King Henry VIII* as the play selected. Between April 23 and the time of the stage production there were lectures arranged for English-speaking organizations of all races. Africans were given talks with an elementary approach to Shakespeare, discussion of the Tudor succession and a description of the style being used for the presentation of the play. For the Asian and Arab audiences the approach was based on plans for the Colony's cultural development, stressing the inter-racial interest in Shakespeare's works and leading up to the play itself. European audiences were given a world picture of Shakespearian interest as a background to the plans for the East African Festival as part of the Coronation Celebrations.

*King Henry VIII* was presented in the National Theatre, which is the first part of the Kenya Cultural Centre to be built. This production was the first Shakespearian play to be given there since the opening towards the end of 1952, and it is believed this was the first production of *King Henry VIII* in the equatorial world. A further inter-racial friendship was established by having pale-skinned Sikhs and Goans among the non-speaking characters as guards and trumpeters. Great help was given by the Governors of the Stratford-on-Avon Shakespeare Memorial Theatre in allowing the Tanya Moiseiwitsch costumes to be sent out for the production, while the music used was the Cedric Thorpe Davie score which had been composed for their production of this play. A permanent set was designed to suit the Theatre. There was the permanent apron stage with two pageant doors and steps coming up from the auditorium. Set at about six feet behind the main curtain was an eight foot upper stage on a lift of two steps curving at its front, a movable 'State' rostrum with three steps was slid on or off as required and a large Tudor arch, with a gallery above, filled the left centre stage. Five steps led to an upper 'walk' set four feet from the back wall rostrum with steps leading down from it to a well which was used for Buckingham's execution procession. Travelling drapes were hung to cut off the two main lift areas, allowing for a rapid continuity of scenes while inner stage furnishings were being changed. The performance was divided into two parts with one interval. There were very few cuts in the text, the only major one being the short scene with Dr Butts. The brief encounter between Buckingham and Wolsey was heightened by bringing Wolsey's train in from the King's side, up stage right, moving to down stage left while Buckingham crossed from down stage right to attract Wolsey's attention centre stage. After the exchange, Wolsey signalled his followers to return the way they had come (back to the King) from whence Buckingham's arrest was made. The Mau Mau State of Emergency duties wrought havoc with the male cast and stage working team, but final desperate appeal was made to the Director of Manpower who delayed further postings from the Company until after the Coronation Celebrations. Twelve performances were given, mostly with the "House Full" notices displayed. The first performance was given solely for English-speaking Africans who responded magnificently to all the comedy and gave the company an encouraging send off. Free matinée performances were given to schoolchildren of all races during Coronation week, the children being received in the foyer by the Mayor of Nairobi in his full robes, attended by the founder of the East African Festival, representatives of the Education Department and the City Mace Bearer. A gala performance was arranged for Coronation night, which was attended by the Governor and his wife, the Lady Mary Baring, with the Government House party. During that evening's performance the interval time was changed to come after Anne Bullen's Coronation Procession so that Her Majesty's world broadcast could be relayed to the audience. The whole production was remarkable for its splendid team work, and East Africa's leading newspaper described it as "worthy of the high occasion". Plans are now being made for the 1954 coming-of-age of these East African Shakespeare Festivals with a further extension of inter-racial partnership.

A. J. R. MASTER

### France

How difficult it is to play Shakespeare in France! Such was Thierry Maulnier's melancholy comment (*Combat*, 27 October 1952) after seeing Julien Bertheau's production of *Romeo and Juliet* at the Comédie Française. A beautiful job, he said, but the magnificence of the show was excessive, and the actors were too steeped in the tradition of Molière and Racine to live before our eyes as creatures of Shakespeare's imagination. Less subtle critics praised the spectacular magnificence (unequalled by the greatest music-halls), the brilliant cast and the two authors of the play, Jean Sarment and Shakespeare (in that order). On the other hand Bertheau and Sarment were severely taken to task by Guy Dumur (also in *Combat*, 17 October 1952). The first had declared: "Sarment has re-invented the text of *Romeo and Juliet*", and the second: "Les Français ne peuvent pas encaisser trop directement Shakespeare" ("encaisser" means "to take a blow" and "je ne peux pas l'encaisser": "I can't stand him"). Dumur pointed out that Sarment was the author of a number of now nearly forgotten prose comedies, and that before him a true poet, Supervielle, had translated (not adapted) *Romeo* with the assistance of Pitoeff.

Yes, Shakespeare's poetic message is difficult to convey to a French audience, and yet young companies and provincial dramatic centres face the problem with intelligence and courage, in spite of their limited means and experience. *Twelfth Night* was given by a suburban company, led by Jean Deninx (at the Théâtre de Rochefort and the Ambigu, April 1952, and at the Œuvre, September to October 1952). Plain curtains were used instead of settings, and costumes hired from a film company. The incidental music was based on old English tunes. Lucien Agostini's French version, and the actors' interpretation received much praise. This was the first production in Paris since Copeau's in 1940.

Copeau's own translation of *Macbeth* (in collaboration with Suzanne Bing) was presented in Paris (Renaissance, June 1952) by Jean Dasté and his comedians, who are doing magnificent service in the industrial city of Saint Etienne. *Macbeth* had not been acted in Paris for the last ten years. It was a conscientious performance, with some weaknesses which critics were ready to excuse as they considered the play especially difficult on account of its Æschylean greatness.

The Grenier de Toulouse (Centre Dramatique du Sud-Ouest) came to Paris in January 1953, and as on their earlier visit of October 1951, received deserved praise for their *Taming of the Shrew*. André Thorent, the translator, and Maurice Sarrazin, the producer, both profess that faithfulness to the text and the spirit of Shakespeare is their constant preoccupation. And since this was a play with a Mediterranean atmosphere, the experience acquired by the company in performing Plautus, Italian comedy and Molière's *Scapin* could be placed at the poet's service. It was good team work with style, verve and a perfect tempo.

Since "a smiling poetry" is the dominant characteristic of the Grenier, *Romeo and Juliet*, which they gave at the Bordeaux Festival (15 and 18 May 1952) did not reach the same level as *The Taming of the Shrew*, though it was efficiently produced. They also played Shakespeare at the Festival des Centres Dramatiques at Aix-les-Bains (August 1952). Maurice Herrand, who was responsible for the dramatic part of the Festival of Angers (13, 15, 17 June 1952), had the bright idea of giving *King John* in the inner court of the castle, so that Angevine citizens of today were able to hear their medieval spokesman from the walls, and laugh at the Bastard's comments on their ancestors' prudence. This was a beautiful and impressive show, with music by Louis Beydts, brilliant colours and a large crowd of actors. Casarès (of the Comédie Française) was particularly moving in the role of Constance.

So Shakespearian drama remains an essential element of France's theatrical life. It is interesting to note that most of the enterprising work is being done outside Paris, though performance in the capital remains the final test for provincial groups. Young companies and imaginative festival organizers are making a brave attempt to bring the audience to the core of Shakespeare's meaning, and challenge the present policy of the Comédie Française which seems to be to make Shakespeare easy with a highly polished but rather conventional technique, lavish scenery and an adulterated text.

JEAN JACQUOT

## Germany

During the period under review no less than twenty-four plays of Shakespeare were given in various productions by German theatres. Of Shakespeare's tragedies *Hamlet* had again the greatest success with the German theatre-going public, one of the more outstanding productions being that at Frankfurt a.M. with more than forty performances. Of his comedies *Twelfth Night*, *A Midsummer Night's Dream* and *The Taming of the Shrew* were most frequently staged.

A very successful production of *A Midsummer Night's Dream* was that of Sellner at Darmstadt with Carl Orff's music. Apart from this remarkable production there were also numerous open-air productions of this play.

*The Merchant of Venice*, a play which for the past twenty years has very seldom been performed in Germany, was successfully staged at Bochum. The company gave fifty performances of this much praised production, ten of them at Hamburg.

*The Winter's Tale*, *Othello* and *Measure for Measure* have also had a wide appeal; and a revived interest in *The Tempest* and *Troilus and Cressida* resulted in a number of noteworthy productions of these plays.

Of the Roman plays *Julius Caesar* was successfully staged at Berlin. The credit of having produced *Coriolanus* in Germany for the first time after the war is due to the Nordmark Landestheater at Schleswig.

A number of producers tried again to replace the traditional Schlegel-Tieck-Baudissin translations by other renderings, old and modern. Thus *Troilus and Cressida* was produced at Essen in the translation by Rudolf Alexander Schröder (President of the German Shakespeare Society) which stresses the tragic character of the play. The very modern rendering of the play by Hans Rothe was chosen by Krefeld and Stuttgart. The traditional translation by Baudissin was presented only at Hanover.

R. A. Schröder's translation of *The Tempest* was given at Bremen, while Essen put on Erich Engel's rendering, which for the last fifteen years has gradually won popularity.

A noteworthy production of *All's Well that Ends Well* at Cologne was in the translation of Walter Josten. Since producers have always considered this play as not easily actable, it is, indeed, remarkable that more than twenty performances have been given.

Of late, Richard Flatter's translations, which by now comprise twenty-five plays, have gained admirers among producers and audience.

Alongside these modern renderings one can also find early translations of Shakespeare's plays in last year's repertories of German theatres. At Bochum *Hamlet* was staged in the translation by Joachim Eschenburg. The production of the play in this prose translation was a great success. The same can be said of *Macbeth* in the translation by Gottfried August Buerger which was played by the Westfaelische Landestheater at Castrop. Eschenburg's translation of *Love's Labour's Lost* was chosen by the students' theatre at Muenster. The production was highly praised at last year's International Meeting of Students' Theatrical Companies at Erlangen.

A Shakespeare event of major importance was the special meeting of the German Shakespeare Society which took place at Duisburg. The programme included several lectures, given by well-known Shakespearian scholars, and the performances of four plays of Shakespeare by four different companies. Apart from the above-mentioned representations of *All's Well that Ends Well, Troilus and Cressida* in the translation by R. A. Schröder, and the Bochum production of *The Merchant of Venice*, the Wuppertal Theatre Company presented *A Midsummer Night's Dream* in the translation by Richard Flatter with the music of Purcell.

L. EHRL<br>W. STROEDEL

## Greece

During the year 1952 two plays by Shakespeare were produced in Athens, both at the National Theatre: (1) *A Midsummer Night's Dream*, translated by J. Economidis, directed by Charles Koun, sets and costumes by S. Vassiliou, music composed by M. Hatzidakis; (2) *The Winter's Tale*, translated by B. Rotas, directed by Alexis Solomos, sets and costumes by S. Vassiliou, music composed by G. Kazasoglou.

GEORGE THEOTOKAS

B. Rotas has recently published a volume entitled *Technologika II*. This volume, in addition to an article on the translating of Shakespeare, is divided into three sections: (1) the relation between the poet's life and his art; (2) a comparison between Athenian and Elizabethan drama; and (3) a discussion of modern plays, considered in the light of Shakespearian technique.

In the first section the author argues that in all his plays, except the very earliest, Shakespeare was concerned to express the struggles and aspirations of contemporary social reality as manifested in the circumstances of his own life. In this respect he differs from Goethe, who, indebted to Shakespeare though he was in many ways, designed his *Faust* rather as a vehicle for the expression of philosophical ideas about life than as a mirror of life itself; and also from Dante, whose mystical outlook belongs rather to the medieval age of faith than to the Renaissance. The author considers that our ignorance of the circumstances of his life constitutes a real obstacle to the full understanding of his plays.

Athenian drama and Elizabethan drama resemble one another in that both express the vitality and confidence of a new social order, which rested in both cases on the rapid expansion of maritime trade, the growth of democratic ideas, and the dissolution of obsolete institutions, in the one case tribal and in the other feudal. This explains why both deal with real life, real people, and real actions; and similarly the lyrical form which is characteristic of them both is related to democracy.

In the third section the author examines further what he calls the "lyrical realism" of Shakespearian drama, which, he maintains, has nothing in common with romanticism but is reminiscent rather of Byzantine paintings. He concludes by contrasting the Elizabethan audience, which was popular, lively, rich in practical experience, with the audience that patronizes the contemporary theatre, which demands romanticism and sensationalism because it consists for the most part of people who know little of the realities of contemporary life except what they have learnt from books.

GEORGE THOMSON

## Italy

What can be considered the best performance of *Hamlet* in Italy in modern times has been given on the stage of the Roman Teatro Valle in the winter 1952-3: Vittorio Gassmann, a young actor of great promise, who impersonated Hamlet, has carried all before him thanks to his elegant, almost Byronic figure, his excellent delivery of the soliloquies, and his generally thoughtful and restrained interpretation (with a notable exception in the crucial scene with Gertrude—Elena Zareschi, a right royal queen—which showed too much of a Freudian bias). The rest of the cast was not on a level with the chief actor, and the presentation of Ophelia (Anna Proclemer) in the character of a mistress rather than a virgin was an unfortunate innovation, but the Italian public has long been accustomed to such disproportions, and the play ran for an impressive number of nights. The translator, Luigi Squarzina, has tried to preserve the vigour of the text, with occasional lapses into modernizing flatness ("this does betoken The corse they follow did with desperate hand Fordo its own life" becomes "dev' essere il feretro d' un suicida"). The performance has offered to Gerardo Guerrieri the occasion to write one of the best pieces of dramatic criticism we have seen for years (in *Lo Spettatore Italiano* for February 1953). Gassmann's success has far outshone the other Shakespearian productions of the year, a rather unsatisfactory *Macbeth* at the Teatro delle Arti (Rome) with Antonio Crast in the role of the protagonist, an even less satisfactory *Winter's Tale* at the Teatro Ateneo (Compagnia Scharoff), and a *Midsummer Night's Dream* at the Teatro Giusti of Verona (July 1952). The translator of the first two plays is Cesare Vico Ludovici, whose Shakespearian versions continue to appear through the press of Einaudi: his trick of interspersing his prose renderings with an hendecasyllabic here and there proves frequently tiresome to the hearers. The Roman Teatro dell' Opera has staged a more successful *Macbeth* set to music by Bloch (first performed in Paris in 1910). Alberto Rossi's version of Shakespeare's *Sonnets*, in prose (a work which has occupied the translator many years, after he had to give up a poetic version in despair), is by far the best Italy has seen; its merits can be appreciated by comparing it with G. Barbensi's *Scelta dai Sonetti*, a work of love unassisted by an adequate metrical skill. *Venus and Adonis* has been translated into Italian prose (together with Marlowe's *Hero and Leander*) by the distinguished young Shakespearian scholar Gabriele Baldini, whose contributions have appeared here and there in Italian periodicals (for instance: 'Lord Bardolph e Sir John Umfrevile nel *Henry IV*', in *Belfagor*, 1952).

MARIO PRAZ

## Malaya

The outstanding production of the year was undoubtedly *A Midsummer Night's Dream* produced in Kuala Lumpur in the magnificent setting of the Lake Gardens by the British Council Arts Theatre Group, under the direction of David Lyttle. This well-spoken and delightfully acted production was like an enchantment to the Asian audience, for whom it seemed to open up a new world.

The Singapore Arts Theatre in a production by Donald Moore presented three colourful and highly creditable performances of *The Merchant of Venice*, while the Arts Theatre Group, again, towards the end of the year acted *Henry V* in an arena production which won widespread approval. A feature of these Groups is that they are composed of people of all races and communities living in the peninsula; and in an address on the occasion of the performance of *Henry V* in the presence of the High Commissioner, General Sir Gerald Templer, the Representative of the British Council related the play to the development of a sense of nationhood in a plural community.

There have been several school performances. Of course many thousands of school children have seen the productions by the Theatre Groups, which are setting good standards of presentation and carrying out valuable educational work in the appreciation of Shakespeare.

ROBERT K. BRADY

## The Netherlands

Shakespeare productions in the Netherlands were concerned mainly with comedy—*The Merry Wives of Windsor*, *The Merchant of Venice* and *Twelfth Night*. The first two were performed in new translations by Bert Voeten, a poet whose renderings of Christopher Fry's plays have also been much admired. The performance of *The Merry Wives* was the most elaborate, staged in an early eighteenth-century style by Michael Langham of the Old Vic, with music by Jurriaan Andriessen.

It would seem that on the whole there is now a tendency for Netherlands actors to take their bearings, so far as Shakespeare is concerned, from England, in spite of continental, mainly French, stage tradition.

Publications include a dissertation submitted at Amsterdam University by H. Röhrmann, *The Way of Life*, the most notable feature of which is perhaps its treatment of Hamlet as a premonition of the isolation suffered by the artistic mind in later times.

J. SWART

## New Zealand

The move towards a professional theatre in New Zealand envisaged in my article in *Shakespeare Survey*, 6 has finally shown some results. This has been partly due to long visits by two first-rate companies from England. Before we had time to forget the impact of the Old Vic Company with Olivier's *Richard III*, the Stratford Company under Anthony Quayle played long seasons in each of the four main cities in *Othello*, *Henry IV* and *As You Like It*. While I write, the tour of the latter Company is not yet complete, but the response of Auckland, the first point of call, has been so wholehearted there is little doubt that the tour will be a financial as well as an artistic success. Olivier and Quayle have both shown that it is possible for a major company to visit Australia and New Zealand for a long Shakespeare season, transport players and scenery twice across the world, and more than pay their way.

Locally the most interesting production was that of *Hamlet*, staged by the Wellington Repertory Society, which is an amateur group. Unlike most of the plays of this Society, it was produced by a young professional New Zealand producer, Richard Campion, recently returned from the Old Vic school. Since that production Campion has organized his own company, which includes two of the *Hamlet* cast and Harold Baigent, the producer for the semi-professional Community Arts Service, whose touring production of *Twelfth Night* was mentioned in *Shakespeare Survey*, 6. This new company, while it is mainly made up of young players, includes several with a fair amount of experience. As New Zealand's first professional company, it has many problems both of organization and support to master. But if it receives even a portion of the encouragement given to our recent visiting companies, the future of acting, and of Shakespearian production, in New Zealand seems likely to inspire quiet confidence.

IAN A. GORDON

### Norway

The year 1952 saw the staging in Oslo of two Shakespearian plays: *Romeo and Juliet* at the National Theatre in May, and *The Merry Wives of Windsor* at the Folketeatret in November. The staging of the former was a real event: the first performance of *Romeo and Juliet* in Oslo in this century.

The performance brought out—very rightly, in my opinion—the rapid development, during those few and hectic summer days, of the emotions of the two lovers. Knut Wigert, in gorgeous Renaissance costumes, looked dazzlingly handsome and spoke in a tender and lyrical voice, never losing, even during the violent outbursts of the end, the intimate appeal, the subtle and revealing inflections. The Juliet of Liv Strömsted made him a fitting partner.

*The Merry Wives of Windsor* was an unqualified success. The theatre was fortunate in possessing an actor, Ingolf Rogde, capable of giving life to the personality of Falstaff. The Slender of Lars Nordrum was also excellent. The whole *mise-en-scène*, by Hans Jacob Nilsen, had speed, gaiety and a disarming grace.

In Trondheim, in October, *Hamlet* was staged at the Tröndelag Teater. I did not see the performance myself, but the critics agree that Georg Lökkeberg created a fascinating and impressive Hamlet.

LORENTZ ECKHOFF

### South Africa

The most important cultural event was the visit of the Old Vic Company to the principal cities, with Tyrone Guthrie's beautiful production of *A Midsummer Night's Dream*, Michael Langham's moving *Othello*, and Hugh Hunt's experimental *Macbeth*, which had the honour of its première in Johannesburg. There was an admirable blend of experienced Shakespearian actors and newcomers to the Old Vic, such as the vivacious Irene Worth, remembered as Celia Coplestone in the Edinburgh Festival production of *The Cocktail Party*. She played Helena with a lovely sense of sportive mischief, Desdemona with true poetic insight, and Lady Macbeth with a fire and dignity that can rarely have been excelled since the days of Mrs Siddons.

In August and September, when G. Wilson Knight was at the University of Cape Town as guest lecturer,

he had the fortune to fall in with Capt. D. M. K. Marendaz, art connoisseur and owner of a Shakespeare portrait purchased in England some years ago. The painting is said to be by Paulus van Somer, who arrived in England from Holland in 1606, and became a court painter to James I. It has not so far been established that the work is either van Somer's or was executed before 1616, as Marendaz claims. He is preparing a book which will make public the facts. The portrait is in oil on an oak panel, measures 9 × 7 inches, and presents Shakespeare three-quarter face, with one large round ear-ring visible, as in the Chandos portrait. It is the picture of an intelligent, vigorous, living man, dressed in large white collar and black doublet, according to the gentlemanly fashion of the time.

Another Shakespeare find was made earlier in the year. It is a portion of an original Second Folio, comprising the complete play *Timon of Athens*. It consists of eleven unbound leaves in a perfect state of preservation, and is owned by F. D. Sinclair, who bought it at a sale of books for 25s. Watermarks and other bibliographical details were verified by the Bodleian Library. There is no doubt of the play's genuineness, though how and when the Folio came to be dismembered is still a matter of conjecture. There are seventeen variants from the Methuen facsimile, mainly concerned with punctuation, and all corrections of errors. On page 107 the correct word *hanging* appears for the erroneous *hunting* of the facsimile. It is a safe assumption that the discovered text represents a corrected state of the text reproduced by Methuen.

A. C. PARTRIDGE

### Sweden

The Swedish theatre has cherished the comedies during the last year. Notable performances have been *Twelfth Night* (Hälsingborg) and *As You Like It* (Malmö). *A Midsummer Night's Dream* and *Twelfth Night* have been favourites with the open-air stages and it is now the fifth summer in succession that the Skansen theatre (Stockholm) has been presenting Shakespeare. The popularity of Elizabethan plays is furthermore shown when we add that Ben Jonson's *Volpone* was acted with great success among the Varberg castle plays.

An interesting recent study is Hans Andersson's *Strindberg's Master Olof and Shakespeare*. It gives us a clear picture of what Shakespeare meant to our foremost dramatist. Per Meurling has increased the not too extensive literature in Swedish on Shakespeare with a volume, mostly biographical. Lastly and long looked for is Helge Kökeritz's work *Shakespeare's Pronunciation*.

It will certainly be found a helpful and, one may hope, an important contribution to the discussion of textual problems.                                    NILS MOLIN

## Switzerland

No book bearing on Shakespeare was published in Switzerland last year (1952). But I should like to repair an omission in my 1951 report, where mention should have been made of Rudolf Stamm's *Geschichte des englischen Theaters* published by Francke (Bern) in that year; this general history of the English theatre contains an excellent up-to-date summary of what is known concerning the conditions under which the dramatists and actors of the Elizabethan-Jacobean age worked; it shows a happy combination of theatrical and dramatic history; though written for a German-speaking public, it should not be allowed to pass unnoticed by English and American students.

In the absence of a Swiss periodical devoted to English philology, Swiss scholars must needs publish what articles they may write in foreign annuals and reviews. The Swiss contributions to the 1952 *Jahrbuch* of the German Shakespeare Society have been particularly numerous. Other papers are to be found in the 1952 volumes of Dutch and American journals.

Several of the plays have been performed in the course of the year, mostly of course in translation. A French company, 'Le Grenier de Toulouse', first founded in 1945, gave in Geneva, Lausanne and Neuchâtel, last October, a spirited rendering of *The Taming of the Shrew* in André Thorent's French version, with Thorent himself in the main part. A Vienna company played *A Midsummer Night's Dream* in German at Fribourg. The Bern Municipal Theatre scored a great success with *The Taming of the Shrew* early in the year and again with *A Midsummer Night's Dream* last winter; the former was given no less than twelve times and the latter ten times. At Bâle, besides *Othello* acted at the Theatre, there was an interesting performance during the summer of *Romeo and Juliet* on an open-air stage in front of the former episcopal palace; there were no stage-properties and no change of scenery; the various scenes were located at different points in the rather large area used for the acting. H. Lüdeke tells me the experiment was a decided success on the whole. In the course of its usual season the Zurich Schauspielhaus produced *The Taming of the Shrew*, *The Two Gentlemen of Verona* and *The Tempest* in German, and for its summer festival, besides giving performances of *Richard II* and, in the open air, of *A Midsummer Night's Dream*, invited the Old Vic

company which acted *Timon of Athens*, in English of course, Madeleine and Jean-Louis Barrault with *Hamlet* in French, and the Piccolo Teatro of Milan with *Macbeth* in Italian: an eloquent demonstration of Shakespeare's international standing.

By way of an introduction to the Zurich festival a series of public lectures was given: 'Shakespeare in England', by H. Straumann, 'Shakespeare in Germany', by E. Staiger, 'Shakespeare in France and Italy', by G. Calgari. Summaries of those lectures were published in the October number of *Hesperia*, the journal issued by the Zurich Institute for the study of foreign cultures, in which, earlier this year, Max Wildi had published a paper on 'London in the Age of Shakespeare'.

The main event last year so far as Swiss interest in Shakespeare is concerned was no doubt the acquisition by Martin Bodmer of Geneva of the great Rosenbach collection of Shakespeariana and its housing in his beautiful library at Cologny, a place already dear to lovers of English literature for its associations with Byron and Shelley, and now turned, thanks to the presence there of that unrivalled collection, into one of its most sacred temples. In point of condition and quality the collection is the largest and by far the best in private hands. The copies of the four Folios are in the finest condition and that of the first is said to be the most perfect in existence. No less than sixty-eight Quartos— thirty-two being first editions, twenty-nine previous to 1623 and twenty-one adaptations by seventeenth-century editors—were bought at the same time by Bodmer, who was already the fortunate possessor of a very fine copy of the first edition of the *Sonnets*. I had the privilege of being shown the whole collection soon after it had been placed in the glass-cases of the sumptuous exhibition-room at Cologny and can testify to the perfection of the arrangements made to give it a home worthy of its supreme value.                        GEORGES A. BONNARD

## Turkey

At least four of Shakespeare's plays have been produced in four outstanding theatres of Turkey since last spring.

The most interesting and original of these productions was *A Midsummer Night's Dream* produced and directed by Carl Ebert at the National Theatre of Ankara in the spring of 1952.

Carl Ebert, who is well known in Britain with his Glyndebourne productions and Festival of Britain performances, had formerly been invited by the Turkish government to start the Drama and Opera departments of the National Conservatoire of Ankara, where he worked for twelve years between 1936 and 1948, and trained almost all the actors and opera singers who now work at the Turkish National Theatre and Opera in Ankara.

The production of *A Midsummer Night's Dream* was excellent, with a beautiful Athenian woodland scenery in pastel green, designed by Sabih Kayan, and a mysterious fairyland lighting by Alberto Milano; Mendelssohn's enchanting music was played by the Orchestra of the National Opera conducted by Hans Hörner; and fairy dances were performed by the Ballet students of the National Conservatoire, formerly trained by Miss Joy Newton and now by Miss Appleyard of Sadler's Wells.

Although a score of Shakespeare's plays had been well known to the average Turkish playgoer since the second half of the last century, this was the first production of *A Midsummer Night's Dream* in Turkish. The verse translation was my own.

The Municipal Theatre of Istanbul, founded in 1914, follows the tradition of opening its curtain every season with a new Shakespearian production. This year's play was *The Tempest*; the Turkish version by Haldun Derin.

Küçük Sahne (a private theatre of Istanbul run by Muhsin Ertugrul, who used to be the Director of the Municipal Theatre of Istanbul) opened with *Twelfth Night*.

In January of 1953 the Drama Department of the National Conservatoire of Ankara started its new stage with *Romeo and Juliet*, directed by myself and produced by Mahir Canova. Although there are several translations of the play, this one is the only verse rendering of *Romeo and Juliet*; it is the work of a young Turkish poet, Yusuf Mardin.　　　　　　NUREDDIN SEVIN

## U.S.A.

Shakespeare ran neck and neck with Shaw in the 1952–3 Broadway sweepstakes, but Shaw won hands down. Each author had two entries, Shaw with *The Millionairess* ridden at break-neck speed by Katharine Hepburn and *Misalliance*, a dark horse, indeed, appearing modestly at the City Center on 55th Street with an excellent cast but no spectacular stars, then moving happily into a Broadway house for what promises to be a long run. Shakespeare entries, both in the City Center repertory, were *Love's Labour's Lost* and *The Merchant of Venice*. It should be noted that the New York City Center is New York's closest approach to a repertory theatre. It offers a season of opera, another of ballet, and a third devoted to theatre, usually second runs or revivals. So hard pressed was the Center financially (it receives no money from the City, though it plays in a barn-like theatre owned by the municipality) that this year it was feared the drama season would have to be omitted, but its new Director, Lincoln Kirstein, was determined to have at least a short theatre season. Joining forces with a group of young actors who had produced several of the plays in Cambridge in previous years, a short season was finally presented. *Love's Labour's Lost* had not been seen in New York since the turn of the century and immediately evoked interest among the critics, if not a wild enthusiasm among the public. The director, Albert Marre, had discovered in his previous experiments with the play that the incongruities of Edwardian costume and an English country-house background, set the stage for fun and games and induced in the audience a mood of playfulness that made the fantastical goings-on of Berowne and the rest acceptable as an excursion into pure make-believe. The action all takes place on a terrace of the English manor-house of the 'King of Navarre' with such odd notions as the arrival of the Princess of France in an early model-T Ford, her entourage bedecked in the 'sportswear' of the period, including bloomers, boaters and motoring veils of fantastic proportions. The costuming of the second act, when all the ladies were in riding habits while the men were correctly turned out in pink hunting coats and high boots, had a dash and elegance of its own. The final scenes gave opportunity for the ladies to appear in evening dresses sufficiently gorgeous to make up for any oddities in their first appearance. A game of croquet between Holofernes and Sir Nathaniel, the smoking of cigarettes and the drinking of innumerable cups of tea were touches which would make the rigid classicist shudder, but which seemed gay enough in this midsummer charade. Joseph Schildkraut as Armado, Philip Bourneuf as Holofernes, and Hurd Hatfield as 'the curate' were thoroughly at their ease in Shakespearian speech—which is more than could be said for most of the cast. The young American actor has no opportunity to learn his trade as it applies to the classics, since there are no repertory theatres offering what one might call post-graduate experience in the art of acting. The lack is acutely demonstrated whenever—as happens all too rarely—a professional Shakespearian production is offered in New York with an American cast.

The City Center's second Shakespeare play, the ever controversial *Merchant of Venice*, suffered from the same handicap. Colloquialism in the reading of poetry, though occasionally revealing, is, in the long run, flat and unprofitable. Shakespeare's verse must spread its wings to lift the hearer to heights which plodding prose cannot achieve. Shylock becomes great because in Shakespeare's poetry he suffers greatly. Under-played, presented as a dignified, baffled, unhappy being, the greatness melts away. In Luther Adler's deliberately quiet, almost evasive interpretation, the agony of suffering, the passion of pent-up fury, the violence of revenge were lacking. The production, again directed by Albert Marre and designed by Lemuel Ayers, was in the traditional Venetian vein, with considerable embellishment of masked revellers and torch-lit dancing. Though neither of these revivals made theatre history, the fact that they were given at all was significant. They mark a renewed effort to establish a classic repertory theatre in New York, and are another step toward that much desired goal.

The only other hopeful sign on the professional Shakespeare horizon is the launching of a drive to build a permanent Shakespeare Festival theatre in Connecticut. The theatre is to be modelled on the old Globe and will have attendant Mermaid Taverns and other Elizabethan trimmings. The project has been launched by Lawrence Langner, co-director of the Theatre Guild, and is an outgrowth of his very successful summer theatre at Westport. So far it has the blessing of the Governor of the State of Connecticut, the Hon. John Lodge (once an actor himself) and of a formidable array of theatre names. All that remains to be done is to raise the money, secure the land, build and endow the theatre, and train the company. When this has been achieved there should be a splendid opportunity for three-way exchange between Stratford-upon-Avon, Stratford in Canada and Shakespeare's youngest 'birthplace', Stratford-on-the-Sound.

ROSAMOND GILDER

# SHAKESPEARE PRODUCTIONS IN THE UNITED KINGDOM: 1952

### A LIST COMPILED FROM ITS RECORDS BY THE SHAKESPEARE MEMORIAL LIBRARY, BIRMINGHAM

**JANUARY**

11    *Much Ado About Nothing:* The Phoenix Theatre, London. *Producer:* JOHN GIELGUD.

21    *The Taming of the Shrew:* The Playhouse, Sheffield. *Producer:* GEOFFREY OST.

28    *Macbeth:* The Playhouse, Nottingham. *Producer:* JOHN HARRISON.

**FEBRUARY**

4    *The Two Gentlemen of Verona:* The Bristol Old Vic Company, at the Theatre Royal, Bristol. *Producer:* DENIS CAREY. (On 19 February opened at the Old Vic Theatre, London.)

16 & 18    *Hamlet:* at Eton College. *Producer:* B. W. M. YOUNG.

**MARCH**

3    *King Lear:* The Old Vic Company, at The Old Vic Theatre, London. *Producer:* HUGH HUNT.

4    *Hamlet:* Oxford University Dramatic Society, at The Playhouse, Oxford. *Producers:* NEVILL COGHILL and DAVID WILLIAMS.

11    *Julius Caesar:* Cambridge University, Marlowe Society and the A.D.C., at The Arts Theatre, Cambridge. (The producer and actors are anonymous.)

13    *Coriolanus:* Shakespeare Memorial Theatre, Stratford-upon-Avon. *Producer:* GLEN BYAM SHAW.

25    *The Tempest:* Shakespeare Memorial Theatre, Stratford-upon-Avon. *Producer:* MICHAEL BENTHALL.

**APRIL**

1    *Henry VI, Part III:* The Repertory Theatre, Birmingham. *Producer:* DOUGLAS SEALE.

19    *The Comedy of Errors:* Morley College Actors, at The George Inn, Southwark. *Producers:* RUPERT DOONE and ROY WALKER. (Edwardian Costume.)

29    *As You Like It:* Shakespeare Memorial Theatre, Stratford-upon-Avon. *Producer:* GLEN BYAM SHAW.

**MAY**

   *Macbeth:* The Bristol Old Vic Company, at The Theatre Royal, Bristol. *Producer:* DENIS CAREY.

17    *Julius Caesar:* First Folio Theatre Company, at The George Inn, Southwark. *Producer:* KENNETH MCCLELLAN.

17    *Henry V:* The Norwich Players, at The Maddermarket Theatre, Norwich. *Producer:* NUGENT MONCK.

26    *Coriolanus:* The Bath Assembly. *Producer:* GLYNNE WICKHAM.

28    *Timon of Athens:* The Old Vic Company, at The Old Vic Theatre, London. *Producer:* TYRONE GUTHRIE.

29    *As You Like It:* Regent's Park Open Air Theatre, London. *Producer:* ROBERT ATKINS.

# SHAKESPEARE IN THE UNITED KINGDOM

**JUNE**

6    *A Midsummer Night's Dream:* Harrow School. *Producer:* RONALD WATKINS.

10    *Macbeth:* Shakespeare Memorial Theatre, Stratford-upon-Avon. *Producer:* JOHN GIELGUD.

17    *Twelfth Night:* Oxford University Dramatic Society. *Producer:* ALISTAIR MCINTOSH.

**JULY**

1    *Cymbeline:* Regent's Park Open Air Theatre, London. *Producer:* ROBERT ATKINS.

21    *The Comedy of Errors:* The Marlowe Theatre, Canterbury. *Producers:* RUPERT DOONE and ROY WALKER. (Edwardian Costume.)

**AUGUST**

4    *The Taming of the Shrew:* The Oxford and Cambridge Players, in the gardens of Blackhall, the British Council's premises in Oxford. *Producer:* GORDON GOSTELOW.

*Romeo and Juliet:* Cambridge University, Marlowe Society, at The Arts Theatre, Cambridge. *Producers:* GEORGE RYLANDS and JOHN BARTON. (August 11, at The Scala Theatre, London. On 25 August opened at The Phoenix Theatre, London.)

12    *A Midsummer Night's Dream:* The Liverpool Repertory Theatre, at The Playhouse, Liverpool. *Producer:* WILLARD STOKER. (Sets and costumes after Botticelli.)

**SEPTEMBER**

10    *Macbeth:* The Mermaid Theatre, London. *Producer:* JOAN SWINSTEAD. (Elizabethan pronunciation).

15    *Romeo and Juliet:* The Old Vic Company, at The Old Vic Theatre, London. *Producer:* HUGH HUNT. (Opened at The Edinburgh Festival, 2 September.)

17    *Much Ado about Nothing:* Smethwick Repertory Company, at The Repertory Theatre, Smethwick. *Producer:* ARTHUR HUNT.

22    *Twelfth Night:* The Playhouse, Kidderminster. *Producer:* ROBERT GASTON.

20    *As You Like It:* The Norwich Players, at The Maddermarket Theatre, Norwich. *Producer:* LIONEL DUNN.

29    *Macbeth:* Arts Council Tour, opening at Cardiff. *Producer:* WALTER HUDD.

29    *Othello:* The Century Theatre on tour, opening at Hinckley, Leicestershire. *Producer:* ABRAHAM ASSEO.

30    *Measure for Measure:* The Bristol Old Vic Company, at The Theatre Royal, Bristol. *Producer:* BASIL COLEMAN.

**OCTOBER**

7    *A Midsummer Night's Dream:* The Windsor Repertory Company at The Theatre Royal, Windsor. *Producers:* LESLIE FRENCH and JOHN COUNSELL.

13    *The Merry Wives of Windsor:* The Arts Theatre, Salisbury. *Producer:* GUY VERNEY.

20    *The Taming of the Shrew:* The Citizens' Theatre, Glasgow. *Producer:* PETER POTTER.

**NOVEMBER**

3    *Henry V:* The Oxford and Cambridge Players, at The Arts Theatre, Cambridge. *Producer:* JOHN BARTON.

8    *The Merchant of Venice:* The Questors Theatre, Ealing. *Producer:* ERIC VOCE.

10    *Julius Caesar:* The Perth Theatre Company. *Producer:* EDMUND BAILEY.

NOVEMBER

18  *Julius Caesar:* Oxford University Experimental Theatre Club. In Marston Hall, Oxford. *Producer:* PATRICK DROMGOOLE.

25  *Othello:* Shakespeare Memorial Theatre, Stratford-upon-Avon. *Producer:* ANTHONY QUAYLE.

DECEMBER

1  *Othello:* Worthing Theatre Company, The Connaught Theatre, Worthing. *Producer:* JACK WILLIAMS.

*Julius Caesar:* The Royalty Theatre, Morecambe. *Producer:* MERVYN R. PINFIELD.

2  *As You Like It:* Shakespeare Memorial Theatre, Stratford-upon-Avon. *Producer:* GLEN BYAM SHAW.

8  *Richard the Second:* Theatre Royal, Brighton. *Producer:* JOHN GIELGUD. (15 December at Shakespeare Memorial Theatre, Stratford-upon-Avon; 24 December at Lyric Theatre, Hammersmith.)

9  *Henry IV, Part I:* Shakespeare Memorial Theatre, Stratford-upon-Avon. *Producer:* ANTHONY QUAYLE.

'The Taverners' (Poetry and Plays in Pubs): Summer Season—*Much Ado about Nothing*; Winter Season—*Othello*. *Producer:* HENRY McCARTHY. (This is a travelling company which gives performances of Shakespeare's plays in public houses and inns.)

PLATE III

A. *King Henry VI, Part One*, Birmingham Repertory Theatre, 1953
Production by DOUGLAS SEALE; Setting by FINLAY JAMES
THE CAPTURE OF JOAN OF ARC

B. *King Henry VI, Part Two*, Birmingham Repertory Theatre, 1953
Production by DOUGLAS SEALE; Setting by FINLAY JAMES
THE DEATH OF CARDINAL BEAUFORT

PLATE IV

*King Henry VIII*, Old Vic Theatre, London, 1953. Production by TYRONE GUTHRIE;
Costumes and Settings by TANYA MOISEIWITSCH

"THERE'S HIS PERIOD, TO SHEATHE HIS KNIFE IN US"

PLATE V

A. *King Henry VIII.* "Who May That Be, I Pray You?"

B. *The Taming of the Shrew*, Shakespeare Memorial Theatre,
Stratford-upon-Avon, 1953

Production by George Devine; Costumes and Settings by Motley
"What You Will Have It Nam'd, Even That It Is"

PLATE VI

*The Taming of the Shrew.* "Strive Mightily, but Eat and Drink as Friends"

PLATE VII

A. *Julius Caesar*, Old Vic Theatre, 1953. Production by HUGH HUNT,
Costumes by ALAN TAGG; Settings by TANYA MOISEIWITSCH

B. *Antony and Cleopatra.* Shakespeare Memorial Theatre, 1953
Production by GLEN BYAM SHAW; Costumes and Settings by MOTLEY
"FROM THIS HOUR THE HEART OF BROTHERS GOVERN IN OUR LOVES"

PLATE VIII

*Antony and Cleopatra.* "Comest Thou Smiling from the World's Great Snare Uncaught?"

# ACTING SHAKESPEARE: MODERN
# TENDENCIES IN PLAYING AND PRODUCTION
## WITH SPECIAL REFERENCE TO SOME RECENT PRODUCTIONS

BY

## T. C. KEMP

One of the most frustrating aspects of theatrical art is the ephemeral nature of the actors' performance. No other art is so urgent as the drama in its impact, and demonstrations in no other art have a more transient existence. The three-hours traffic of the stage is an insubstantial pageant: once it has faded, the watcher is left with nothing but a memory. We go to the theatre to enlarge our experience in an emotional and intellectual exercise of more vitality and liveliness than is possible in any other medium, yet this very fullness of experience makes it difficult to communicate that experience to others.

We have all met the veteran playgoer who saw Irving, the not-so-aged who remembers Benson, and the comparative youngster who has seen a performance by Olivier. We have heard them trying to share their experiences with others, and we have seen how not one particle of the real quality and essence of the performance has been communicated. Efficient comment on the nature and quality of an actor's performance is a difficult exercise. Yet without it your theatre historian is unable to discern tendencies, for it is only by comparing present performances with past achievements that we are able to detect the changes in style and fashion that take place on our stages: and it is only through the written records of those who saw the great actors in their prime that we can savour the quality of past players. The painter suffers from no such limitation: the canvasses of Rembrandt glow as richly for us as they did for the burghers of Amsterdam three hundred years ago. The poet is assured of permanence in the printed page. The player's performance is a mere memory at curtain-fall.

Yet here and there we come across a record, left by some member of an audience with the gift of tongues. Then, so far as the printed word can invoke the past, we catch a fleeting glimpse of the departed player and get a peep at genius in action. I had such an experience fifteen years ago, when for the first time David Garrick became for me a living presence justifying legend. In 1938, the Clarendon Press published *Lichtenberg's Visits to England, as described in his letters and diaries.* These were translated and annotated by Margaret L. Mare and W. H. Quarrell. Lichtenberg was twice in England, first in 1770 and then in 1774 until 1775. In his letters home, afterwards reprinted in the *Deutsches Museum*, he recorded his visits to the London theatre, and his account of Garrick as Hamlet is a perfect piece of reporting that seats us in the pit at Old Drury in the year 1775:

Hamlet appears in a black dress, the only one in the whole court, alas! still worn for his poor father, who has been dead scarce a couple of months. Horatio and Marcellus, in uniform, are with him, and they are awaiting the ghost; Hamlet has folded his arms under his cloak and pulled his hat down over his eyes; it is a cold night and just twelve o'clock; the theatre is darkened and the whole audience of some thousands are as quiet, and their faces as motionless, as though they were painted on the walls of

I

the theatre; even from the farthest end of the playhouse one could hear a pin drop. Suddenly, as Hamlet moves towards the back of the stage slightly to the left and turns his back on the audience, Horatio starts, and saying: "Look, my lord, it comes", points to the right, where the ghost has already appeared and stands motionless, before anyone is aware of him. At these words Garrick turns sharply and at the same moment staggers back two or three paces with his knees giving way under him; his hat falls to the ground and both his arms, especially the left, are stretched out nearly to their full length, with the hands as high as his head, the right arm more bent with the hand lower, and the fingers apart; his mouth is open: thus he stands rooted to the spot, with legs apart, but no loss of dignity, supported by his friends who are better acquainted with the apparition and fear lest he should collapse. His whole demeanour is so expressive of terror that it made my flesh creep even before he began to speak. The almost terror-struck silence of the audience, which preceded this appearance and filled one with a sense of insecurity, probably did much to enhance this effect. At last he speaks, not at the beginning but at the end of a breath, with a trembling voice: "Angels and ministers of grace defend us!" words which supply anything this scene may lack and make it one of the greatest and most terrible which will ever be played upon the stage. The ghost beckons to him; I wish you could see him with eyes fixed on the ghost, though he is speaking to his companions, freeing himself from their restraining hands, as they warn him not to follow and hold him back. But at length, when they have tried his patience too far, he turns his face towards them, tears himself with great violence from their grasp, and draws his sword with a swiftness that makes one shudder, saying: "By Heaven! I'll make a ghost of him that lets me." That is enough for them. Then he stands with his sword on guard against the spectre saying: "Go on, I'll follow thee", and the ghost goes off the stage. Hamlet still remains motionless, his sword held out so as to make him keep his distance, and at length, when the spectator can no longer see the ghost, he begins slowly to follow him, now standing still, and then going on, with sword still on guard, eyes fixed on the ghost, hair disordered, and out of breath, until he too is lost to sight. You can well imagine what loud applause accompanies this exit. It begins as soon as the ghost goes off the stage and lasts until Hamlet also disappears. What an amazing triumph it is.

Lichtenberg's account not only describes Garrick's performance but also recreates the atmosphere of the theatre, that silence and tension which great acting generates. He also remarks on Garrick's talent for giving individuality to everything:

Garrick will sooner thrust his left hand into his right hand pocket, if need arise, than let go a pinch of snuff that he has between the fingers of his right hand. And if he were representing, for example, a great glutton, and wanted to feel with his fingers whether his capon or pheasant on the spit was done to a turn, I dare swear that he would probe it with the fourth finger of his left hand. In all the others there would be too much strength and too little feeling.

This individuality has been the constant feature in great actors of every age. Recalling Irving, James Agate wrote:

The voice of the greatest actor I ever saw or ever shall see, was a staccato, raven croak, his walk an ungainly halting limp, his speech a mass of slurred consonants and unintelligible vowels. And did not Mr. Shaw say of this great player that he "had no voice, and when you looked closely at him, no face". Yet I remember an educated man, a professor at Owens College, telling me that when the play had been *Louis XI*, he had to stay the night in town because he could not endure the mile-long walk along a lonely country road for fear of that dead face following.

Why had Richard Tarleton only to put his head "the tire-house doore and tapestrie betweene" to set the multitude in a roar? What spell was woven by that master comedian of the late-Victorian music-hall which led Max Beerbohm to declare:

I defy anyone not to have loved Dan Leno at first sight. The moment he capered on, with that air of wild determination, squirming in every limb with some deep grievance, all hearts were his. That face, so tragic, with all the tragedy that is writ on the face of a baby-monkey, was ever liable to relax its mouth into a sudden wide grin and screw up its eyes to vanishing point over some little triumph wrested from Fate, the tyrant.

These snatches from the records, these attempts to preserve the actor's moments of triumph, all suggest that the secret of the great players' success lay in the individuality with which they endowed their characters. To be a successful player is not to say thus, or thus. It is to set a character apart from his fellows by those individual quirks of personality that bring life and variety to the human pattern: and the modern tendency in acting is to infuse this individuality in subsidiary as well as in leading characters. Shakespeare is the prime author for this exercise. Those mountains of "raw material for acting", as Granville-Barker called them, are such that a playgoer may see twenty Hamlets and still be ready to visit Denmark again on a twenty-first invitation.

There was a time, some fifty or sixty years ago, when the playing of Shakespeare had hardened into a ritual except in the hands of a few star players. Among stock companies there was an official prompt copy which laid down the undeviating line for a Shakespearian production. There were approved methods of recital and declamation. Certain actions were attached to certain lines, and business had become traditional. A visitor to London in Kemble's day has recorded that in his production of *Hamlet*, Kemble permitted the old gravedigger's business with the waistcoats. As the dialogue proceeded, the First Gravedigger paused in his digging and took off a waistcoat; then another and another: this performance was repeated a dozen times. A variation was sometimes introduced by allowing the Second Gravedigger to put on the waistcoats as the First took them off. Today your Shakespearian actor would scorn to use so hackneyed a piece of business. He is all for individuality, for the fresh approach, even for the topical touch: anything that will build up the character and give it actuality. I remember that in the Old Vic production of *The Taming of the Shrew* in 1947, Peter Copley played Tranio in a 'wizard-prang' accent and in the fulsome moustache of 'Flying Officer Kite', a character popular at the time on the radio. The search for new facets of old treasure goes on. What brings visitors in their hundreds of thousands to the Memorial Theatre and sends playgoing London across the river to the Old Vic is the hope that in addition to expected excitements some actor may spring a surprise in a familiar character or that some alert producer may discover a new route to the Shakespearian summit.

In the 1952–3 season no startling new discoveries were made, but the most important Shakespearian productions showed the questing spirit at work; actors striving to make individuals of characters; producers playing for speed and continuity. Hugh Hunt's production of *Julius Caesar* at the Old Vic went at a sufficient pace against Tanya Moiseiwitsch's setting, a convenient arrangement of columns and balustrated recesses, which provided peeps at a classical vista and at the same time allowed the mob to surge by devious channels. Alan Tagg's costumes were classical-Elizabethan, and Hugh Hunt's direction achieved a crowded robust Rome, resounding with noise. Entrances were loudly trumpeted and the storm roared to long reverberations of thunder. The players, almost to a man, were obviously anxious to get away from the set piece, from the formal recital of familiar rhetoric. More than usually these Romans were closely and personally concerned with all that was going on: the plotters were deep in conspiracy, not merely immersed in seditious speech. William Devlin, as Brutus, forwent any attempt at that loftiness of spirit that so often turns the patriot into a prig, and showed instead the man impelled by political considerations yet still holding firm to ethical principles. In the same idiom of deliberate, direct action, Paul Rogers set Cassius working at insurrection as well as talking about it. He urged his speeches with a compulsion that came as much from the head as from the heart, though in the quarrel with Brutus there was passion enough. Robin Bailey made a new approach to Mark Antony. Here was a fellow calculating his chances down to the last move, and not always concealing his nervousness at the strength of the odds against him. He was plainly apprehensive as he argued his way out of that tight blood-stained corner in the Capitol; and by showing the mob that he had many qualms about the whole business, he prepared them for the reading of the will by a pretended anxiety that hid his artfulness. Douglas Campbell's Caesar was a pompous shallow thing, asking to be deposed: and Helen Cherry and Yvonne Coulette presented a conventional pair of anxious Roman matrons. Casca is one of those minor characters on whom an enterprising actor can always place a splash of colour. Here William Squire touched him with a defensive smile that revealed more than it concealed.

The first performance of the Old Vic production of *King Henry VIII*, a salute to Coronation Year, was attended by Her Majesty the Queen and the Duke of Edinburgh. In it Tyrone Guthrie followed the lines of his Stratford Festival arrangement of the play in 1951. An extended description and critical analysis of this Stratford production was written by Muriel St Clare Byrne and appeared in *Shakespeare Survey*, 3. An excellent idea, this close and lengthy concentration on the details of a production: such analyses are useful as historical records. None of our practising dramatic critics can command the space necessary to deal so fully with a single production. At the Old Vic Tyrone Guthrie again took the bright way with the Tudors. He put some of the bishops on the bottle: furniture was kicked about in crises: tardy choristers scrambled frantically into their places: the King chaffed Cranmer at inappropriate moments. Some of the fun was forced; but no real harm was done to the play or the period by these latter-day antics: on the contrary, the Guthrie touch helped along a play that often lags if left entirely to itself. It was especially interesting to see a fresh team of actors fitting itself into the producer's fixed pattern. Here was an opportunity to observe how the individuality of the actor can change the colour and sometimes even twist the pattern of a play. The changes of hue and shape were here slight. The figure of Henry VIII is too solid and formidable to allow of much variation in the actor. Shakespeare's King is a stock figure. At the Old Vic, Paul Rogers found himself faced with the author's limited view of this many-sided monarch. He showed us the quick irascible temper, the sudden gushes of pawky humour; the autocrat battering bluntly at circumstance was in full view, but the man of alert and informed mind was missing for the very simple reason that Shakespeare himself had kept him out of the play. Nothing was missing, however, in Gwen Ffrangcon-Davies's performance of Queen Katharine. This is not usually considered a great part, but Miss Ffrangcon-Davies showed us how many qualities may be brought to it. Her steadfastness in trial was both stirring and moving, and the ringing challenge to her judges sounded magnificently. Her matronly dignity in court, her quiet resolution before the visiting cardinals, and her lingering faith in her cause even during those declining days at Kimbolton were beautifully suggested in a performance of much tenderness. Alexander Knox took an unexpected way with Wolsey, one that avoided the able administrator, the ecclesiastical fox, and the experienced diplomat, and achieved instead merely a cheerful ordinariness. Here was a smiling Wolsey, apparently highly pleased at having got on so well in the world. With the Cardinal in power, Mr Knox never came to grips: with the Cardinal in disgrace he was quite at ease. As Buckingham, Leo Genn went to the "long divorce of steel" simply and eloquently, carrying with him—as all good Buckinghams should—the full-flowing sympathy of the audience.

In July 1953, London was agreeably surprised by the visit of Sir Barry Jackson's Birmingham Repertory Theatre Company to the Old Vic in the three parts of *King Henry the Sixth*. The complete trilogy had already been performed in Birmingham as proof of Sir Barry's long-held conviction that all three parts are eminently actable. The event proved him to be right. As a play, Part 1 turned out to be the least satisfactory, but even here the players found ample raw material for acting. The producer, Douglas Seale, aimed at continuity, vigour, and clarity. He had no star actors to call upon, for Sir Barry has always encouraged youth and preferred zest and loyalty to the mannerisms of the famous. This young team, standing "like greyhounds in the slips, straining upon the start", went through the civil wars of York and Lancaster at a fine pounding pace. Youth rushed to the service of the young Shakespeare and showed these early neglected plays to be thoroughly stageworthy. Jack May, as the unhappy Henry, gathered round him the woes of one born to be king but resenting the destiny thrust upon him. This figure of the boy-king grew in pathos through the triple tragedy. Rosalind Boxall, as Margaret, came from France to be bride to the much-mocked monarch, and remained to develop into the fighting Amazon, an interpretation that grew in vituperative power as the trilogy unfolded. Edgar Wreford showed Richard Crookback limping towards the throne; Nancy Jackson presented the witch that Tudor audiences looked to see in Joan of Arc; and Alan Bridges, Richard Pasco, Bernard Hepton, John Arnatt and Alfred Burke adapted themselves to the barons, cardinals, dukes and commoners that turned Plantagenet England into a bear-garden. By masterly contrivance, Douglas Seale kept the changing pageant of war and riot on the move in a permanent setting. Under a gothic arch, designed by Finlay James, the councils and the conflicts, the triumphs and the defeats of the warring houses waxed and waned. The players spoke clearly and forthrightly. The producer had encouraged them to achieve a dramatic beat in this surge of action by remaining still when not actually speaking. This discipline achieved an undisturbed concentration upon the lines. The revival of this rarely performed trilogy was an example of the British repertory theatre at its best.

The 1953 Stratford Season included *The Merchant of Venice*, *Richard III*, *Antony and Cleopatra*, *The Taming of the Shrew* and *King Lear*. For Glen Byam Shaw's production of *Antony and Cleopatra*, Motley devised a pillared open space with steps to varying levels, a place of free air and a wide sky under which Peggy Ashcroft established Cleopatra's domination beyond all questioning. Miss Ashcroft is not regarded as a powerful actress, though she has always compelled attention by her quiet artistic authority. There was some question as to whether she would be able to achieve the courtesan who—as Quiller-Couch put it—was a courtesan in grain, born a liar, and born also royal Egypt: we must accept her, without faltering, for the naked, conscienceless, absolute, royal she-animal that she is. Cover the courtesan in mistaken ruth, and by so much you hide out of sight the secret of her majesty.

As soon as Miss Ashcroft began to speak we knew that she was going to justify Plutarch's assertion that "her voice and words were marvellous pleasant". To this she was soon adding a steady assertion of the wanton's will. This was no rip-roaring hussy, no spiteful kitten, but a mature woman who knew exactly what she was doing and exalted quietly in every moment of it. Again and again she unloosed those quiet gushes of seduction by which Antony is irretrievably overwhelmed. In the monument-scene Miss Ashcroft rode tragedy superbly to its climax, calm and lofty, almost detached in the royalty of her leave-taking. Michael Redgrave made a noble ruin of Antony. He suggested the shagginess, the sensuality, the incipient coarseness of the man who is running to seed. Here and there, he made fine and fervent play with those turbulent regrets for departed reputation: these recesses for remorse were made all the more effective by the abandon with which he went swinging back to Cleopatra: the completeness of his surrender indicated the fervour of the passion that carried him. Marius Goring, as Octavius Caesar, was the perfect patrician, with a mind and a will of his own; all brain and no heart. Only in his leave-taking of Octavia did this lawyer of the purple allow emotion to peep out. Harry Andrews made Enobarbus the prototype of the hardened campaigner of every war. Here was the careful watcher of generals in council, the deep drinker at banquets, the old soldier who walked in leather and lived by steel, the keeper of many a rendezvous with danger at a score of disputed barricades. Glen Byam Shaw achieved a fine production. His regulation of the busy traffic between Rome and Egypt was swift and orderly. The scene in which the sentries hear the unearthly music to which the god Hercules takes his departure from Antony, went for little: but in that notable recess for recreation in which the captains carouse aboard the galley and even Caesar unbends, the scene rose splendidly to riot.

George Devine's production of *The Taming of the Shrew* took a new way with the old farce. We were kept always informed that we were watching a play within a play, on this occasion in the handsome hall of an Elizabethan mansion, designed by Vivienne Kernot. The towers of Padua were to be glimpsed through the windows, but we were aware that the English alehouse was on the heath just around the corner. Marius Goring took a civilized way with Petruchio. Here was no heavyweight champion battling for a wench, but a fellow of some sensitiveness and perception. He had his own humorous values and his own sense of the dramatic. He gave the impression that Petruchio was watching this taming business with the anxious eye of an artist. When Katharina was unusually rampageous, he had a moment of hovering anxiety lest he should not be able to bring her to heel again. When he had so achieved, he let out his triumph on a fine flow of rolling speech. This was a whimsical trainer teaching his pupil how to behave for her own good. By the time that he and Katharina were on their way back to Padua and that perverse argument about the sun and the moon was being thrashed out, we realized that this couple had fallen deeply in love, and Petruchio's "Kiss me, Kate!" was not so much a command as an invitation. Yvonne Mitchell's Katharina consorted consistently with this particular Petruchio. She was attracted by her would-be trainer, and watched him with sulky feminine interest. When she realized that she was beginning to fall in love with this unpredictable but masterful gallant from Verona, she gave him a smile which promised that the armistice, once signed, would be permanent. By reducing the whip-cracking to a minimum and keeping the circus tricks at a reasonable distance from the customary bear-baiting, the producer touched the training quite firmly with romance. This new feeling for the old farce was most agreeable.

In spite of Lamb, Bradley, Hazlitt and other objectors, *King Lear* generally justifies its place in the theatre. Its demands are heavy, but when these are met generously, if not completely, the play gives a rich yield in power and poignancy. Sufficient of these came from George Devine's production at the Shakespeare Memorial Theatre to justify the play's place in the 1953 programme. *King Lear* has been produced a dozen times during the seventy-four years of Festival at Stratford. There is no point in comparing one production or one performance with another. Granville-Barker suggested that the greater the play the less likelihood there is of its perfect performing, yet strangely enough, the less need for it. Certain it is that not more than once in a generation there arrives an actor who can do justice to the whole of Lear. Success is therefore a matter of degree and Michael Redgrave achieved a fair degree at Stratford. His imposing presence and impressive figure set us anticipating an Olympian fury, instead of which Redgrave suggested fury held in check. This extremely intelligent actor can suggest an intensity of thought, an inner turmoil that indicates passion suppressed: but in *King Lear* we wait for passion to run in full flood. That Redgrave checked it was obviously a matter of choice, not of inability, for in the speech "I will do such things, what they are yet, I know not, but they shall be the terrors of the earth!" he voiced the full-throated anger and allowed us to see Lear as the oak riven by thunderbolts. With Lear mad and groping in the ruins of his former pride and state Redgrave was most moving. If the royal rage had been as vehement as the royal sorrows were intense this would have been a great Lear. It seems that most actors are limited either to the King rampant in wrath or to the King couchant in sorrow. Michael Redgrave chose the pathetic way yet gave hints that the other, too, was within his range.

George Devine used a full text and kept it moving. The setting by Robert Colquhoun recreated the customary megalithic landscape, but curved its columns into reminders of Henry Moore. Unless the scenery is fantasticated no artist can do much with those chilly windswept heights and those inhospitable castle gates round which the royal rages shrill and weep. That group of mad, half-mad or shamming mad people on the heath is one of the most pitiable assemblies ever contrived. Kent (reliably played by Harry Andrews) is a counter to the prevailing delirium: but in the Fool, Shakespeare created something much more subtle. The sorrows of the King are linked with the homelier lot of common humanity by the pathetic humour of the Fool. Marius Goring showed us this anxious, frightened jester fighting a losing battle. His attendance upon Lear was close, urgent and sympathetic. He delivered the pregnant sarcasms and the chiding homilies with an impertinent courage that gradually waned as his master's woes deepened. Slowly the pert spirit drooped; despair and silence enveloped it; all quips were finally muted and all mirth was forever quenched as he sank out of sight. Marius Goring's suggestion of gradual decline was delicately made in fine gradations of feeling. It has been suggested that the Fool can never be to us what he was to the play's first audience. To them he was a stage stock character. But at Stratford, Marius Goring gave this traditional figure a new authority by vesting him with that individuality which alone can quicken a legend to present life.

# THE YEAR'S CONTRIBUTIONS TO
# SHAKESPEARIAN STUDY

## I. CRITICAL STUDIES

### reviewed by CLIFFORD LEECH

"Probably", says R. W. Babcock,[1] "the most important type of modern criticism of Shakespeare is historical criticism." There is indeed no denying that it can help us to understand the meaning of the plays; but when he goes on to describe it as a co-operative activity, as if all its practitioners were at one in their methods and aims, and to speak as if our knowledge of the Elizabethan scene were growing ever surer, we must marvel at his ability to reconcile contradictions and to give his blessing to conjecture. Such claims, too, may overlook the special contribution made to his immediate world by any artist of stature: he will inevitably think in terms of that world, and if he is a dramatist he must work through other men, his actors, whose responses are not likely to be much out of the ordinary; he must offer an interpretation of living that can be graspable, if not fully comprehensible, to an audience haphazardly assembled; but ultimately he will possess standing because he is not quite as others are. He will offer more than is expected, more perhaps than his very interpreters realize. In the last few years a remembrance of this may have led us to some loss of faith in 'historical criticism'. In so far as it establishes fact (as, for example, in the history of the dramatic companies), or cogently suggests the prevalence of certain thought-patterns or forms of technique, we do of course still welcome it with full hearts. Yet we come also to value the critics who use these findings while at the same time realizing that Shakespeare is so much our concern because of his difference from his fellows, that he is not merely a skilled expositor of current Elizabethan notions, that no single critic can tell us all that the plays contain. When Joseph Gregor[2] tells us:

Die Möglichkeit, die Angst des Daseins zu überwinden, die Reinheit der Gesinnung bis auf das Letzte zu bewahren, und sei es mit der Gefahr des Untergangs, dem *Geist*, dem massgebendsten Licht über den Menschen, wieder sein Recht auf Erden zu geben—das ist uns Hamlet,

we may feel that this is indeed a Hamlet for the moment, but shall also recognize that the personal interpretation derives in part from the inexhaustible richness of the play Shakespeare made. So too we may welcome Kenneth Muir's[3] critical but generally sympathetic account of certain Freudian interpretations of the plays, for in its better examples this approach puts at our disposal a newer and sometimes clearer terminology. From a different standpoint, L. C. Knights[4] has noted that the political ideas in *Julius Caesar* and *Coriolanus* are to be related not only to

---

[1] 'Historical Criticism of Shakespeare', *Modern Language Quarterly*, XIII (March 1952), 6–20.

[2] 'Was ist uns Hamlet?', *Shakespeare-Jahrbuch*, LXXXVII–LXXXVIII (1952), 9–25.

[3] 'Some Freudian Interpretations of Shakespeare', *Proceedings of the Leeds Philosophical Society (Literary and Historical Section)*, VII (July 1952), 43–52.

[4] 'Shakespeare and Political Wisdom: A Note on the Personalism of *Julius Caesar* and *Coriolanus*', *Sewanee Review*, LXI (Winter 1953), 43–55.

Elizabethan theory but to perennial truths concerning social organization, in particular to the vitiation of political behaviour when human beings are regarded only as ciphers or groups. Of wider scope is the British Academy lecture of H. V. D. Dyson,[1] who gives a sensitive presentation of Shakespeare's tragic world, bringing out the affinity it seems to possess with our own experience, when that is most organized and seen most clearly. Here indeed there is a scrupulous refusal to impose on Shakespeare's tragedies a neat doctrinal cloak.

But these contributions are of a special and limited character. An extended or detailed study of any aspect of Shakespeare's work must today be securely based on patient investigation. Too often, however, one's own or another's *trouvaille* presents itself as a talisman. Then 'historical criticism' may claim that it offers the last word, it will correct our errors and bid us have done with dreams. Of recent examples of this kind of writing, the most notable is Henri Fluchère's *Shakespeare, dramaturge élisabéthain*, now translated.[2] In this book there is much that is admirable, for when free to use his own judgement the writer is excellently capable of seeing the complexities of Shakespearian writing: he knows there is no simple explanation to be offered as a 'meaning' of *Henry V*, or the light and dark comedies, or *Coriolanus*, and he is well-informed on Seneca and Machiavelli, and sensitive to Ford. But his reading of recent criticism has been inevitably selective and he has found its air of authority difficult to withstand. He is lavish of space in attacking the study of 'characters', fails to distinguish adequately between the handling of character in *The Two Gentlemen* and in *Lear*, and yet at times he can respond to a dramatic figure in a way not so different from Bradley's. Anxious to see Shakespeare in his age, Fluchère is yet impatient of research: perhaps that is why he can tell us that "Shakespeare began to be bowdlerized in the eighteenth century" (forgetting the Restoration prunings) and can imply that the Swan drawing shows an inner-stage. Of previous criticism he can wave aside much: until some twenty-five years ago "Shakespearian criticism...had made no serious progress since Coleridge". And though good things are likely to come up at any moment, we have also to read that Gloucester's blinding is but horror for horror's sake, that apparently Cleopatra is to have her wished eternity of love, and that perhaps Prospero will take Caliban to Milan. The book offers a clear demonstration both of the critic's need of help from the historical investigator, and of the dangers of over-rapid historical generalization. It is only fair to add that the translation is nowhere felicitous and at times falls into grotesque error.

There is much more consistency of method in J. V. Cunningham's examination of Shakespearian tragedy.[3] He explores the meaning of 'tragedy' from Donatus onwards, and has an interesting list of Shakespearian uses of 'tragedy' and 'tragic', arriving, however, at the disappointing equation of tragedy and death. Doubtless the two notions were closely intertwined for the Elizabethans, but Cunningham does not allow for the emergence, during composition, of an effect or attitude not dictated by convention. He shows Shakespeare using Thomistic machinery in displaying a character coming to a point of decision, but leaves us strangely dissatisfied when he presents Hamlet as wholly resolute and reasonable: in Act v he is forced to see him abandoning all rational schemes and relying on "the tide of circumstance which is the Special Providence of God", which could be interpreted as an argument against the rationality

---

[1] *The Emergence of Shakespeare's Tragedy* (Geoffrey Cumberlege, 1953).
[2] *Shakespeare* (Longmans, Green, 1953). The French edition was reviewed in *Shakespeare Survey*, 3.
[3] *Woe or Wonder. The Emotional Effect of Shakespearean Tragedy* (Denver: The University of Denver Press, 1951).

Cunningham has previously displayed for our admiration. What he has to say about the tragic function of "resignation to death in the Christian sense" would be more satisfactory if he took *Othello* into account. The book would more surely help us to understand the Elizabethans if it did not try to keep the poet's imagination within a Thomist cage. There is a curious reference to "Brutus' suicide" at the end of *Lucrece*.

Similar simplifications are to be found in several short studies. Karl F. Thompson[1] sees in the romantic comedies a use of ideas and devices taken from the courtly love code. This, Thompson feels, raises the status of the plays. We may, however, decide that their continuing vitality is due rather to our surprising impression that 'real' people are involved in the action. S. L. Bethell[2] interestingly sees Shakespeare unique among writers of histories in making his comic manner serve as a vehicle for the governing idea of the play, the logical fallacies used by disordered persons underlining their function in the dramatic structure. From this perceptive beginning, he proceeds to a remarkable presentation of Falstaff as a hypocritical Puritan. Similarly, in examining the "diabolic images" in *Othello*,[3] he sees that play in morality terms: it shows a temptation and fall, ending in fact in Othello's damnation. Quieting our doubts, he tells us that Elizabethans expected most people to be damned. Bethell is not afraid of consistency, and we must assume that Brutus and Antony too are, in Shakespeare's mind, among the damned: like Othello, they killed themselves. It seems strange, therefore, that the plays should end with the expression of high admiration for all these characters. It would be better to recognize a human inconsistency in Shakespeare's thought than to christianize him to the point of monstrosity. A morality contention between Justice and Love is presented as the key to *Othello* by Miss Winifred M. T. Nowottny.[4] Love, she suggests, should override Justice, as faith should override reason. Othello's tragedy is that he demands from Love the testimony that is the concern only of Justice. This interpretation does not seem to distort the play, but we may doubt whether any Jacobean tragedy can be presented in these well-ordered terms. Francis Fergusson[5] sees the first three acts of *Measure for Measure* as a series of masquerades, the last two as presenting "the underlying truth of the human situation", and finds in this the explanation of the change in style. In Act v, he tells us, we have first a series of trials according to the letter of the law: then, with the reappearance of Claudio, 'mercy' operates. The Duke represents Shakespeare, who probably played him, perhaps before an Inns of Court audience. Lucio cannot be forgiven, perhaps because he represents "treachery" and has been "using his imagination in the service of darkness". One wonders what would have happened to Claudio without Lucio's help, what the connexion is between the Duke's 'mercy' and his apparent acquiescence in Angelo's rigour until Isabella's virtue comes in question, what explanation there is for the sadistic touches ("this new-married man") from the hand of mercy. This might be regarded as an extreme example of interpretation *via* hypothesis, were it not for S. F. Johnson's[6] piece of argumentation that Hamlet came in Act v to a Christian acceptance of the workings of Providence. Whether or not

---

[1] 'Shakespeare's Romantic Comedies', *PMLA*, LXVII (December 1952), 1079–93.

[2] 'The Comic Element in Shakespeare's Histories', *Anglia*, LXXI (1952), 82-101.

[3] 'Shakespeare's Imagery: The Diabolic Images in *Othello*', *Shakespeare Survey*, 5 (1952), 62–80.

[4] 'Justice and Love in *Othello*', *University of Toronto Quarterly*, XXI (July 1952), 330–44.

[5] 'Philosophy and Theatre in *Measure for Measure*', *Kenyon Review*, XIV (Winter 1952), 103–20.

[6] 'The Regeneration of Hamlet. A Reply to E. M. W. Tillyard with a Counter-Proposal', *Shakespeare Quarterly*, III (July 1952), 187–207.

the conclusion is justified, we need have no hesitation in rejecting the props with which it is here supported. Johnson tells us that Hamlet and Horatio "reach a joint conclusion" in v, ii that Claudius must be killed: let him look again at Horatio's speeches. Hamlet's behaviour at Ophelia's grave is not to be taken into account, because "the passion there is personal and not in direct relation to his chief aim": thus Johnson disposes of the clearest indication that the old Hamlet is back in Denmark. When Hamlet speaks to Osric about the duel, he says "the King" but means 'God' (a secret, doubtless, to everyone until Johnson found the key). Hamlet is sure he will win the duel because Providence has so decreed: in the text we read, "since he went into France, I have been in continual practice". If all this were offered as a personal fancy, it would do no harm; but it suggests a forcing of the issue in the interest of *Gleichschaltung*.

The period under review has, however, seen the appearance of a number of studies where the Shakespearian complexity is recognized. This, indeed, provides the basis for Robert Fricker's [1] treatment of characterization. In broad outline, Fricker sees Shakespeare as moving from effects of simple contrast (through confusion of one character with another, as in *The Comedy of Errors* and *Twelfth Night*, through disguise, hidden origin, deception) to a 'polarity' which arises from a contradiction deep-set in a character's being. The distinction between contrast and polarity is itself not simple, for the pretences of Beatrice in her antagonism to Benedick and of Prince Hal in his good-humour at the Boar's Head represent also genuine inclinations. Later Shakespeare draws characters that, either through changes of mood, changes of personality, or character-development, display to us different facets of their being in different parts of the play. Fricker draws attention to Montaigne's realization of the contradictions within himself, and on this and on medieval notions of inner conflict he bases an elaborate structure composed of different types of contrast and polarity. He indicates that there is much overlapping, yet the planning of his book suggests an orderly pigeon-holing of characters difficult to credit. Moreover, he leaves us with a sense that the mystery remains: how, with so many variations in behaviour and outlook, does a Shakespearian character yet give us the sense of an organic being? Frequently Fricker points out that the contrasts and polarities do not destroy psychological verisimilitude, but the plain statement seems only to by-pass the problem. It may well be, as appeared from J. I. M. Stewart's *Character and Motive in Shakespeare*, that the sense of wholeness is to be explained only in terms of more recent notions of psychological possibility, and Fricker has done well to draw attention to the extraordinary range of conduct and attitude within a single character. Where his passion for orderliness takes him too far is perhaps in such cases as Cloten and Polonius, where Shakespeare may well have used the figure variously, having a different purpose to serve in different scenes. This is a substantial book, and it would take much space to indicate Fricker's comments on a considerable number of major characters: not all would win general assent, but incontestably there is a free recognition here of the God's plenty that has kept Shakespeare on our stage. Moreover, this critic sees the principle of contrast as an essential part of Shakespeare's dramatic structure, thus relating his characterization to his whole dramatic method and to his view of the nature of things. There are curious blemishes in the treatment of Shakespeare's successors: Webster is quite inadequately mentioned, and wrong dates are given for Marston's *Antonio* and Chapman's *Bussy*. But this is a book to be welcomed, and one hopes that an English translation will appear.

[1] *Kontrast und Polarität in den Charakterbildern Shakespeares* (Bern: A. Francke Ag., 1951).

Ernst Theodor Sehrt[1] has devoted a thoroughly documented work to Shakespeare's presentation of forgiveness and mercy. While cautious in attributing particular religious notions to the dramatist, Sehrt sees in him an early preoccupation with the idea of forgiveness, which becomes gradually more serious until, in *Measure for Measure*, it is an essential part of the play's thought. The forgiveness of Proteus and Bertram is, he thinks, perfunctory, a convenient means of achieving a fortunate ending: on the other hand, *Measure for Measure* and *The Tempest* are plays in which forgiveness is central. The handling of individual plays is shrewd and well-balanced. Sehrt is willing, for example, to see inconsistencies in *Measure for Measure*, and brings out the unchristian complacency of the Venetians in their 'forgiveness' of Shylock. But perhaps the most fruitful part of the book is its thorough investigation of the idea of forgiveness in antiquity, the Middle Ages, and the sixteenth century. In particular, the demonstration of a greater sternness in the sixteenth-century moralities, influenced by the reformers, is an important contribution to our understanding of pre-Shakespearian drama. The kind of Christian feeling found in certain of Shakespeare's plays is seen to contribute to, rather than explain, their atmosphere. Sehrt admits, moreover, that in no Shakespearian play is there a satisfactory consideration of the place of mercy in a Christian commonwealth. As in Fricker's book, there is no attempt here to apply a simple formula. We must hope that this too will be widely read.

Among other general studies there are books by the Editor of this *Survey*, by F. P. Wilson and H. Röhrman. Nicoll's[2] primary concern is to introduce the general reader to the various approaches to Shakespearian study that have been followed in recent years, and justice is widely and manifestly done within a very few pages. Wilson[3] and Röhrman[4] have considered Shakespeare along with Marlowe. In his comments on Shakespeare, Wilson startles and convinces when he says "that for all we know there were no popular plays on English history before the Armada and that Shakespeare may have been the first to write one". This may be the most important sentence written on Shakespeare during the year. Röhrman's approach to Renaissance drama is to see it as reflecting the Renaissance passion for individual power, which is for him the root of much later trouble. He is aware of a sceptical element in Marlowe, sceptical of his own rebelliousness, and he sees *Hamlet*, *Troilus* and *Macbeth* as, in different ways, comments on the evil of power. His interpretation romanticizes Troilus, and takes away a good deal of Hamlet's liveliness. Röhrman shows an independence of mind, and a readiness of response, but his dislike of the Renaissance determines too abruptly his attitude towards the plays. Here also should be noted three articles: R. A. Foakes[5] valuably indicates much current confusion in the use of the term 'image', makes an important distinction between the 'subject-matter' and the 'object-matter' of an image, sees dramatic imagery as also including visual and auditory effects, iterative words, and historical and geographical placing, and keeps foremost in his mind the effect of the play as a play; T. W. Baldwin[6] has noted the recurrence in Shakespeare of the image 'nature's moulds' and finds that its development confirms the accepted chronological order for

[1] *Vergebung und Gnade bei Shakespeare* (Stuttgart: K. F. Koehler, 1952).
[2] *Shakespeare* (Methuen, 1952).
[3] *Marlowe and the Early Shakespeare* (Oxford: Clarendon Press, 1953).
[4] *Marlowe and Shakespeare. A Thematic Exposition of Some of their Plays* (Arnhem: Van Loghum Slaterus, 1952).
[5] 'Suggestions for a New Approach to Shakespeare's Imagery', *Shakespeare Survey*, 5 (1952), 81–92.
[6] 'Nature's Moulds', *Shakespeare Quarterly*, III (July 1952), 237–41.

the plays in which it occurs; Rigoberto Cordero y Leon [1] has explored the atmosphere of Shake-spearian tragedy and its concern with death.

In addition to Bethell's article noted above, there have been several concerned with the histories. Georges A. Bonnard [2] has emphasized Richard II's pleasure in acting a part, while Leonard F. Dean [3] claims that Bolingbroke too is a persistent actor. Dean relates the behaviour of Richard and Bolingbroke to More's comparison between life and the theatre. The sickness in the body politic is symbolized by its theatrical inclinations: there is a dualism in the pretence and the consciousness of it. Dean is less convincing when he claims that Henry V "will miraculously resolve the dualism in the theatrical state". W. Gordon Zeeveld [4] sees Hotspur and Falstaff as representing, not excess and defect of honour, but a false honour and a rational denial of that honour. Hal's "food for worms" (a sympathetic comment on Hotspur's death) is seen as an echo of Falstaff's "food for powder", each implying the falsity of Hotspur's 'honour'. The suggestion is useful, if we do not see it as providing the 'meaning' of the play. Samuel B. Hemingway [5] argues that the 'Stoll-Falstaff' appears on the stage, the 'Morgann-Bradley-Falstaff' in the study, and that our reactions to Hal are similarly variable. But our attitudes to the characters are surely complex however we meet them, and the article does not recognize any difference between the effects of Part I and Part II. Stuart M. Tave [6] has provided useful comments on Morgann's predecessors and influence.

Some of the comedies have received special notice. J. W. Lever [7] sees the opposition of Shylock and Portia as representing a conflict between Usury and Love. He notes the many shortcomings of the Venetians, and interprets the bond as an application to usury of the matter of Jacob's sheep —an ironic twist arising out of the debate in I, iii. Norman Nathan [8] replies that this strain is not dominant in the play, which has much of the fortuitousness characteristic of romantic comedy. Yet our discomfort in the play may arise from a sense that something important is in debate: Sehrt, as noticed above, sees the treatment of mercy here as inadequate and fragmentary, and the views of Lever and Nathan can be reconciled if we admit a confusion in the play. Kerby Neill [9] takes on the defence of Hero's Claudio, pleading for him as a genuine lover. Though the argumentation is skilful, we may yet be puzzled by Claudio's question about Hero's money: it may have been the usual thing with Elizabethans, but why does Shakespeare go out of his way to tell us of it here? Neill further says it is the belief in the slander, not the repudiation, that is the heart of the matter, but we may regard as equally important the extraordinary callousness of Claudio's and Pedro's behaviour after Hero's apparent death. Probably Shakespeare did not give Claudio so much attention as his commentators have done, but when for a moment he

[1] 'Figuras de Shakespeare', *Annales de la Universidad de Cuenca*, VII (October–December 1951), 69–83.

[2] 'The Actor in Richard II', *Shakespeare-Jahrbuch*, LXXXVII–LXXXVIII (1952), 87–101.

[3] '*Richard II*: The State and the Image of the Theater', *PMLA*, LXVII (March 1952), 211–18.

[4] '"Food for Powder"—"Food for Worms"', *Shakespeare Quarterly*, III (July 1952), 249–53.

[5] 'On Behalf of that Falstaff', *ibid.* III (October 1952), 307–11.

[6] 'Corbyn Morris: Falstaff, Humor, and Comic Theory in the Eighteenth Century', *Modern Philology*, L (November 1952), 102–15; 'Notes on the Influence of Morgann's Essay on Falstaff', *Review of English Studies*, n.s., III (October 1952), 371–5.

[7] 'Shylock, Portia and the Values of Shakespearian Comedy', *Shakespeare Quarterly*, III (October 1952), 383–6.

[8] 'Rejoinder to Mr Lever's "Shylock, Portia, and the Values of Shakespearian Comedy"', *ibid.* 386–8.

[9] 'More Ado about Claudio: An Acquittal for the Slandered Groom', *ibid.* III (April 1952), 91–107.

considered the man he perhaps did not much like him. L. C. Knights[1] links *Troilus* in its general tone with *2 Henry IV*, and offers an unusually convincing contrast between Greeks and Trojans, the Greeks standing for an impersonal "reason", the Trojans for "intuition". But both, he says, are presented critically. Though the dramatist's approach was "not philosophical", he was at this time seeing human experience in relation to large concepts. Less thoughtfully, Robert K. Presson[2] presents this play as showing reason temporarily overcome by passion: at the end, he thinks, Troilus "is completely enlightened" and Ulysses's wisdom becomes, for Achilles, "the midwife to his better self". It was thus, one presumes, his better self that murdered Hector.

*Hamlet* and *Othello* have received more attention than the other tragedies. William Empson[3] has written a highly speculative article, based on the theory (supported apparently only by extant references to the *Ur-Hamlet*) that revenge-plays were commonly laughed at around 1600: Shakespeare therefore in his first draft made his hero unable to explain the delay which the audience regarded as the ridiculous thing in the *genre*: Hamlet lecturing the players turns topsy-turvy the over-theatrical figure that, as a revenger, he inevitably was. The play, says Empson, was further complicated by additions in a second version (1601). The length of the extant play is due to the fact that it was played at varying lengths according to the audience's response on a particular occasion: "The soliloquy 'How All Occasions' is a sort of encore planned in case an audience refuses to let the star go." In this whimsical affair there are one or two interesting points. Empson notes Hamlet's sureness of his power in the "How all occasions" soliloquy, though his comment that here Hamlet was "(presumably) surrounded by guards" is not borne out by the Q2 stage-directions. More striking is the comment on Hamlet's punctilious behaviour to Laertes after the graveyard-scene: Empson observes that Hamlet there seems indifferent to the deaths of Laertes's father and sister. Brents Stirling[4] sees in Hamlet a realization of "an incapacity for emotion" and a "recoiling...from a capacity for over-emotion". Hamlet, he shows, reproaches himself for both dullness and display. This explains the Ghost's coming to whet his "almost blunted purpose" just when he has been showing himself apparently most active; it underlines the futility of his graveyard-ranting. The article well brings out the barriers between Hamlet and other people, which coexist with his striving after courtesy. Yet we are left seeking the explanation for this 'polarity', which apparently had not always been evident in the man, and Stirling has to regard the last scene as a mere winding-up. William Robbins[5] sees the Queen, Ophelia and Horatio, representing normality, juxtaposed with three figures "obsessed, distorted, fanatical"—the Ghost, the King, Hamlet. The first group is led to destruction (or, in Horatio's case, to a thought of suicide) through its involvement with the second group. Yet, in a deeper sense, Hamlet belongs to both groups because of the conflict within him. The argument is strained in its use of Horatio's impulse to suicide, and we have the impression that Robbins has dug into his own mind for this neat pattern. Unlike some attempts at 'meaning', however, it does not damage the play. Hardin Craig[6] presents Hamlet as acting in the capacity

[1] '"Troilus and Cressida" Again', *Scrutiny*, XVIII (Autumn 1951), 144–57.

[2] 'The Structural Use of a Traditional Theme in *Troilus and Cressida*', *Philological Quarterly*, XXXI (April 1952), 180–8.

[3] '*Hamlet* When New', *Sewanee Review*, LXI (Winter 1953), 15–42.

[4] 'Theme and Character in *Hamlet*', *Modern Language Quarterly*, XIII (December 1952), 323–32.

[5] '*Hamlet* as Allegory', *University of Toronto Quarterly*, XXI (April 1952), 217–23.

[6] 'A Cutpurse of the Empire: On Shakespeare Cosmology', *A Tribute to George Coffin Taylor*, ed. Arnold Williams (University of North Carolina Press, 1952), pp. 3–16.

of a prince, dealing justice for the good of the state: inevitably, Craig is puzzled as to why he has to die, like an unprincely revenger. Miss Josephine Waters Bennett[1] makes a strong case for seeing the *Ad Demonicum* of Isocrates as the source of Polonius's advice to Laertes. As the original was well-known in Tudor schools, Polonius is not here speaking out of character, but as an old man reciting precepts known to every schoolboy. This is a useful article, which suddenly takes our breath away when we read: "Shakespeare was concerned...to minimize, as far as possible, Hamlet's crime in killing him." Also on *Hamlet*, we should note Max Lüthi's[2] interesting comparison of the play with a Gascon folk-tale taken down in the nineteenth century. The articles on *Othello* are slighter: John Robert Moore,[3] replying to the contention of H. J. Webb,[4] defends Othello and Cassio as soldiers, largely by imagining a background of event for which the play gives little warrant and by overlooking Othello's yielding to Desdemona's petition for Cassio; Elmer Edgar Stoll[5] protests against Theodore Spencer's view[6] that Iago is a 'malcontent', finding his manner of public speech and conduct altogether different from Hamlet's and Malevole's: yet Iago has a certain roughness of tongue, and he certainly views himself as a 'displaced person': Stoll's argument seems to depend on an assumption that Elizabethan 'types' were self-contained, which Spencer was careful to warn us against; Philip Butcher[7] suggests that 'Moor' and 'negro' were interchangeable terms for Shakespeare, referring to the Peacham drawing of Aaron and distinguishing Aaron and Othello from other North Africans in the plays: one is not quite convinced that this distinction was clear to Shakespeare; Ernest Brennecke[8] notes the modifications that Shakespeare apparently made in the traditional 'Willow Song' and the skilful and moving interruptions of Desdemona's singing; Michel Poirier[9] reconsiders the time-problem in *Othello*, noting Johnson's reference to it but forgetting Rymer's. On *Lear*, D. A. Traversi[10] has noted the anticipations of later event in the dialogue of the first two acts, and has interesting observations on Lear's not being alone on the heath (in contrast to Timon) and on the triangle of ideas represented by the Fool's 'head', 'heart' and 'codpiece'. John F. Danby[11] presents *Lear* as a demonstration of Christian patience, and thus perhaps confuses part of Shakespeare's material with the whole of his effect. One is surprised to find him seeing the "punishments" in this play (including Gloucester's) as agreeing "in proportion and quality" with the sins. Miss E. Catherine Dunn[12] sees the storm in *Lear*, III, ii, as the expression of an Empedoclean conflict of Love and Hate, precipitated by ingratitude. Rightly noting that Lear invokes destruction on himself and on the cosmos, she misses in the second apostrophe his note of protest against his own suffering.

[1] 'Characterisation in Polonius' Advice to Laertes', *Shakespeare Quarterly*, IV (January 1953), 3–9.

[2] 'Hamlet in der Gascogne', *Shakespeare-Jahrbuch*, LXXXVII–LXXXVIII (1952), 48–57.

[3] 'Othello, Iago, and Cassio as Soldiers', *Philological Quarterly*, XXXI (April 1952), 189–94.

[4] Noted in *Shakespeare Survey*, 6.

[5] 'Iago not a "Malcontent"', *Journal of English and Germanic Philology*, LI (April 1952), 163–7.

[6] 'The Elizabethan Malcontent', *Joseph Quincy Adams Memorial Studies* (1948), pp. 523–35.

[7] 'Othello's Racial Identity', *Shakespeare Quarterly*, III (July 1952), 244–7.

[8] '"Nay, That's Not Next!" The Significance of Desdemona's "Willow Song"', *ibid.* IV (January 1953), 35–8.

[9] 'Le "Double Temps" dans *Othello*', *Etudes Anglaises*, V (May 1952), 107–16.

[10] '"King Lear" (I)', *Scrutiny*, XIX (October 1952), 43–64; '"King Lear" (II)', *ibid.* (Winter 1952–3), 126–42.

[11] *Poets on Fortune's Hill. Studies in Sidney, Shakespeare, Beaumont & Fletcher* (Faber and Faber, 1952). Other aspects of this book are referred to in the following paragraphs and in the next section.

[12] 'The Storm in *King Lear*', *Shakespeare Quarterly*, III (October 1952), 329–33.

R. M. Smith[1] enjoys quoting some fierce denunciations of Goneril's steward, and shows that he was, in a sense, for Shakespeare a human being. There is an article on *Macbeth* from William Empson,[2] who argues against the view that the first two acts have been seriously cut. He claims that, as it stands, the play is psychologically acceptable. The element of confusion is needed: "So far from being a cut version of a tidy historical play now unfortunately lost, it is a rather massive effort, very consistently carried out, to convey the immense confusion in which these historical events actually occur." This is convincing, but what remains puzzling is that, while we need for the play a sense of the 'normality' that Macbeth destroys (which is indeed referred to in "This castle hath a pleasant seat" and in Macbeth's mention of "troops of friends"), we never in the early scenes feel that the world shown is other than bloody and confused. This may point to a dichotomy in the thought of the play: on the one side, Macbeth the destroyer of order; on the other, Macbeth an inhabitant of a disordered world (like Webster's Vittoria), rashly trying to overtop others. This may explain why Dover Wilson feels it necessary to imagine the play as more deliberate, less chaotic, than its present form allows.

There has been little separate comment on the Roman plays. John F. Danby[3] has written a judicious chapter on *Antony and Cleopatra*, in which he shows that Shakespeare's purpose is not to be found in an easy direction of sympathy either to Rome or to Egypt. We cannot resolve the play's dichotomy, he says, "unless we are prepared to take the delusions of either party as a resolution". One may feel a little uncertain when he speaks of Shakespeare as here deliberately constructing "a world without a Cordelia", deliberately excising "the Christian core of his thought". It would make the play into a carefully planned exercise, with Shakespeare above this particular battle. Significantly, perhaps, Danby misses the sense of the grotesque which is as strong here as in any tragedy and which hints at Shakespeare's involvement and concern. Irving Ribner[4] presents Coriolanus as a character drawn with an extreme consistency, as he never escapes from pride, never acquires true vision. Ribner sees this as marking an advance in Shakespeare's artistry, but it is perhaps Coriolanus's rigidity of character—the almost complete absence of 'polarity', in Fricker's sense—that repels many audiences. Edwin Honig[5] sees *Sejanus* and *Coriolanus* as 'tragical satires', and makes the point that Jonson, in his final picture of the mob, carries the satire home to his audience.

Several articles have dealt with one or other of the romances, and may thus help us to avoid the simple formula that claims to dispose of the whole group. *Pericles*, according to J. M. S. Tompkins[6] in a sensitive examination of the play, is a study of patience—not stoical, but gentle and accepting even when most moved. In the plays that followed, he suggests, this theme is repeated but in a subordinate place. He notes that Pericles does not have to learn this virtue, it is part of his given nature: this, it might be added, links him with those characters in the later plays whose behaviour is, through much of the action, independent of external influence. Adrien Bonjour[7] is concerned with Shakespeare's unobtrusive preparation of his audience for the

[1] 'A Good Word for Oswald', *A Tribute to George Coffin Taylor*, pp. 62–6.

[2] 'Dover Wilson on *Macbeth*', *Kenyon Review*, XIV (Winter 1952), 84–102.     [3] *Op. cit.*

[4] 'The Tragedy of *Coriolanus*', *English Studies*, XXXIV (February 1953), 1–9.

[5] '*Sejanus* and *Coriolanus*: A Study in Alienation', *Modern Language Quarterly*, XII (December 1951), 407–21.

[6] 'Why Pericles?', *Review of English Studies*, n.s., III (October 1952), 315–24.

[7] 'The Final Scene of *The Winter's Tale*', *English Studies*, XXXIII (October 1952), 193–208.

statue-scene in *The Winter's Tale*, with the much greater neatness of construction in the play as a whole than Shakespeare found in Greene, and with the difficulty of accepting Wilson Knight's view of the statue-scene as a symbolic expression of immortality, which hardly coheres with the moving reference to the ageing of Hermione. Bonamy Dobrée[1] suggests that *The Tempest* differs from the other romances in its perfunctory treatment of forgiveness and reconciliation. The themes that here interested Shakespeare most were those of reality and appearance, destiny and freedom. Dobrée warns us against dissecting, and rightly draws attention to the sense of fusion that the play gives. It is evident, however, that some passages in the play jar upon him. The romances as a whole are the concern of John F. Danby[2] and D. S. Bland.[3] Danby parts company with some recent critics in seeing these plays as less serious than their predecessors, having 'an *ironia* of their own'. His picture of a relaxed Shakespeare is not, however, completely maintained: he sees well enough how important a threat the plain words of Boult can be. Bland offers an embroidery on Wilson Knight's frame, seeing the storm in these plays as "the means by which the agent of regeneration is taken out of the tragic centre and set apart until the time is ripe for her return". The article includes the statements that "the hero is purged of his error by suffering, as Pericles is" (what error, one wonders), that Prospero's art destroys the wickedness in Antonio (a point on which Shakespeare is reticent), and that in the tragedies, unlike the romances, "we are not immediately conscious of a larger society being involved".

There are two interesting articles on the non-dramatic poems. Robert P. Miller[4] sees the Courser-Jennet episode in *Venus and Adonis* not only as an ironic presentment of romantic courtship, with the implication that it is a disguise for lust, but as emphasizing the irrationality of the whole procedure: moreover, the use of the word "breeder" for the Jennet implies that, in her following of instinct, she stands above Venus, who in full consciousness seeks only enjoyment. Miller recognizes that Shakespeare's presentation of the episode is "delightfully humorous", and that the poem is by no means didactic in tone. J. V. Cunningham[5] convincingly traces the imagery of *The Phoenix and the Turtle* to the scholastic presentation of the doctrine of the Trinity, noting also the use of "essence" as 'intellectual soul' in *Measure for Measure* and *The Two Gentlemen*.

A special aspect of the history of Shakespeare criticism is surveyed by Robert Gale Noyes.[6] He gives a spirited account of the references to Shakespeare and Shakespearian performances (London and provincial) in the novels of 1740–80. The novelists' attitude to Shakespeare reflects that of the more formal critics, though we must agree with Noyes that the novelists often entertain us more successfully. George Winchester Stone, Jr,[7] has continued a similar inquiry into eighteenth-century periodicals. Heinrich Straumann,[8] Emil Staiger,[9] and Guido

---

[1] 'The Tempest', *Essays and Studies*, n.s., v (1952), pp. 13–25.  [2] *Op. cit.*

[3] 'The Heroine and the Sea: An Aspect of Shakespeare's Last Plays', *Essays in Criticism*, III (January 1953), 39–44.

[4] 'Venus, Adonis, and the Horses', *ELH*, XIX (December 1952), 249–64.

[5] '"Essence" and the *Phoenix and Turtle*', ibid. 265–76.

[6] *The Thespian Mirror. Shakespeare in the Eighteenth-Century Novel* (Providence, Rhode Island: Brown University, 1953).

[7] 'Shakespeare in the Periodicals 1700–1740. A Study of the Growth of a Knowledge of the Dramatist in the Eighteenth Century', *Shakespeare Quarterly*, III (October 1952), 313–28.

[8] 'Shakespeare in England', *Hesperia*, III (October 1952), 173–82.

[9] 'Shakespeare in Deutschland', ibid. 183–90.

K

Calgari[1] have traced Shakespeare's influence on critical ideas in England, Germany, and France and Italy respectively. R. W. Zandvoort[2] has surveyed Shakespeare criticism in this century: he observes that each generation seems to approach Shakespeare as if his plays are related to the most esteemed literary *genre* of the time, so that for the Victorians the plays were hardly distinguishable from novels, for the 'new critics' they are close to twentieth-century poetry. In particular he praises Granville-Barker, who saw the plays as belonging to the theatre, "niet het wolken-koekoeksheim der moderne pseudo-mystiek".

## 2. SHAKESPEARE'S LIFE, TIMES AND STAGE

### reviewed by HAROLD JENKINS

Books of the past year include one, by M. M. Reese,[3] which covers the whole of our field—life, times and stage—in a manner which seeks to "mediate" the conclusions of scholarship "in terms acceptable to ordinary men". The author shows that he can do this lucidly, readably, and, except in the rather unnecessary chapter on the University Wits, without superficiality. Though taking most of his facts at second hand, he interprets them with skill and judgement. His sane balance in many controversial matters is shown especially in the biographical sections. Arguing the probability of Shakespeare's grammar-school education, he reminds us of the lack of evidence for it; he reviews the theories about the "hidden" years without adding to them; a first-rate reconstruction of Shakespeare's working life as playwright for an acting company ends with a sensitive recognition of how little as well as how much in his work this can explain. All the same, more than a little learning does not entirely avoid the dangers of relying upon secondary authorities: it cannot have been Peele himself who specified the three vials of blood and the sheep's gather called for by the playhouse 'plot' of one of his plays, and the occurrence of variants in the First Folio does not show it to have been poorly printed by the standards of its day. Some slight doubts about the author's security in textual matters come to a head when bad quartos are wrongly defined. Occasional statements which go beyond the evidence are made more dangerous by the confidence which the author's usual scrupulousness is likely to inspire. Contrary to a common assumption, one must be less not more ready to risk a conjecture when writing for the uninformed, who from this book will suppose it probable that Heminge and Condell had to decline offers from Ben Jonson to improve the Folio text, almost certain that on the Elizabethan stage actors sometimes made their entry on horseback through the yard, definitely established that Shakespeare sold his theatre shares before his death. Such things mar a book which nevertheless gives as full and fair an impression of Shakespeare's personality as the common reader is likely to find.

No other work this year has attempted to cover the whole life. The mythical biography, one may note in passing, is represented by A. W. Titherley's laborious work proving Shakespeare to have been the pen-name of the Earl of Derby.[4] To believe this is of course to follow in the steps

[1] 'Fortuna di Shakespeare in Italia e in Francia', *Hesperia*, III (October 1952), 191–9.
[2] *Shakespeare in de Twintigste Eeuw* (Groningen: J. B. Wolters, 1952).
[3] *Shakespeare: his World and his Work* (Arnold, 1953).
[4] *Shakespeare's Identity: William Stanley 6th Earl of Derby* (Winchester: Warren and Son, 1952).

of Abel Lefranc, whose latest volume has received some consideration from F. L. Schoell.[1] Connoisseurs in Shakespearian claimants may be referred to a Swedish pamphlet[2] which surveys a field ranging from the Earls of Derby, Oxford and Rutland to Anne Whateley and John Florio's father.

One of the more reputable attempts to extend our knowledge of Shakespeare's circle is Katharine Esdaile's suggestion, in her careful account of the Jannssens, or Johnsons, of Southwark,[3] that Shakespeare may have known this family of stonemasons, to one of whom we owe the monument in Stratford church. Though it is not quite "reasonable" to believe that Shakespeare met the Johnsons when they were working on the monument to Southampton's father at Titchfield in 1593, the curious antiquarian may take pleasure in this link. There is no evidence for Barbara D. G. Steer's idea[4] that Shakespeare may have learnt about the Italian drama from the Bassano family, who were musicians at the English court, and small profit in the biographical conjectures which continue to come from H. A. Shield.[5] Accepting the theory that Shakespeare was a player in the house of Sir Thomas Hesketh, he would identify the Dark Lady with one Jane Harsnape, who also lived there. Identifying Mr W. H. with William Hughes of Holt, which is eight miles from Chester, where there lived a brother of the publisher, Thomas Thorpe, he supposes this the route by which the Sonnets reached print.

Leslie Hotson's attempt to date the Sonnets in 1589, though opinion has hardened against him, is still having repercussions. The Comtesse de Chambrun[6] has taken the opportunity to reiterate her own theories that the "mortal moon" sonnet celebrates Southampton's release from prison after Elizabeth's death and that Mr W. H. is his stepfather, Sir William Hervey. Her view that Mr W. H. is not wished but wishes happiness seems syntactically untenable. J. M. Nosworthy[7] wittily exposes the folly of basing any theory upon alleged topical allusions, sensibly reminds us that to date one sonnet is not necessarily to date the rest, and tentatively proposes a vocabulary test which—though it is hard to see significance in words like 'mortal' and 'eclipse'—may well have something in it. An able essay by Patrick Cruttwell,[8] watching the Sonnets pass from a straightforward adoration of the young Adonis to a perception of human sorrow and social injustice, interprets them as a spiritual autobiography which epitomizes also the crisis of a generation.

Problems of the dates and authorship of plays are central for the Shakespearian biographer, whose principal task must be to trace the dramatic career. Hence the New Cambridge edition of the *Henry VI* plays[9] is of considerable biographical as well as textual interest. It is tolerably orthodox in dating Parts II and III, and with them Shakespeare's 'arrival' as a playwright, not later than the winter of 1591–2; much more controversial when Dover Wilson continues to

---

[1] 'Deux études récentes sur Shakespeare', *Etudes Anglaises*, VI (February 1953), pp. 28–34.

[2] Harald Gyller, *Shakespeare eller icke Shakespeare det är frågan* (Stockholm: Sällskapet Bokvännerna, 1951).

[3] 'Some Fellow-Citizens of Shakespeare in Southwark', *Essays and Studies*, n.s., V (1952), 26–31.

[4] 'Shakespeare and Italy', *Notes and Queries*, CXCVIII (January 1953), 23.

[5] 'Links with Shakespeare IX–X', *ibid.* CXCVII (12 April and 30 August 1952), 156–7, 387–9.

[6] 'Une Critique de la Critique: Mr Leslie Hotson et la date des "Sonnets" de Shakespeare', *Etudes Anglaises*, V (February 1952), 44–9.

[7] 'All Too Short a Date: Internal Evidence in Shakespeare's Sonnets', *Essays in Criticism*, II (July 1952), 311–24.

[8] 'A Reading of the Sonnets', *Hudson Review*, V (Winter 1953), 554–70.

[9] *King Henry VI*, ed. J. Dover Wilson, 3 vols. (Cambridge: the University Press, 1952).

promote the old theory that Greene's attack on Shakespeare as an upstart crow implies a charge of plagiarism.[1] With Malone and against most of our contemporaries, he maintains that Shakespeare in *Henry VI* was only the reviser of plays largely written by Greene with assistance from Peele and Nashe. Dissent will be forthcoming from those who lack Dover Wilson's confidence about what the immature Shakespeare could not have written; but his case has been accepted by at least one reviewer,[2] and some of his arguments are impressive, especially those for Nashe's hand in Part I, which it will be more difficult, I think, in future to ascribe to Shakespeare alone. A vigorous argument in favour of his single authorship has nevertheless come meantime from L. Kirschbaum.[3] The possibility of Shakespeare's hand in *Edward III* is relevant to the general question of how far in his earlier years he may have given himself to revising other men's plays, and on this Kenneth Muir[4] has assembled a good deal of internal evidence, which needs fuller scrutiny and more precise evaluation, perhaps, than he has given it. At the other end of Shakespeare's career the case for his collaboration with Fletcher is strengthened by M. Mincoff's powerful argument for his part-authorship of *The Two Noble Kinsmen*.[5]

There are one or two illuminating discussions of books that Shakespeare used. In particular, an excellently presented argument by J. W. Lever[6] shows John Eliot's *Ortho-epia Gallica* to be the likely source of more details in the plays than was hitherto suspected. Margaret T. Hodgen,[7] without denying that Gonzalo's commonwealth is probably based upon Montaigne's description of the cannibals, shows that both draw upon a traditional conception of primitive society. Otherwise there is little new on Shakespeare's intellectual background; even on his political ideas the stream of articles, recently in spate, shows signs of—no doubt temporarily—drying up. In introducing an account of the histories at Stratford in 1951 with an exposition of the Elizabethan attitude to English history,[8] Dover Wilson goes over ground that he has helped to make familiar. Irving Ribner,[9] finding the Lancastrian "tetralogy" less concerned with the ethics of rebellion than "the type of ruler who should succeed Elizabeth", does no more than shift an emphasis. Karl Brunner[10] suggests that the ideals of "peace and order" which Shakespeare expressed in the history plays were peculiarly those of "the middle class to which he belonged".

Important aspects of the social life of the period—the education of girls, marriage customs, domestic occupations—are treated in Carroll Camden's study of *The Elizabethan Woman*.[11] It makes good use upon occasion of letters and diaries—to show Dorothy Selkane claiming a patent to mine coal or Lady Anne Clifford losing twenty-seven pounds at cards; but in drawing upon his wide reading in the didactic, satiric, and fictional kinds of literature, the author only sometimes allows for literary convention or recognizes that theory is not practice. He will cite a legal

---

[1] Cf. his revival of this view in 'Malone and the Upstart Crow', *Shakespeare Survey*, 4 (1951).

[2] G. Blakemore Evans, in *Shakespeare Quarterly*, IV (January 1953), 84–92.

[3] 'The Authorship of *1 Henry VI*', *PMLA*, LXVII (September 1952), 809–22.

[4] 'A Reconsideration of *Edward III*', *Shakespeare Survey*, 6 (1953), 39–48.

[5] 'The Authorship of *The Two Noble Kinsmen*', *English Studies*, XXXIII (June 1952), 97–115.

[6] 'Shakespeare's French Fruits', *Shakespeare Survey*, 6 (1953), 79–90.

[7] 'Montaigne and Shakespeare Again', *Huntington Library Quarterly*, XVI (November 1952), 23–42.

[8] J. Dover Wilson and T. C. Worsley, *Shakespeare's Histories at Stratford 1951* (Reinhardt, 1952).

[9] 'The Political Problem in Shakespeare's Lancastrian Tetralogy', *Studies in Philology*, XLIX (April 1952), 171–84.

[10] 'Middle-Class Attitudes in Shakespeare's Histories', *Shakespeare Survey*, 6 (1953), 36–8.

[11] Cleaver-Hume Press, 1952.

authority in the same breath as a romance by Greene, amatory verses along with handbooks of household management, as though their evidence were of equal worth. Similarly, the value of the numerous illustrations varies with their source. Delighted no doubt by incidental details, the reader yet learns less than he is led to hope about women's "place in a rapidly changing world".

The relation between an Elizabethan poet's work and his position in society is the theme of J. F. Danby's *Poets on Fortune's Hill*.[1] The poets begin with Sidney, who enjoys independence on the summit, while Spenser must cling to patronage, which Donne fails to find. Lower down Shakespeare rests secure on the ledge of theatrical success, which Jonson uses to climb up from; but Beaumont and Fletcher are on ground which is beginning to shift. This nicely conceived pattern is rich in suggestions for the critic, but attains coherence at the risk of some distortion. And in order to establish it convincingly one would have to examine both the Elizabethan social structure and works by more than three poets. A quite excellent essay on *Arcadia* tells us much about the Elizabethan ethos, but the Shakespearian chapters[2] seem to depend for their relevance upon some sleight of hand.

The most important book in this section, not only because of the breadth and detail of its survey but because of the new perspective in which it regards familiar material, is one which relates Shakespeare to the dramatic traditions of his day. In it Alfred Harbage[3] maintains that there were in fact, in the public and the private playhouses, two sharply divided traditions: the "theatre of a nation", originating in the performances of the craft guilds and strolling players and vitally related to popular dramatic performances in every shire, and the "theatre of a coterie", descending from the entertainments of schools, universities, and the court. The facts of theatrical organization are solidly arrayed, and it is estimated that round about 1600 three popular play-houses had between eighteen and twenty-four thousand spectators a week through nine months of the year while the boy actors in their indoor theatres had only six or seven hundred a week through six months. The changed perspective which, in emphasizing such figures, Harbage seeks to enforce, two examples may rapidly illustrate: the so-called landmarks of the early drama —*Ralph Roister Doister, Gorboduc*, and the rest—do not, it is suggested, belong to the main tradition at all; and the impression that the drama after 1600 shows a spirit of disillusion is a fallacy due to the prominence of the coterie theatre in the crucial years. There seems a danger in quantitative rather than qualitative assessments, but Harbage's extensive examination of the rival repertories affords evidence of a "split in philosophical outlook" which it is his book's main purpose to describe. Briefly, the popular theatre used romantic and historical material to provide actions mingling heroism, pathos and buffoonery in plays upholding a Christian humanism which placed man at the centre of a divinely planned universe of law. By contrast the coterie plays—a pertinent count shows eighty-five per cent of them to have been comedies—were witty, licentious and satirical, replacing feelings of family or national solidarity with the standards of a social and intellectual élite, who despised the vulgar and found their highest philosophical ideal in the stoic who defends his individual integrity against a hostile community. This very interesting argument of course invites one to pick holes. While the continuity of the coterie tradition from Lyly to Marston is more assumed than demonstrated, the line through Jonson,

[1] Faber, 1952.  [2] See above, pp. 135 ff.
[3] *Shakespeare and the Rival Traditions* (New York: Macmillan, 1952).

Marston, Tourneur and Webster, cutting across the dividing line of theatres, is scarcely acknowledged. The harsh voice of Marston is too readily taken to be representative of the select drama. Along with Chapman and Jonson he provides a preponderance of the instances; and notwithstanding the self-assertiveness of these three writers, they seem to emerge as less responsible than the coterie audience for the character of their plays. Moreover Harbage, who does not like satire, will be thought to depreciate their work; and conversely, he does not always stress how much the supremacy of the popular drama depends on the overshadowing figure of Shakespeare. Nevertheless it is the glory of the public play-houses, as this book well shows, that they were "the only possible nursery...for the kind...of artist that Shakespeare was". And when all qualifications and exceptions have been noted, there remains a broad moral antithesis between the two theatres, shrewdly discerned and skilfully expounded, which must surely be accepted.

There is also valuable work to be recorded on individual dramatists among Shakespeare's contemporaries. Two who have not been edited since last century are having this neglect redeemed. While the first volume of Dekker, by Fredson Bowers, is announced, the first volume of Peele, by David H. Horne,[1] makes what can be made of the scattered fragments of Peele's biography, defends him from charges of dissoluteness, and gives the text of the poems and pageants. The fullest study of Chapman to date, covering all but the translations, has been written by Jean Jacquot:[2] though it does not sufficiently relate the plays to the contemporary theatre, it is elaborate on the philosophy they express. Eugene M. Waith[3] gives the best description I have read of the peculiar quality of Beaumont and Fletcher. While begging some questions of how they are to be valued, his book should revive interest in them after some recent critical disparagement; and though of late we have probably heard too much of formal rhetoric in connexion with the drama, the comparison of Beaumont and Fletcher's technique with the rhetorical methods of the Roman *controversia* is certainly illuminating.[4] Finally, F. P. Wilson has outlined the main problems in Marlowe:[5] with—rarest of virtues—the courage to "have no opinion" on many of them, he yet shows a fresh critical approach in warning us against subjective interpretations of Marlowe's plays and corrects some common assumptions about their lack of variety and dramatic power. All this makes a little surprising his ready rejection of large tracts of *Faustus* and *The Jew of Malta*.

A small group of articles has studied particular conventions of dramatic action. Muriel Bradbrook's discussion of disguise[6] is less concerned with clothes than with those double roles—exemplified in Hamlet's antic disposition or Angelo's combination of judge and tempter—which afforded Shakespeare a dramatic means of expressing the problem of 'seeming' and reality. Joseph T. McMullen's somewhat mechanical examination of mad songs[7] goes to show that these

[1] *The Life and Works of George Peele*, ed. C. T. Prouty, vol. I, *The Life and Minor Works of George Peele*, by David H. Horne (New Haven: Yale University Press, 1952).

[2] *George Chapman (1559–1634): sa vie, sa poésie, son théâtre, sa pensée* (Paris: Société d'Edition *Les Belles Lettres*, 1951).

[3] *The Pattern of Tragicomedy in Beaumont and Fletcher* (New Haven: Yale University Press, 1952).

[4] Cf. also the same author's '*Controversia* in the English Drama: Medwall and Massinger', *PMLA*, LXVIII (March 1953), 286–303.

[5] *Marlowe and the Early Shakespeare* (Oxford: Clarendon Press, 1953). See also above, p. 132.

[6] 'Shakespeare and the Use of Disguise in Elizabethan Drama', *Essays in Criticism*, II (April 1952), 159–68.

[7] 'The Functions of Songs aroused by Madness in Elizabethan Drama', in A. Williams (ed.), *A Tribute to George Coffin Taylor* (Chapel Hill: University of North Carolina Press, 1952), 185–96.

were more often organic than incidental excitements. His account of scenes using "games of cards, chess, dice, and backgammon"[1] would be more instructive if it did more to analyse the nature of a "noteworthy dramatic convention". A. Bronson Feldman's assemblage of Low-Country men in the drama,[2] if it has any point, confirms one's impression that Dutchmen tended to be figures of fun.

A material addition to our knowledge of the London stage at the very beginning of Elizabeth's reign results from Charles T. Prouty's researches[3] in the churchwardens' accounts of St Botolph without Aldersgate, which show that a hall in the parish was frequently let to players. There is an estimate of over a hundred performances between 1557 and 1568, and a conjecture that the facilities for an upper and an inner stage afforded by a gallery at one end of such a hall might have influenced the structure of the regular playhouses. Creizenach's theory that English playhouse structure was directly indebted to the outdoor stages of the Netherlands has been revived by Feldman,[4] still searching for Dutch contacts; but whatever one makes of a Dutch joiner in James Burbage's employ and the possible Dutch origin of Peter Street, builder of the Globe and Fortune, it will not be disputed that the evidence is "certainly meager". How Peter Street would proceed in erecting the Globe from the timbers of the Theatre is expertly considered by Irwin Smith,[5] who believes that in their "essential frame" these two houses must have been exactly alike. It would obviously be dangerous, however, to draw inferences about one from what is known of the other. Richard Southern's interpretation of the De Witt-Van Buchell description of the Swan[6] seizes on details usually overlooked: a timber frame was filled with flint conglomerate and the pillars supporting the galleries were painted to imitate marble. The Renaissance design betokened by such marbling might strengthen the hypothesis, considered by Walter Hodges,[6] that the underside of the 'heavens' was painted with stars and allegorical signs to represent the sky. The capacity of the second Globe is noted by F. R. Saunders,[7] who draws attention to a contemporary estimate that it held an audience of over three thousand for Middleton's *A Game at Chess*. That there were Catholics, including priests, in the Jacobean audiences is clear from the Catholic controversy about attendance at playhouses, which is discussed, not for the first time, by I. J. Semper.[8]

A common fallacy about Elizabethan costume has been corrected in a lively book by Leslie Hotson,[9] who shows conclusively that the Elizabethan fool normally wore not a hood, jerkin and hose, but a long coat; and that the 'motley' of which this was made did not consist of differently coloured patches but of cloth speckled with differently coloured threads. This is important not only for the proper dressing of the part but for the interpretation of many passages of dialogue. It explains Feste's "I did impeticos [empetticoat] thy gratillity" and enriches Duke

---

[1] 'The Use of Parlor and Tavern Games in Elizabethan and Early Stuart Drama', *Modern Language Quarterly*, XIV (March 1953), 7–14.

[2] 'The Flemings in Shakespeare's Theatre', *Notes and Queries*, CXCVII (21 June 1952), 265–9.

[3] 'An Early Elizabethan Playhouse', *Shakespeare Survey*, 6 (1953), 64–74.

[4] 'Dutch Theatrical Architecture in Elizabethan London', *Notes and Queries*, CXCVII (11 October 1952), 444–6.

[5] 'Theatre into Globe', *Shakespeare Quarterly*, III (April 1952), 113–20.

[6] Richard Southern and C. Walter Hodges, 'Colour in the Elizabethan Theatre', *Theatre Notebook*, VI (April–June 1952), 57–60.      [7] *Times Literary Supplement*, 14 November 1952, p. 742.

[8] *The Month*, n.s., VIII (July 1952), 28–39. Cf. *Shakespeare Survey*, 6 (1953), 162.

[9] *Shakespeare's Motley* (Hart-Davis, 1952).

Senior's lament for the "poor dappled fools"; while the use of a similar cloth for cloak-bags gives point to Prince Hal's calling Falstaff a "stuffed cloak-bag of guts". Hotson's observation is brilliant and penetrating. But it overlooks inconvenient evidence, like the "motley jerkin" of the fool in *Patient Grissell*. And it sees some that is not there: when, to take one example, Sir Thomas More's man in his master's apparel is reproved with "Fool, painted barbarism", this does not imply that he is More's jester or anything about a jester's clothes. Elsewhere[1] Hotson has collected some striking quotations which prove that the stage-keepers sometimes appeared on the stage wearing masks; and this discovery too enables him to reveal new meanings in familiar passages. But again he entangles fact and conjecture and surrounds his valid quotations with others which seem to swell the evidence but do not. The evidence that the stage-keepers were responsible for keeping order and drawing the curtain on the inner stage is slender (and has met objection on the first point from H. H. Schless);[2] I find none that they remained on stage throughout the performance.

Richard Southern's big work on the little-studied subject of *Changeable Scenery*[3] deals mostly with things outside our period. Yet of course the movable scenes which were introduced on the public stage at the Restoration were fully evolved in the court masques before the Civil War; and the first third of the book traces this evolution in scholarly detail from the moving cloud in a court entertainment in 1574 to the shutters, wings, borders, and 'scenes of relieve' of the 1630's. Southern acutely sees that the purpose of these things is not dramatic but spectacular and that Inigo Jones's quarrel with Ben Jonson epitomizes the rivalry between words and spectacle in theatrical art. In this aesthetic issue he asserts the rights of the showman. But his subject is less aesthetics than mechanics, without which the show cannot exist. The real hero of his history is the groove which allows the shutter to move. On all such technicalities of scenery he writes with a technical expertness which makes this a unique and authoritative contribution to the history of the stage.

Between the scholars who investigate how Shakespeare's plays were staged in his own time and the producers who seek to stage them now Cécile de Banke[4] has laudably tried to build a bridge. But her bridge is secure at one end only. She has a good native sense of the principles of stage-illusion and her experience can help the amateur producer in his practical problems. Her scholarship, alas, rests on sand; or even, as when attributing the "greater part" of *Pericles* to Fletcher, apparently on air. Any conjecture about the staging of the plays her eager *naïveté* translates into "well-established" fact. She talks of the wall down the centre of the stage in *Romeo and Juliet* and lists thirteen roles that Heminge "undoubtedly played". So she falls a natural victim to the fallacies put about by Cranford Adams's reconstruction of the Globe, beguiled by his kind of literalism, which confuses the stage with the imaginary world it represents, into tying interiors to the alcove and bedrooms to the upper stage (with consequent troubles with the property bed). Such mistakes are avoided by Warren D. Smith[5] in his examination of Shakespeare's dialogue for indications of place and setting. Contrary to expectation he finds

---

[1] 'False Faces on Shakespeare's Stage', *Times Literary Supplement*, 16 May 1952, p. 336.

[2] *Ibid.*, 6 June 1952, p. 377.

[3] *Changeable Scenery: Its Origin and Development in the British Theatre* (Faber, 1952).

[4] *Shakespearean Stage Production: Then and Now* (New York: McGraw-Hill, 1953).

[5] 'Stage Settings in Shakespeare's Dialogue', *Modern Philology*, L (August 1952), 32–5.

that by far the majority of specified settings are exteriors; but I hardly think it follows that the Elizabethan stage gave the impression of a room, which Shakespeare was often concerned to counteract. Close scrutiny of the dialogue can also, of course, yield clues to the stage-action; but Richard Flatter[1] does not achieve complete conviction with his attractive argument that Hamlet in the play scene draws his sword upon the King.

The year's contributions to the stage-history of individual plays begin with two attempts to cast doubt on accepted performances during Shakespeare's lifetime. C. A. Greer[2] questions whether it was Shakespeare's *Richard II* that was acted on the day before the Essex rebellion; and Sydney Race,[3] bent on including them in his growing list of Collier fabrications, once more challenges the journal-entries which record performances of *Richard II* and *Hamlet* on board the *Dragon* in 1607–8. In neither case are scholars likely to be seriously perturbed. If they could accept Joan Rees's suggestion[4] that a passage in the 1607 version of Daniel's *Cleopatra* derives from an eyewitness account of *Antony and Cleopatra*, they would know something of how the actors managed the hoisting of Antony into the monument. C. B. Hogan[5] has compiled, principally from newspaper sources, a list of Shakespeare performances in the first half of the eighteenth century. Though its bulk is due more to an uneconomical arrangement than to the amount of new material, this will be a useful reference-book, especially for its account of the textual adaptations and its indexes of actors and their roles. An interesting appendix giving figures for each play shows before 1740 a neglect of the romantic comedies remarkably at variance with the author's notion that the relative popularity of the plays was much the same then as now. Particulars given by W. O. S. Sutherland[6] of how eighteenth-century actors played certain Shakespearian roles include some picturesque details for Polonius and an account of Wilks's Hamlet. J. Yoklavich[7] describes the Hamlet of Thomas Sheridan, whose impressiveness in the graver contemplative speeches brought a new conception to the part. Charles Kean's painstaking historical accuracy in stage-production is nicely demonstrated by Wilbur D. Dunkel[8] in quoting from a letter in which Kean defended the costume he wore as Wolsey against objections from Cardinal Wiseman's secretary.

The full series of designs for Kean's "archaeological" production of *Hamlet* in 1850 is one of the notable things included by Raymond Mander and Joe Mitchenson in their pictorial stage-history of the play.[9] Though pictures can suggest little enough of acting, this volume is an interesting experiment in telling the history of the theatre's visual art with the minimum reliance upon verbal description.[10] Its range is from Rowe's frontispiece of 1709 to television,

[1] 'The Climax of the Play-Scene in "Hamlet"', *Shakespeare-Jahrbuch*, LXXXVII–LXXXVIII (1951–2), 26–42.

[2] 'The Play Performed at the Globe on 7 February, 1601', *Notes and Queries*, CXCVII (21 June 1952), 270–1.

[3] 'The Authenticity of the Keeling Journal Entries', *ibid.* (26 April 1952), pp. 181–2.

[4] 'An Elizabethan Eyewitness of *Antony and Cleopatra*?', *Shakespeare Survey*, 6 (1953), 91–3.

[5] *Shakespeare in the Theatre 1701–1800* (Oxford: Clarendon Press, 1952). The present volume, the first of two projected, covers only 1701–50.

[6] 'Polonius, Hamlet, and Lear in Aaron Hill's *Prompter*', *Studies in Philology*, LXIX (October 1952), 605–18.

[7] 'Hamlet in Shammy Shoes', *Shakespeare Quarterly*, III (July 1952), 209–18.

[8] 'Kean's Portrayal of Cardinal Wolsey', *Theatre Notebook*, VI (July–September 1952), 80–2.

[9] *Hamlet Through the Ages* (Rockliff, 1952).

[10] A discussion of the importance of the film for this purpose is in R. H. Ball, 'The Shakespeare Film as Record: Sir Herbert Beerbohm Tree', *Shakespeare Quarterly*, III (July 1952), 227–36.

taking in Japan and Uzbekistan. Further witness to Shakespeare's far-flung dominion is given by such articles as those recounting performances of his plays among the pioneers of the American west[1] and, strangest of all, by negro actors in La Ceiba, Honduras,[2] where a continuous tradition from the slaves of seventeenth-century English colonists still preserves *Henry VI*, Part III, and *Richard III* as a living folk drama. Nearer home Sir Barry Jackson[3] notes some "puzzles" which engaged the Birmingham Repertory Theatre when they staged Parts II and III of *Henry VI*, while the number and tone of articles reviewing Stratford plays signify Stratford's newly acquired prestige as—oddly enough—the theatrical metropolis of Shakespeare. Things have changed there since the Benson Company did seventeen plays in a three-week festival nearly half a century ago. What these were one can learn from a lively new history of the Memorial Theatre,[4] in which Matheson Lang forgetting his lines or Frank Benson, late for a cue, rushing on as Leontes in grey flannels, do not interrupt the useful year-to-year record of plays and casts. From reviews of recent Stratford productions one may pick out the searching criticisms of the 1952 series by D. J. Enright and Clifford Leech,[5] whose united voice raises issues fundamental to all theatrical production. Their complaints are of "extra attractions" imported into Shakespeare or a "constant search for novelty", which manifests itself in "the elaborateness of the stage-machinery" or in a slight tendency "towards the world of technicolour", which in turn betrays an embarrassment at Shakespeare's "naked power" or an "impulse to compromise with a suspect public taste".[6]

[1] Levette J. Davidson, 'Shakespeare in the Rockies', *Shakespeare Quarterly*, IV (January 1953), 39–49.

[2] Louise W. George, 'Shakespeare in La Ceiba', *ibid.* III (October 1952), 359–65.

[3] 'On Producing *Henry VI*', *Shakespeare Survey*, 6 (1953), 49–52.

[4] T. C. Kemp and J. C. Trewin, *The Stratford Festival* (Birmingham: Cornish, 1953).

[5] Enright, 'Substitutes for Shakespeare: Reflections on the Stratford Season 1952', *The Month*, n.s., VIII (October 1952), 232–5; Leech, 'Stratford 1952', *Shakespeare Quarterly*, III (October 1952), 353–7. The history cycle in 1951 is well described by T. C. Worsley (J. Dover Wilson and T. C. Worsley, *Shakespeare's Histories at Stratford 1951*, Reinhardt, 1952) and Richard David ('Shakespeare's History Plays—Epic or Drama?', *Shakespeare Survey*, 6 (1953), 129–39).

[6] Here both sides of the Atlantic are at one. Similar criticism of a technical display which, instead of assisting the imagination, comes between it and Shakespeare is made by G. E. Dawson of an American production ('The Catholic University *Macbeth*', *Shakespeare Quarterly*, III (July 1952), 255–6). Among other articles on recent productions are those in which performances in Germany are reported by Wolfgang Stroedel ('Bühnenbericht 1950–2', *Shakespeare-Jahrbuch*, LXXXVII–LXXXVIII (1951–2), 174–80) and in Austria by Doris Eisner ('Sieben Jahre Shakespeare in Oester-reich 1945–51', *ibid.* pp. 180–97). The 'International Notes' in *Shakespeare Survey*, 6 (1953, pp. 117–25) are of productions during 1951 in nineteen countries. The Olivier-Vivien Leigh *Antony and Cleopatra*, the Gielgud *Winter's Tale*, and the Orson Welles *Othello* provoke some literary virtuosity from George Rylands ('Festival Shakespeare in the West End', *ibid.* pp. 140–6), the Shakespearian film-work of Olivier and Welles enthusiasm from René Lalou ('Shakespeare et le Cinéma', *Etudes Anglaises*, V (November 1952), 309–18). It remains to recognize belatedly some salutary views on staging, along with some odd ones on the plays, in *Producing Shakespeare*, by C. B. Purdom (Pitman, 1950): he demands a stage which will facilitate continuous action but neither the antiquarian reconstruction of an Elizabethan playhouse nor the permanent set which compromises with the picture-stage.

## 3. TEXTUAL STUDIES

*reviewed by* JAMES G. McMANAWAY

This has been a notable year in textual studies; perhaps later generations will call it revolutionary. When has scholarly tradition been called so sharply in question as in F. P. Wilson's lecture, 'Marlowe and Shakespeare'?[1] "Was it Shakespeare and Marlowe", he inquires, "who first gave dignity and coherence to the historical play and raised it above the level of a chronicle? So we have always been taught to believe; but when we look for these early chronicle plays written before the Armada, where are they?...Many play-titles have survived [from the 1580's], and a few plays, and if we go by these we are forced into this surprising conclusion: that there is no certain evidence that any popular dramatist before Shakespeare wrote a play based on English history." And after dismissing the pretensions of *The Famous Victories of Henry the Fifth* and several of its ilk, he continues: "My conclusion is, though I am frightened at my own temerity in saying so, that for all we know there were no popular plays on English history before the Armada and that Shakespeare may have been the first to write one." This is heady wine of a new orthodoxy with which to fortify oneself before venturing into the mazes of collaboration and revision that are detailed in the plays recently edited by John Dover Wilson.

In the introduction and notes on the copy, Dover Wilson sets out his beliefs about the composition and date of the three parts of *Henry VI*[2] with the same audacity that has characterized his work in the other volumes of this edition. Part I, he thinks, was plotted by Robert Greene in 1591 and, as "harey the vj", was performed by Strange's Men on 3 March 1591/2 to compete with Pembroke's *First Part of the Contention* and *The True Tragedie of Richard Duke of York*. When Greene's fraudulent sale of *Orlando Furioso* to the Queen's Men and also to Strange's came to light, Henslowe and Alleyn paid him off and took over the unfinished play, which already contained scenes by Thomas Nashe and possibly George Peele. Shakespeare was then employed to complete the play and whip it into shape. That a mere player should have been brought in to finish a play of his devising is what led to Greene's infuriated attack on the "Upstart Crow" (p. xlix). Wilson seems to be of two opinions about Nashe: on pp. xlviii–xlix, Greene is represented as planning the play with Nashe, but on p. l Wilson concedes that all the passages he attributes to Nashe may have been written after the play was taken out of Greene's hands.

It seems to me unlikely that Strange's should have employed both Shakespeare and Nashe, and I find it incredible that Greene could have addressed Nashe in friendly terms in *A Groatsworth of Wit* if he had ever been a collaborator of the detested "Shake-scene". In the light of H. T. Price's insistence that one mind and hand wrought the design of *1 Henry VI*, it is interesting to find Wilson writing (p. xxxi): "At any rate it was certainly plotted by one mind, as a consideration of the sources utilized in the various scenes will now make clear."

Among the features of the play that have troubled critics are shifting attitudes towards Joan of Arc, the Talbot death scenes, indecision whether Henry Beaufort is a bishop or a cardinal,

[1] *Marlowe and the Early Shakespeare* (Oxford University Press, 1953), pp. 105, 106, 108.
[2] *The First Part of Henry VI, The Second Part of Henry VI, The Third Part of Henry VI* (Cambridge University Press, 1952).

and changes in versification. The first two are used by Leo Kirschbaum in his argument[1] that *1 Henry VI* was written by Shakespeare alone and at one time as the first play of his trilogy. One may find merit in his thesis that the death of Talbot is the bitter fruit of the quarrel in the Temple Garden scene and that there is no shift in attitude towards the Maid of Orleans and yet disagree about the date of composition. Kirschbaum ignores the probability that *2* and *3 Henry VI* were written for one company and *1 Henry VI* for another. The finer poetry in certain passages that link the latter to the other two and help carry Shakespeare's theme throughout can best be explained as a revision after the three plays came into the possession of the Chamberlain's Men.

Discussion of the authorship of *2* and *3 Henry VI* begins inevitably with Greene's attack upon Shakespeare in 1592, which Dover Wilson continues to interpret as an accusation of plagiarism.[2] With this I cannot agree until evidence is produced that Elizabethan playwrights took offence when acting companies had play manuscripts revised or augmented. It is difficult to find in Greene's words (supposing that Chettle did not tamper with them) more than anger that an actor should be so presumptuous as to write plays; indeed, it is possible that Shakespeare has suffered less from Greene's attack than from Chettle's ambiguous apology: "diuers of worship have reported his uprightnes of dealing, which argues his honesty"—that is damning with faint praise!

It is Wilson's position that *The First Part of the Contention* and *The True Tragedie of Richard Duke of York* are reported texts, as Peter Alexander has maintained, but not of *2* and *3 Henry VI*, as printed in the Folio. These are, rather, Shakespeare's revisions of two plays of Pembroke's Men plotted and in large part written by Greene. Even the Jack Cade scenes are not pure Shakespeare, he argues, but rather a confection of Nashe with Shakespearian garnishing. All this occurred early in 1591 or 1592, prior to the performance of "harey the vj" by Strange's. As in his attributions of authorship in Part I, Wilson relies principally on vocabulary tests, supplemented by comments on versification and imagery. The section headed, 'Shakespeare's Early Dramatic Style' (III, pp. vii–xvi), indicates what Wilson expects from Shakespeare's pen in this early period.

The first thoroughgoing examination of Wilson's editions, and a review of major importance, is that of G. Blakemore Evans.[3] Accepting Wilson's interpretation of the episode of the "Upstart Crow", Evans confesses at the outset that he is a moderate disintegrationist. But he rejects Wilson's identification of *1 Henry VI* with Strange's "harey the vj" for two weighty reasons: (1) the Bad Quartos of *2* and *3 Henry VI* draw upon *1 Henry VI* even more than first noted by Alexander; and (2) the Bad texts of *1* and *2 Troublesome Raigne of John King of England* are heavily indebted to *1 Henry VI* in phrase and the handling of situation. Since *John* was published in 1591, *1 Henry VI* must have been performed even earlier. Evans offers the following tentative chronology:

(1) The original of *1 Henry VI* about 1589–90 (very shortly before *The Troublesome Raigne*, published in 1591).

(2) *2* and *3 Henry VI*, not planned as direct continuations of the *Ur-1 Henry VI*, but themselves clearly a consecutive two-part play, about 1590–1.

[1] 'The Authorship of *1 Henry VI*', *PMLA*, LXVII (1952), 809–22.
[2] *1 Henry VI*, pp. xiv ff.; see *Shakespeare Survey*, 4, pp. 56–68.
[3] *Shakespeare Quarterly*, IV (January 1953), 84–92.

(3) The first revision of the *Ur-1 Henry VI* by Greene, to fashion it into a more or less regular prologue for Parts 2 and 3, just before the break-up of the Strange-Admiral alliance in May of 1591.

(4) The final revision of all three plays, by Shakespeare, in early 1592 (before Greene's death on 3 September 1592) for the company recently formed around Richard Burbage (see Wilson's interesting suggestion on the origin of the mysterious Pembroke company, *op. cit.* II, pp. xii–xiv).

He disagrees with Wilson, and with Alexander, about the Talbot scenes and contributes additional evidence of Greene's participation in *Henry VI*.

What special problems confront the editor of a play that survives in both a Bad and a Good Quarto, and upon what principles should he base his text? A remarkably lucid and penetrating answer to these questions is attempted by Richard Hosley,[1] as they relate to *Romeo and Juliet*, the Good Quarto of which was printed from Shakespeare's foul papers with occasional reference to the Bad Quarto. Neither Hoppe nor Duthie has understood all the dangers of corruption inherent in the situation, as Hosley shows in his discussion of typical passages. His conclusions are valuable for the study of every play of which there are Bad and Good texts, and all future editors will bear a heavier burden of responsibility and enjoy a somewhat greater freedom in making their texts.

After an interval of nine years, another volume of the New Variorum Shakespeare has come from press—*Troilus and Cressida*,[2] edited chiefly by H. N. Hillebrand but brought to completion and seen through the press by T. W. Baldwin. After Hillebrand's failure in health, Baldwin made the final revision and added some material of as recent date as 1951. Unfortunately this did not include the important articles by Greg, Alice Walker, and Philip Williams on the copyright of *Troilus*, the proof that the Folio was printed from a corrected copy of the Quarto, and the nature of the manuscript by which the Quarto was corrected. This might not have altered the editorial decision to reprint the Folio text, but it should have modified the discussion of the early texts and their relative authority. The Variorum volumes afford such a wealth of material in small compass that it is to be hoped others will be published at short intervals.

The latest volume in the New Arden series is *King Lear*,[3] edited by Kenneth Muir. The Introduction and Appendices supply valuable information about date, sources and interpretation, not all of it quite up to date: Greg, for example, does not now consider that the text of the Quarto was obtained by stenographic report. Much more serious is the editor's uneasiness in dealing with textual and bibliographical matters. There is no explicit statement, but one is left to infer that the text may differ very little from the one prepared by the editor about 1935 for an amateur production (p. xi). The statement about the presence of uncorrected and corrected formes in the First Folio (p. xi) and that about sophistication and deliberate changes in the manuscript (p. xix) suggest that Muir has only a vague idea about the varieties of text printed in the Folio, as revealed in the textual history of the individual plays, and may not have formulated clearly his opinions about the textual position of *Lear*. His text, in any event, seems to have been formed on the basis of personal preference—"we shall accept Quarto readings not only where the

---

[1] 'The Corrupting Influence of the Bad Quarto on the Received Text of *Romeo and Juliet*', *Shakespeare Quarterly*, IV (January 1953), 11–33.

[2] *A New Variorum Edition of Shakespeare*, '*Troilus and Cressida*' (Philadelphia: J. B. Lippincott, 1953).

[3] London: Methuen, 1952.

Folio readings are manifestly corrupt, but also where Quarto seems palpably superior" (p. xix)—without indication of the way in which the text may have been modified by the agents of transmission: the actors' memories, the scribe, the Quarto compositor, the editor (i.e. the agent who collated a copy of the Quarto with a theatrical manuscript), and the Folio compositor. This is unfortunate, because *Lear* is one of the most difficult plays in the canon. The general reader will scarcely detect these imperfections, but a sounder text would give the volume greater utility in schools and colleges.

In three closely reasoned articles[1] Fredson Bowers addresses himself to several matters of more than casual interest. The importance of facsimile editions is undisputed, but what kind of facsimile should an editor produce? Except for the use of the general reader, it is no longer sufficient to reproduce the pages of one exemplar, unless it be unique, for every copy of an early book consists of an indiscriminate collection of uncorrected and corrected sheets. The ordinary conditions of proof-reading were such, however, that the so-called corrected formes give a text that in the essentials may be less faithful to the author's intention than the compositor's first setting of type. In most cases, then, if it cannot be proved that the author is responsible for alterations in the type or that the press-corrector consulted the manuscript copy, an editor can, paradoxically, give the best facsimile text by reproducing the uncorrected states of the formes. Shakespeare Folios and Quartos not being generally accessible, most detailed study has to be based upon facsimiles. It is urgent, therefore, as I pointed out fourteen years ago, that publishers of facsimiles should modernize their policies in order to meet the needs of modern scholarship.

In the second paper, Bowers states concisely the editorial position in each of the plays of Shakespeare and then demonstrates with ease that not a single play now exists in print with as sound a text as it is possible to establish. If this proposition astounds the lay reader, it should not dismay the scholar. In two score years, so much has been learned about the nature of dramatic manuscripts and printing house methods that editorial practice has lagged. This is particularly true of the last ten years, when so many new discoveries have been made about the spelling habits of compositors, the methods of proof-reading, the nature of printer's copy, and the choice of the most authoritative text. This paper should be read by everyone who has a serious interest in Shakespeare and especially by every college and university teacher and every prospective editor.

The third paper is an *apologia*, intended to dispel the anxieties of those who suspect that the current elaboration in bibliographical description "may so widen the division between the bibliographer and the student of literature that it will be impossible even for the textual critic to use without difficulty some of the technical devices now employed in the analysis of the physical makeup of a book" or those others who fear the establishment of "a conception of pure bibliography, written by bibliographers for bibliographers".

Bowers defines (1) enumerative or compilative bibliography, (2) historical bibliography, (3) analytical bibliography, (4) descriptive bibliography, and (5) critical or textual bibliography; affirms the right and duty of the bibliographer to discover and record everything that can be

[1] 'Bibliography, Pure Bibliography, and Literary Studies', *Papers of the Bibliographical Society of America*, xlvi (1952), 186–208; 'The Problem of the Variant Forme in a Facsimile Edition', *The Library*, 5th series, vii (December 1952), 262–72; and 'A Definitive Text of Shakespeare: Problems and Methods', *Studies in Shakespeare* (University of Miami Press, 1953), pp. 11–29.

ascertained about the production of a book, whether or not it has immediate utility; and asserts the interdependence of bibliographical and textual investigation and the necessity to employ both in literary study.

Once the most neglected in the canon, Shakespeare's History Plays now engage almost as much attention as the Tragedies, not only for their political ideas and imagery, but for their dates of composition and their relation to the extant or hypothetical plays that are their supposed sources. Dover Wilson's study of *Richard III* is a good example.[1] It is agreed that Shakespeare wrote *Richard III* about 1592 or 1593, shortly after *Henry VI*, and that *The True Tragedy* is a reported text, printed late enough to contain reminiscences of *Richard III*. Wilson adds to the evidence collected in 1900 by G. B. Churchill and reinterprets it as proving that several of the more striking similarities between the two plays may best be explained as a borrowing by Shakespeare directly from *The True Tragedy* or from the unknown play of which it is a reported text. This is exactly the relationship that some critics have agreed upon for the *Shrew* plays; did the same thing happen twice? Was Shakespeare, perhaps, the author of both hypothetical source plays? If so, how early did he write them? Wilson suggests that the *Ur-Richard III* must have been acted about 1588, for otherwise Peele could not have echoed, "A horse, a horse", in *The Battle of Alcazar*.

When he edited the newly discovered White (now Folger) copy of the Third Quarto of *Richard II*, A. W. Pollard suggested that the Folio text of the play was printed from a marked copy of this Quarto that lacked two leaves, the imperfection being supplied by the corresponding leaves of the Fifth Quarto. Later commentators have wavered between the Third Quarto and the Fifth Quarto as the source. The doubt is resolved by Richard E. Hasker's exhaustive collation of the texts[2] that proves Pollard correct. As Hasker reconstructs the story, at some time between 1598 and 1608 (when the Fourth Quarto appeared), a copy of the Third Quarto was marked for prompt use. Between 1615 (the date of the Fifth Quarto) and 1622, its last two leaves were lost or defaced, and the corresponding pages of the Fifth Quarto, suitably marked, were inserted to complete the text. This prompt book itself was given to Jaggard for printing the Folio. Now the passage in IV, i containing the deposition of Richard was first printed in the Fourth Quarto in a reported version; the Folio gives a vastly better text, but Hasker finds no evidence whether it was printed from corrected leaves of the Fifth Quarto or a transcript of the prompt book. He would like to think, however, that the text was supplied in manuscript and that the Fifth Quarto leaves were inserted while the play was still in production. His postulate that the manuscript prompt book was lost or destroyed by 1622 is, I think, wrong; it contained the licence of the Master of Revels and would have been preserved, in whatever state of decay. If it had not been in existence, the actors would scarcely have risked sending their prompt book to a printer. It might be argued, of course, that a quarto was marked for prompt use while the company was on tour and that in 1622 two prompt books were in existence.

The eighth volume in the invaluable series of collotype facsimiles published by the Shakespeare Association is *Troilus and Cressida* (1609).[3] In its first state, as Sir Walter Greg explains in

[1] 'Shakespeare's *Richard III* and *The True Tragedy of Richard the Third*, 1594', *Shakespeare Quarterly*, III (October 1952), 299–306.

[2] 'The Copy for the First Folio *Richard II*', *Studies in Bibliography*, V (1952), 53–72.

[3] London: Sidgwick and Jackson, 1952.

his introduction, the title-page states that the play has been performed by the King's Men. In the process of publication, this title was replaced by a two-leaf cancel (printed integrally with the final leaves M 1 and M 2 of the text). In this second state, the title-page omits the reference to the King's Men, while the address to the reader boasts that there has been no public performance. It concludes with the remarkable prophecy that "when he [Shakespeare] is gone, and his Comedies out of sale, you will scramble for them".

Within nine years after publication, the First Folio was out of print, and the market seemed to call for a second edition. This was issued in 1632, and though it has no textual authority it has long been considered a desirable book, not only because it provides an early text of Shakespeare, but also because one of the commendatory verses is the first appearance in print of John Milton. Scholars and collectors have noted the names of the booksellers concerned, have speculated on the priority of the various imprints, and bid high for the rare ones. Their easy assumptions are now upset by William B. Todd, whose examination of the paper used in printing the title-page and its conjugate leaf and of the other bibliographical evidence has led to the recognition of a new order of issues and states.[1] The article is highly technical but it cannot be ignored. For students of Milton it means that he wrote "starre-ypointing Pyramid". For Shakespearians, it fixes the order in which the title-pages were printed off and also indicates approximately how many copies went to each of the undertakers; it also throws light on the vexed problem of copyright and the speed with which the market absorbed the edition. Collectors and booksellers will learn with some consternation that variant title-pages they have prized for their supposed priority were actually printed at two separate times about 1641.

The determination to approach as closely as possible to Shakespeare's fair copy of a play has driven more than one student to live laborious days. One variety of such drudgery is the tabulation of spelling variants in the effort to discover which of two (or more) compositors set a given passage of text in a Quarto or Folio. This is far from profitless speculation. The Pide Bull *Lear*, for example, is thought by many to be a reported text; the Folio was printed from a copy of the Quarto which had been collated with the prompt book. But Jacobean compositors did not always follow copy meticulously. How many variants in the Folio represent manuscript readings and how many owe their existence to the habits of the Folio compositor? If a study of how each of the Folio compositors treats his printed and manuscript copy enables an editor to make a proper discount for compositorial interference (or shall we say corruption?), we come one stage nearer the true text. Such a contribution to knowledge is the report of I. B. Cauthen, Jr.[2] He extends the list of words used previously by Satchell, Willoughby, and Hinman, decides that compositor B set all of *Lear*, and supplies new information about several other plays in the Folio.

Studies of the habits of Jaggard's compositors A and B may seem to fall into the category of vermiculate scholarship, but not as they are pursued by Alice Walker. In the seventh and latest volume in the series of 'Shakespeare Problems',[3] she continues to examine the minutiae of six plays which survive in two or more relatively independent texts and further develops her theory

---

[1] 'The Issues and States of the Second Folio and Milton's Epitaph on Shakespeare', *Studies in Bibliography*, V (1952), 81–108.

[2] 'Compositor Determination in the First Folio *King Lear*', *Studies in Bibliography*, V (1952), 73–80.

[3] *Textual Problems of the First Folio*: '*Richard III*', '*King Lear*', '*Troilus and Cressida*', '*2 Henry IV*', '*Hamlet*', '*Othello*' (Cambridge University Press, 1953).

that Jaggard had a marked preference for printed over manuscript copy, especially after the long interruption from 1621 to 1623 in printing the First Folio. The little book is packed with so much matter—one is tempted to say dynamite—that it is necessary to select only a few illustrative details and leave the rest for thoughtful reading. The 1622 Quarto of *Othello*, she believes, "was a memorially contaminated text, printed from a manuscript for which a book-keeper was possibly responsible and based on the play as acted"; a copy of it was collated with a more authoritative manuscript for use in printing the Folio. Through Act I, the Good Quarto of *Hamlet* (1604/5) was printed from a corrected copy of the Bad First Quarto; then the printer turned directly to Shakespeare's foul papers. Before the Folio was begun, the original prompt book had been replaced by a transcript, which, being at one further remove from the foul papers, deviated yet more from Shakespeare. A copy of the Second Quarto, already contaminated by the First Quarto readings, was collated with this second prompt book for Jaggard's use in the Folio, but it was not given the same responsible, scrupulous treatment that *Lear* received, for the reason that the King's Men had at this date no manuscript comparable in authority or accuracy to Roberts's Quarto of 1604/5. In the case of *Lear*, Miss Walker joins Kirschbaum in rejecting Duthie's notion that the text of the Pide Bull Quarto was the product of a communal act of memory by Shakespeare's Company and proposes an entirely new theory: that most of the Quarto represents a transcript of Shakespeare's foul papers, dictated by one minor actor to another (the boys who played Goneril and Regan are prime suspects) and recorded in a horribly illegible hand. In I, i, II, iv and v, iii, where these actors appear prominently, the text is not only debased as described above but contaminated by reliance of the culprits upon very fallible memories. Later a copy of the Quarto was collated with the prompt book for use in printing the Folio. If all this be true, the Pide Bull Quarto has much greater potential authority than now accorded it and editors must rid themselves of their timorous distrust and more boldly conflate the two texts to recapture Shakespeare's lines.

The treatment of *Richard III* is extensive and startling. Miss Walker agrees with Patrick, Greg, and McKerrow that the Quarto was printed from a manuscript based on a memorial reconstruction by the King's Men. There is intimation that the prompt book was lost prior to 1602. In 1621, a Shakespearian autograph of the play was found defective and pieced out with segments of the Third Quarto; but when Jaggard resumed printing the Folio in 1623 it was decided to supply him with printed copy, the Sixth Quarto as it happened, collated with the author's manuscript and patched with the same fragments of the Third Quarto mentioned above. Along with these theories about the transmission of the text is a detailed study of the kind of errors habitually made by compositors A and B and a calculation of the corrupt readings in the Second to the Sixth Quartos which the collator failed to alter by reference to his manuscript. The number is shocking—approximately 140. By contrast, modern editors emend only about ten readings. It is instructive to see how these figures are arrived at. It is more important to understand their implications and the general trend of Miss Walker's arguments. Their moral is that in future editors must ever more be bold. Editorial work must henceforth be characterized by a new kind of liberty of emendation. This will differ from the eclecticism indulged in by the great editors of the eighteenth century and their less robust imitators. Supported by modern bibliographical and textual criticism, it will demand of editors the exercise of the finest critical discrimination, especially in those areas where substantive texts are suspect.

L

# BOOKS RECEIVED

BANKE, CÉCILE DE. *Shakespearean Stage Production* (New York: McGraw-Hill Book Company, 1953).

CAMDEN, CARROLL. *The Elizabethan Woman. A Panorama of English Womanhood 1540–1640* (New York and Houston: The Elsevier Press; London: Cleaver-Hume Press Limited, 1952).

CUNNINGHAM, J. V. *Woe or Wonder. The Emotional Effect of Shakespearean Tragedy* (Denver, Colorado: University of Denver Press, 1951).

DANBY, J. F. *Poets on Fortune's Hill. Studies in Sidney, Shakespeare, Beaumont and Fletcher* (London: Faber, 1952).

DYSON, H. V. D. *The Emergence of Shakespeare's Tragedy.* Annual Shakespeare Lecture of the British Academy, 1950; from *Proceedings of the British Academy*, XXXVI (London: Geoffrey Cumberlege, 1953).

*Essays and Studies,* 1952. Collected for the English Association by Arundell Esdaile (London: John Murray, 1952).

FLUCHÈRE, H. *Shakespeare.* Translated by Guy Hamilton (London: Longmans, Green, 1953).

FRICKER, ROBERT. *Kontrast und Polarität in den Charakterbildern Shakespeares. Swiss Studies in English,* XX (Berne: A. Francke, 1951).

GYLLER, HARALD. *Shakespeare eller icke Shakespeare det är frågan* (Stockholm: Sällskapet Bokvännerna, 1951).

HARBAGE, ALFRED. *Shakespeare and the Rival Traditions* (New York: The MacMillan Company, 1952).

HOGAN, CHARLES BEECHER. *Shakespeare in the Theatre 1701–1800. A Record of Performances in London 1701–50* (Oxford: Clarendon Press, 1952).

HORNE, DAVID H. *The Life and Minor Works of George Peele* (New Haven: Yale University Press, 1952).

HOTSON, LESLIE. *Shakespeare's Motley* (London: Hart-Davis, 1952).

JACQUOT, JEAN. *George Chapman (1559–1634): sa vie, sa poésie, son théâtre, sa pensée. Annales de l'Université de Lyon,* XIX (Paris: Société d'Edition Les Belles Lettres, 1951).

KEMP, T. C. and TREWIN, J. C. *The Stratford Festival. A History of the Shakespeare Memorial Theatre* (Birmingham: Cornish Bros., 1953).

MANDER, R. and MITCHENSON, J. (Compilers). *Hamlet through the Ages. A Pictorial Record from 1709.* Edited by Herbert Marshall (London: Rockliff, 1952).

NICOLL, ALLARDYCE. *Shakespeare.* Home Study Books (London: Methuen, 1952).

NOYES, ROBERT GALE. *The Thespian Mirror. Shakespeare in the Eighteenth-Century Novel* (Providence, Rhode Island: Brown University Studies, XV, 1953).

PURDOM, C. B. *Producing Shakespeare* (London: Pitman, 1950).

REESE, M. M. *Shakespeare his World and his Work* (London: Edward Arnold, 1953).

ROHRMAN, H. *Marlowe and Shakespeare. A Thematic Exposition of some of their Plays* (Arnhem: Van Loghum Slaterus, 1952).

ROTAS, B. *Technologika II* (Athens, 1952).

# BOOKS RECEIVED

ROWSE, A. L. *A New Elizabethan Age?* Presidential Address of the English Association, 1952.

SEHRT, ERNST THEODOR. *Vergebung und Gnade bei Shakespeare* (Stuttgart: E. F. Koehler Verlag, 1952).

*Shakespeare Quarterly*, vol. III (New York: Shakespeare Association of America, 1952).

SHAKESPEARE, WILLIAM. *Henry VI*, Part I; *Henry VI*, Part II; *Henry VI*, Part III (three volumes). The New Shakespeare. Edited by John Dover Wilson (Cambridge University Press, 1952).

SHAKESPEARE, WILLIAM. *King Lear*. The Arden Edition of the Works of William Shakespeare. Edited by Kenneth Muir (London: Methuen, 1952).

SHAKESPEARE, WILLIAM. *Troilus and Cressida*. Shakespeare Quarto Facsimiles no. 8. Introduction by W. W. Greg (London: The Shakespeare Association and Sidgwick and Jackson, 1952).

SHAKESPEARE, WILLIAM. *Troilus and Cressida*. The New Variorum Shakespeare. Edited by Harold N. Hillebrand; T. W. Baldwin Supplemental Editor (Philadelphia and London: J. B. Lippincott, 1953).

SOUTHERN, RICHARD. *Changeable Scenery. Its Origin and Development in the British Theatre* (London: Faber, 1952).

WALKER, ALICE. *Textual problems of the First Folio. A Study of Richard III, King Lear, Troilus & Cressida, 2 Henry IV, Hamlet and Othello.* (Cambridge University Press, 1953).

WILSON, F. P. *Marlowe and the Early Shakespeare*. The Clark Lectures, 1951 (Oxford: Clarendon Press, 1953).

WILSON, JOHN DOVER and WORSLEY, T. C. *Shakespeare's Histories at Stratford 1951.* Photographs by Angus McBean (London: Max Reinhardt, 1952).

# INDEX

L*

# INDEX

# INDEX

# INDEX

# INDEX

# INDEX

# INDEX

# INDEX